OBJECT-ORIENTED SPECIFICATION AND DESIGN WITH C++

THE McGRAW-HILL INTERNATIONAL SERIES IN SOFTWARE ENGINEERING

Consulting Editor

Professor D. Ince
The Open University

Titles in this Series

OBJECT-ORIENTED SPECIFICATION AND DESIGN WITH C++

Peter Henderson

University of Southampton

McGRAW-HILL BOOK COMPANY

London · New York · St Louis · San Francisco · Auckland · Bogotá · Caracas
Lisbon · Madrid · Mexico · Milan · Montreal · New Delhi · Panama · Paris
San Juan · São Paulo · Singapore · Sydney · Tokyo · Toronto

Published by
McGRAW-HILL Book Company Europe
Shoppenhangers Road, Maidenhead, Berkshire, SL6 2QL, England
Telephone 0628 23432
Fax 0628 770224

British Library Cataloguing in Publication Data
Henderson, Peter
Object-oriented Specification and Design
with C++. – (McGraw-Hill International
Series in Software Engineering)
I. Title II. Series
005.133
ISBB 0–07–707585–4

Library of Congress Cataloging-in-Publication Data
Henderson, Peter
Object-oriented specification and design with C++/Peter Henderson.
p. cm. — (The McGraw-Hill international series in software engineering)
Includes bibliographical references and index.
ISBN 0–07–707585–4
1. Object-oriented programming (Computer science) 2. C++
(Computer program language) I. Title. II. Series.
QA76.64.H46   1993
005.1'1—dc20

93–17756
CIP

2345 CUP 9654

Typeset by Pentacor PLC, High Wycombe, Bucks
and printed and bound in **Great Britain at the University Press, Cambridge**

CONTENTS

PREFACE

When I set out to write this book, my plan was simple. I would cover the basic ideas of object-oriented analysis and design, introduce C++ and develop one or two complete, working programs covering the entire development from start to finish. Thus I would illustrate how effective object-oriented methods are and how suitable C++ is as a language for hosting them. But there was one major, additional idea that I wanted to explore. I have long been an advocate of modelling early in the software design life-cycle. I program a great deal, and always follow a process of first building a model in some suitable modelling language before beginning the detailed steps of program design. Typically I will use a modelling language such as LISP or Smalltalk; these languages provide very high-level abstractions which make the building of a complete working model very cheap – so cheap that one can afford to refine one's model iteratively and thus explore the problem domain in a way which would be too expensive once real coding had begun. Thus it was that my plans for the book evolved to include the use of a modelling language, an executable object-oriented specification language called Enact. An implementation of this tool for the PC is provided with the book. Other implementations are available from the author by electronic mail and file transfer.

This modelling language complements the object-oriented methods we shall introduce and, convincingly we hope, illustrates the facility with which a design can be turned into correct C++ with few if any bugs remaining to be sorted out. One major objective has been to illustrate the entire design process so completely that all the design considerations right down to working C++ code have been openly discussed, alternatives have been considered and their relative merits described. Four not entirely trivial examples are given. One is a program to maintain records for a library. As well as developing the library's main functions we also deal with a menu-driven user interface for it and with the persistence of its data over time (and over machine failure). Another program is an editor/browser for data about a hierarchically structured product, again with user interface and persistence. In the spirit of object-oriented methods we also develop a generic application of which the library and the hierarchy editor are specific examples.

The book is designed to teach object-oriented methods, to give an introduction to C++ and to illustrate a modelling (or rapid prototyping) methodology for software development. It is intended for use by professional engineers and by students either as part of a course or for self-study. Professional engineers will use the book to teach themselves about object-oriented methods and about the ways these methods are supported by C++. My expectation is that such readers will adapt the techniques presented here to fit into their own way of working and indeed this approach is encouraged from the outset. To support it, a short annotated bibliography is included as Appendix 3.

The book can be used as part of a course on object-oriented methods. The main chapters include exercises which support such a course, and additional materials are available from the author by electronic mail. The book can also be used to teach C++. Unlike most other introductory C++ books, a method of program design is given which (whether or not the prototyping is used) leads quickly to effective C++ code. For a complete C++ course, additional material would be required, such as the programming manuals which support the compiler being used. The author has used the book on a more general software engineering course. It was partly my frustration with the superficial way that general software engineering texts deal with their subject that led me to prepare the material in the book. Of course, to do justice to a class in software engineering, it is necessary to cover many more topics than I have covered here. What I have done in class is to present a wide range of topics from one of the traditional texts on software engineering and present the material from this book as an extensive, worked example. The class can then be engaged in discussions on the relative merits of various methods and on the nature of the development life-cycle, using this book as a suitable case for treatment.

Finally, for self-study, the book is designed to be worked through from beginning to end, with or without a PC to run the Enact software and with or without a C++ compiler to support the practical work. But the ideal, of course, is to have access to an implementation of both Enact and C++, to try out the examples, and to do the exercises. If you do this, then, if I have been successful in the design of the book, everything will fall into place and you will understand what the reasoning has been behind some of my design decisions. And shortly after that I expect you will realize that you can now do a better job yourself than I have done. That of course is what I hope, for it is that which will mean that I have succeeded as a teacher and transferred my understanding to you.

While it is true that the book has been designed to be read in the order presented, that should not discourage you from sampling later chapters before you begin. For example, the C++ chapter (Chapter4) is stand-alone, but the order in which it presents topics and the examples it uses are the same as the preceding chapter, and so it may be a little simpler if tackled in that order. To get a feel for the book as a whole, you can skip through the figures, which together describe all the main ideas and present all the main examples.

Chapter 1 gives some background and sets the context for what is to follow. Chapter 2 presents the design method from analysis to coding on a simple example. The idea is that you then have a map of the territory in your head and are thus better equipped to navigate the ensuing pages. In Chapter 3 we get down to details and present the basic object-oriented concepts and ideas. In this chapter also we introduce the modelling language Enact. Chapter 4, as we have mentioned earlier, is an introduction to C++. In this chapter we have made various choices, not least of all which aspects of the language to emphasize and which to leave out. The chapter is written for the beginner but is sufficiently terse, partial and idiomatic that, we trust, the experienced reader will nonetheless be interested by it.

Chapters 5 to 8 are devoted to increasingly complex examples which are completely worked out. Chapter 9 is a small indulgence which relates the methods discussed here to some of the author's other interests, specifically formal specification and functional programming. The hope is that these ideas will also interest you and send you off, via the bibliography, to study these issues too. Chapter 10 reprises Chapter 1 and discusses what has been achieved and what remains to be done. The appendices give details of Enact, of the C++ libraries on which we depend and a candid description of the books which constitute my reference library for my current approach to programming.

If I have achieved my objective in writing this book then I will have convinced you, by the end, that object-oriented techniques are important, that careful modelling is useful and that C++ is an excellent host for the object-oriented paradigm. But more importantly, I will have convinced you that these topics are worthy of more of your time and you will go on from here and develop methods of your own which expand upon mine.

ACKNOWLEDGEMENTS

I wish to thank my colleagues and students in the Department of Electronics and Computer Science at the University of Southampton who have helped me to develop the material presented here by providing a lively and interesting environment in which to work. They have always been prepared to discuss ideas in a constructive manner. Similarly I have been helped over recent years by collaboration with International Computers Ltd (ICL) who have involved me in many projects which have had a significant impact on my attitude to software engineering. To all of them I am grateful. But the responsibility for the ideas presented here is entirely my own.

Peter Henderson
Southampton

UNIX is a trademark of AT and T.

1

ON WHAT WE HOPE TO ACHIEVE

1.1 OBJECTIVES

This is a book about the whole of the software development process. It is a book which describes and discusses methods of software development and demonstrates their use on realistic examples. It is also a book about C++. It sets out to illustrate some contemporary methods of software development and uses C++ as the target language for eventual delivery of the product. The reader is not expected to know C++ before reading this book. Sufficient description of the language is included that the detailed development of the code can be understood.

Most of the book is devoted to one, reasonably large, example. This is an interactive program to maintain a record of who has borrowed books from a library. Eventually, by the end of Chapter 7, we will have developed a complete working C++ program which has a reasonable user interface and a simple database component. In developing this program we will learn methods of object-oriented software development and how C++ is particularly well suited to the support of software developed in this way. The object-oriented software development methods which we choose to describe, however, are not unique to C++. Rather, C++ is a good language to illustrate the methods.

Of course, we aim to develop software of high quality. There are many dimensions to quality, correctness and robustness being the obviously most important. Performance is a quality which cannot be ignored even now, despite the fact that computers are becoming very powerful indeed. We shall also consider delivery of adequate performance to be an important quality to be achieved in the software we shall develop. But the dimension of quality with which we shall be most preoccupied in this book is the ability of the software we develop to survive a lifetime of change as requirements change and as technology evolves. It has always been the case that software, once delivered, needs to be modified throughout its life to fit into an ever-changing world. The cost of modification of this sort has come to dominate the cost of the development as a whole. The reasons for this are many and varied, but one important factor is that the code itself is not easy to understand and the supporting documentation is never complete and never entirely consistent with the code.

The consequence is that much too much time is spent trying to understand old code. Perhaps the code was written by someone else. Perhaps it was written by yourself long ago. The code represents an investment which is more cost-effective to reuse than to rebuild. But the quality of the code in respect of its openness to change is perhaps not as high as it could be. The object-oriented methods which we shall describe and demonstrate in this book are targeted primarily on making the eventual design and the eventual code as flexible as possible with respect to unanticipated future change. We shall, of course, not ignore the qualities of correctness, robustness and performance, but we will encourage also due consideration of the quality of flexibility in the delivered product.

1.2 A VIEW OF THE SOFTWARE DEVELOPMENT PROCESS

We are concerned with the whole of the software development process and we are concerned particularly with the flexibility (openness to unanticipated change) of the software products which we develop.

The methods which we propose are object-oriented because such methods are particulary well suited to our objective of flexibility. The reason for this is that the object-oriented methods encourage the creation in the machine of a model of the real world where there is a very direct relationship between the machine model and the real world artefacts. Each entity in the real world will be represented by a single object in the machine. But before we go into detail about the particular methods to be described and before we justify the concentration on object-oriented methods we need to study the software development process a little more closely.

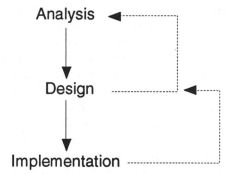

Figure 1.1 The three stages of software development.

First we will look at the initial development of a new piece of software, then at its evolution. We shall see that these are just two different ways at looking at the same process. Figure 1.1 shows the three main stages of a software development activity. Suppose we have been set the task of developing a simple program. For the sake of argument let us anticipate the example to be used later in this book, the program which will allow us to record the borrowing of books from a library. The analysis stage is when we are working on understanding the customer's requirements: precisely what information is to be held, how is it to be updated and queried? The design stage is when we decide how the desired information is to be organized and processed by the computer. Here we would choose a suitable implementation platform, normally under strict commercial constraints which may force the choice to be less than ideal from other points of view. The implementation stage is when we set about the production of code and the careful testing which measures and ensures qualities of correctness, robustness and performance.

If our library maintenance program is to be stand-alone, it might be sufficient for us to go through this development process once from top to bottom, delivering the first version of the product at the end of the implementation stage. Realistically, we would expect to have to iterate a little and retrace our steps as we discover later in the development process that there are details which we have neglected to consider in the earlier stages. But we can still consider the model in Fig. 1.1 to apply. There may be one or more developers involved in the entire development. We can consider them as working at different times in different roles, depending upon whether the activity they are performing at any particular time is appropriately identified as analysis, design or implementation. That is to say, the consequence of doing some analysis is sufficient information to be able to do a bit of design. So we do some design which leads to a reconsideration of the analysis. If we are to discover incompleteness in the analysis, then we will return to that activity and so we iterate between analysis and design. This is true even in quite formal situations where the process of development to be followed by a team is strictly laid down with reviews and various statutory documents to be produced. The analysis activity anticipates the design activity as much as possible, but never perfectly.

We proceed to the implementation stage when analysis and design between them have determined a sufficiently precise description of the required code. We build code components, in most programming languages, as collections of subroutines. Each component is tested individually and in conjunction with the others against a progressively more demanding set of tests. The consequence of this is that we discover inadequacies in our coding. We correct them. But we also discover inadequacies in our design. Correcting these may be more expensive, because the changes required may well affect components which we have already considered completed. Changes in the design may reach into every component in the system. The implementation stage is the ultimate arbiter of completeness and consistency of our analysis and design. The more care and attention we have lavished on the earlier stages, the more likely we will be able to avoid expensive revision of design or code late into the implementation stage. So we need methods which will encourage care in the early stages of software development. This is our objective.

So far we have only discussed the development of a stand-alone program built effectively from scratch. Yet we have already encountered the need to subject some of our software components to change, caused by the fact that we may have been less than perfect in analysis and design. If the design we had made had, from the outset, been targeted on being as flexible as possible, then the discovery of changes would perhaps be less costly.

Let us now consider a more typical scenario for our software development. Rather than develop a stand-alone program from scratch, imagine our development to be either the revision of an already existing, but now inadequate, version of the program. Or imagine that it has to interface with an already defined system, such as a graphical user interface. This is of course how all real software engineering really is, and always has been. But nowadays the element of revising and reusing existing components is becoming the major part of each software development activity.

Even for this more elaborate, but more typical, development process our sample model of Fig. 1.1 still applies. Now we take analysis to be the activity of understanding the problem, the real world system to be supported, and also to be the activity of understanding what computer systems already exist to be reused and to be interfaced to. Design involves capturing more precisely the description of the new components to be built, the existing ones to be reused and where necessary the existing ones which require revision before they can be reused.

So we see the development process as a kind of production line, where we are shipping products, the products being evolving versions of the software which our customer requires. We may have a requirement for change coming from evolution in our customer's business or from an evolution in technology. Or we may have a requirement for change coming from the fact that late in the development process we recognize a failing in some of the earlier stages which we must now repeat. Whichever reason causes the requirement for change we will wish it to be as inexpensive as possible. It is reasonable to expect that the earlier we can detect a requirement for change the cheaper it will be to incorporate it. This is particularly true where the change is in fact to correct an error. So we require methods which will enable us to anticipate change as early as possible in the development process. And we need methods which enable our product to survive a lifetime of change because we know that we cannot anticipate all the changes which may be required of it.

1.3 THE METHODS TO BE DESCRIBED

The nature of any software development process, including the one we have described, is that it proceeds from the informal to the severely formal. It is not possible to be more formal than a program. It has a precise meaning, which is the behaviour which it evokes in the machine which runs it. But we begin the development in a very informal way. We have to understand the requirements. We capture the requirements using English and maybe a few *ad hoc* diagrams. Then we have to proceed, step by step, and add more and more formality until the entire product is committed to the formal statement of our collection of coded components.

Early in this process, diagrammatic methods are useful because they provide a framework for capturing knowledge about the problem and the product which we propose will solve it, without being pedantic about which details should be recorded. Later in the process as we become more precise, we might make use of formal or semi-formal notations, such as pseudocode, to capture the evolving design. Ultimately we will expect to arrive at a design which decomposes our product into manageable components and we will expect to possess a reasonably formal description of the interface to each component. Implementation would then produce coded components each of which has an obvious relationship to the corresponding design component.

This much would be true of any methods we chose to adopt. In this book I will describe a set of object-oriented methods which are not original. Neither are they in any sense a perfect set or a panacea for the software development problems described in the previous section. But they are a set of methods which I have found work together well. You should study them in the spirit of deciding how you could adopt such methods yourself, how you could adapt them to your own or your company's style, and how you could use them alongside other methods which you have found valuable. Perhaps more significantly, you should look at the way I have assembled this set of methods, and how I have targeted them on a particular language (C++) and a particular way of using this language. Then you may develop your own methods in a similar way.

The emphasis will be on developing software which can cope with change. Object-oriented techniques have made substantial progress in that direction, so we will adopt those ideas as central. We also want to detect inadequacies in the development as early as possible, because that is when they are cheaper to correct, so we will try to introduce precision and formality as early as possible and so check consistency.

I shall introduce the notion of an *abstract system* and provide a means for building a working model of the abstract system as a way of checking consistency in the evolving design.

A software design problem will be solved by developing an abstract system for it. Initially we will use the object-oriented analysis techniques of Coad and Yourdon (see bibliography) to determine the objects and operations of our abstract system. In particular we will use the augmented entity relationship diagrams of Coad and Yourdon to give one description of the abstract system. The interface to the Abstract System and to the objects it describes will be defined by *protocols*, for which we will define both a textual and diagrammatic form. Each has merits. So far, we are still in the analysis stage of the development process. In moving to the design stage we will use a diagram of the actual layout of objects in our model of the real world. We will introduce diagramming techniques for making such diagrams visually most helpful. This diagram we will call the *object diagram*.

By the time we have assembled some or all of the above descriptions we are already part of the way into design. We need to complete the design by determining the details of how each object will be represented and how each operation will be performed. This is where we would normally resort to pseudocode – not a bad idea. But we will recommend a more formal step. We will build a *working model* using a prototyping tool, the Enact modelling language. Enact is not the only language we could use for this purpose: Smalltalk is an obvious alternative. Enact is, however, sufficiently simple that it can be learned in a few hours. An interpreter for Enact, which runs on a PC, is supplied with the book. Building a model in Enact is rather like writing pseudocode, but one has to be that little bit more complete so that the model can be executed. The Enact interpreter will tell you a lot about your model as it evolves. In fact, it will discover inconsistencies in your design at a very early stage in the development. We shall see that the aim of arriving at a sufficiently general but simple abstract system will be greatly aided by the feedback we get from working with Enact models. In fact, the expectation is that building an Enact model is only a few hours' work, so that discovering inadequacies in the design can be very cheap indeed. This discovery occurs at a stage when we can still afford to put it right, so we can afford to refine the design and the Enact model iteratively until we are happy that we have dealt with all the inadequacies.

The Enact model, we shall see, is some way short of being an actual program. But, having built it, we can be reasonably confident that the implementation stage will have few surprises for us. In this book we have chosen to go to C++ for implementation. This is for many reasons. It is important that we take our methods all the way through to implementation because the requirements of the computer impose some very definite constraints upon us as designers. C++ is a good target for object-oriented designs. Some would say C++ was an object-oriented language. Some would say it falls short of providing all the facilities we might expect of an object-oriented language. In fact, C++, like the language C upon which it is based, is a good host for many different programming styles. It does have additional features beyond C which make it even better at hosting different styles of programming, so we can expect that it will accept our object-oriented designs as well as almost any language. But an overwhelming consideration in the choice of C++ is the massive and increasing commercial interest in it. There is little doubt that in the fullness of time it will replace C as the language of choice for system programming. This of course is enormously facilitated by the fact that it has (or very nearly has) ANSI C as a proper subset, so old code can easily be transported to C++ and used in conjunction with new code taking advantage of some of C++ unique features.

There are a great many programming languages which vie for our attention when we come to choose which is best for a particular application. Pascal, BASIC, LISP and the 4GLs that accompany database systems are languages that might be chosen, rather than C or C++, for a particular application. The methods described in this book will be equally applicable to those languages, especially when taking the versions of those languages which include object-oriented extensions. The method we will demonstrate of deriving the implementation from the abstract system will involve deriving *coding rules* for using the target language (in our case C++) in an idiomatic way. This has many advantages: it reduces the variety of features used in the target language; it makes constructions in that language more instantly recognizable (an important feature in making the code easier to change), and it makes the relationship between the design, recorded in the diagrams and protocols of the abstract system and in the Enact model, and the code easier to determine, an essential feature of our ability to handle the code economically in the future.

1.4 OUTLINE OF THE BOOK

The book is based on the development of a single, fairly large example. In an attempt to set the scene and to introduce you to all of the methods to be recommended, Chapter 2 is devoted to a first attempt to take this example through all stages of development, right through to working C++ code. This, as it were, tells the story in outline, asking you to accept that detailed descriptions and reasoning are postponed until the development proper which occurs later in the book. Thus by the end of Chapter 2, you have seen a little of everything that is to come.

Chapter 3 can then go into detail on the object-oriented method and on the diagramming techniques which support its use. We define the notion of abstract system as a generalization of abstract data type and discuss how the object-oriented method supports the development of abstract systems, which in turn supports the need for software which is flexible in that it is open to future change. In Chapter 3 we also define the Enact modelling language and describe its use. There is a user manual for Enact in Appendix 1 which has a 'Getting Started' section for readers who wish to get the feel of it before reading Chapter 2. After Chapter 3 we expect that some readers will wish to follow the text by using the Enact tool to experiment with the models developed in later chapters.

Next we turn to C++. Chapter 4 is an introduction for the reader who has not encountered the language before. We assume some familiarity with programming, such as would be gained from having used C, BASIC or Pascal, but do not assume previous knowledge of any of these languages. Since our use of C++ will be idiomatic we believe that experienced C++ programmers will still find the chapter interesting as they discover which parts of the language we emphasize and which we ignore. The description of C++ is simplified because we have already studied object-oriented ideas in Chapter 3. Some C++ features are left undescribed at this stage and described as needed in the remaining chapters. Eventually, towards the end of the book we return to a discussion of our idiomatic use of C++ as an encouragement to you to develop your own idioms. At that time we also discuss how the methods of the book can be applied to other programming languages.

Chapters 5, 6, 7 and 8 are devoted to the main example. Chapter 5 discusses the need for a satisfactory user interface and then takes an excursion into developing one. Chapter 6 attaches this user interface to our main example. Chapter 7 then turns to the need for persistence, the ability of our library data to survive over time, including shutdown or breakdown of the machine. We solve this problem in a simple way. Chapter 8 returns to the issue of flexibility and develops a more generic version of the library example.

In Chapter 9 we allow ourselves to discuss the relationship between the methods described in the earlier part of the book and other methods of software design. In particular, we look at the influence of mathematical methods of specification and at the relationship between object-oriented methods and the abstract data type much loved of mathematical methods. Our objective here is not so much to suggest that mathematical methods have a major role to play in software development as that they are a good guide to which methods are simple and sound. In Chapter 9 too we return to the discussion of C++ as a host for other programming styles than the object-oriented style. In particular, we look at the extent to which C++ is suited to functional programming and to the hosting of user-defined application-oriented languages.

Chapter 10 concludes by once again expanding the thesis of this chapter, that flexibility is a necessary additional quality for contemporary software. Having studied the methods and seen them applied, we are in a position to judge the extent to which we have achieved what we set out to achieve. If you are encouraged to use the methods described here or to adapt your own methods to meet the same objectives or simply to consider your own methods in the context of the objectives set out here then the book will have achieved as much as its author can hope.

2

THE METHOD APPLIED – A FIRST EXAMPLE

2.1 OBJECTIVES

In this chapter we introduce all the key elements of the development method and illustrate them with a complete, worked example. The diagramming and information gathering required by the analysis step is introduced first. Then we demonstrate the design step by building a working model of the proposed system using the Enact design language. Finally, to exemplify the implementation step, we take this model through to some C++ components. Later chapters will deal with each of these steps in detail.

2.2 PROBLEM STATEMENT

In my office I have a few hundred books. Outside my office I have a few dozen colleagues. Often my colleagues ask if they may borrow a book. I graciously acquiesce. I try to remember who has which book. As often as not I can remember, but every so often (it seems increasingly often) I just cannot recall who it was took a particular book. So the exercise we will undertake here is to design a computer system which can keep track of the whereabouts of my books.

This example is simple enough that we can hope to complete all three stages of the development of a first prototype in a single chapter. It is also sufficiently complex to allow us to introduce the first stratum of ideas behind the development methods which we propose. It is not, however, a typical problem for these methods. In fact, if the problem we were tackling were simply as we have stated it, we would immediately recognize that all we require is a database package (such as dBASE III). We wouldn't ever need to do any programming, just set up a few tables. A more typical problem for the methods we propose would be the development of the database package itself. Nevertheless, our exercise will serve its purpose and introduce us to the basic ideas of object-oriented development.

Returning to the exercise we have set ourselves, since the method requires us to model the real world, we need perhaps to look a little more closely at what happens in the real world of my personal library.

I am not pedantic about my books. I refer to them by short names, usually the surname or surnames of the author or authors, occasionally by an abbreviation of the title. So I may lend 'Stroustrup' to one colleague, 'Chandy and Misra' to another and 'Smalltalk80' to a third. Similarly, my colleagues are 'David' and 'Hugh' and so on. The computer system we are to design will be one which allows me to say, for example, 'David has borrowed Stroustrup', 'which books does David have?', 'who has Stroustrup?' and 'David has returned Stroustrup'.

We might envisage a user interface to our product which presents lists of books and lists of people and offers its user the opportunity to record borrowings and make simple queries. In this chapter, we shall only go as far as designing the basic objects needed to record this information. In later chapters we shall pick up the challenge of the user interface.

2.3 ANALYSIS

We carry out the systems analysis by a method derived from Coad and Yourdon (see bibliography). As they explain, this analysis will generally be an iterative process, refining the choice of objects until a simple yet adequately powerful architecture is discovered. Our exercise is so simple that little iteration will be required in this chapter. We shall, however, see such iterative refinement in later chapters.

Stroustrup

Figure 2.1 An object which represents a book.

The analysis step requires us to build a conceptual model of the real world. The real world has books and colleagues. Books have location, either in my room or with a colleague. The development method suggests that we build a model of the real world in the computer system, having for each relevant real-world entity a corresponding object in the computer system. As the real world evolves ('David' borrows 'Stroustrup'), so the computer-based model evolves to keep step and hence record the relevant facts.

We choose objects to model the real-world entities. At the analysis stage, an object is something which has attributes and upon which we can perform operations to inspect and change these attributes.

Let us have an object to represent a book. Figure 2.1 shows an object representing the book which I refer to as 'Stroustrup'. In such a diagram, an object is represented by a box with the type of object clearly marked. The name of the object is written below, or alongside, the box.

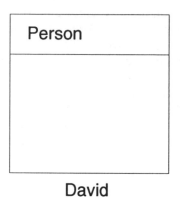

David

Figure 2.2 An object which represents a person.

For my colleagues I will have an object to represent a person. Figure 2.2 shows an object representing the person which I refer to as 'David'.

For each real-world entity, our object model will contain exactly one object. Drawing a diagram of a typical state of (our model of) the real world will be a considerable help in understanding the extent of the design problem which will face us when taking the computer representation into account. We will use some methods for diagramming our model which will be fully described in Chapter 3. Suppose 'David' borrows 'Stroustrup'. This we will draw as in Fig. 2.3. An arrow from 'Stroustrup' to 'David' indicates that 'David' is the borrower of 'Stroustrup'.

An arrow from 'David' to 'Stroustrup' indicates that 'Stroustrup' is one of the books in 'David's' collection. Since 'David' can have many books, this second arrow is potentially multi-headed, as we have tried to indicate on the diagram. Figure 2.4 shows a more elaborate model, where various colleagues have borrowed various books. 'David' has two books, 'Hugh' has one and 'Stephen' has none. Some of my books are not borrowed by anyone.

This type of diagram, which I will refer to as an *object diagram*, uses some conventions for arrows which are designed to make the diagram tidy. However, the benefits of diagramming, as we briefly discussed in Chapter 1, are largely to do with the extent to which they are able to capture a whole-model view, as opposed to an accurate description of detail. The diagramming conventions, described in the next chapter, are therefore more appropriately considered as guidelines or suggestions than as hard and fast rules.

It is not premature at the analysis stage to write down such possibly concrete representations of objects. It is, however, important to capture some of the more abstract properties of the objects. The importance lies in the extent to which we are to be successful in creating an architecture for our system which is going to be adequate to our purpose, valid, and potentially be able to evolve as we evolve our requirements. We have said in Chapter 1 that the cost of design flaws is least at the analysis stage and greatest at

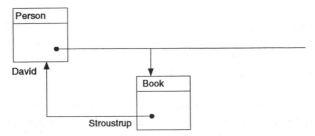

Figure 2.3 David has borrowed Stroustrup.

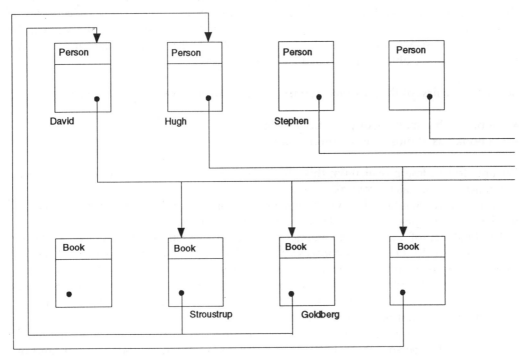

Figure 2.4 A library with four persons and four books.

the implementation stage. It is important therefore that we construct both abstract and concrete views of our proposed architecture at this stage so that we are led to consider as many of the properties of our proposal as we can.

The abstract view comes with the consideration, not of individual objects, but with the classes to which they belong. In the next chapter we shall go carefully through the object-oriented concepts which we are introducing here. Meanwhile, we shall use them consistently with their eventual definitions. *Class* and *object* are important concepts. They are not the same. The distinction is fundamental. An object will always be an instance of a class. It is therefore possible to refer to all the instances of a particular class.

Implicitly we have introduced two classes, `Book` and `Person`. When the eventual system is built we would expect to have a few hundred objects which were instances of `Book`, one for each book which I own and a few dozen objects which are instances of `Person`, one for each of my colleagues.

Figure 2.5 An Entity Relationship diagram for the library classes.

Each book may be in my room or allocated to one person. Each person may have zero, one or many of my books. These possibilities are recorded on an ER diagram as shown in Fig. 2.5. The relationship between *Person* and *Book* is shown as a line. The classes (used to represent real-world entities) are shown as boxes. The crow's feet at the *Book* end of the relationship means there can be (zero to) many books in a person's collection. The absence of crow's feet at the *Person* end of the relationship means that there can be (zero or) at most one person allocated to each book. The ER diagram captures the same information as the object diagram in a more concise way.

So we list the first of the (abstract) properties which we wish our system to have:

- a person has many books (the books which he or she has borrowed)
- a book has at most one person (the borrower)

Writing down these properties in this way is forcing us to fix our terminology and hence our concepts (such as borrower).

Although we shall take this system much further, in this and later chapters, at this stage we shall settle on just these two classes of objects as sufficient to our purposes.

The final step of analysis is to enumerate the events which may take place to alter the state of the world. Our world consists of a number of books and a number of persons. These are represented by objects which are instances of the classes *Book* and *Person*. If the representation reflects the real world correctly then each book will be allocated to one person, or to no one, and each person will have a number of books. If a book is allocated to a person then that person will have said book in his or her collection. Conversely, if a person has a certain book in his or her collection, then that book is allocated and indeed allocated to that person. We will return to a discussion of the redundancy built into our design, and its ramifications for correctness (good and bad), in a later chapter.

The events which can cause the real world to change and which must be reflected in the system are

- a person borrows a book
- a book is returned

Both events affect both the book and its borrower. So we expect to have operations on each object which correspond to the actions to be taken on the occurrence of these events. It is possible to go further at the analysis stage into the details of such operations. Indeed it would be essential for a more elaborate system. But for us, the next step, which is to begin design by building a working model, is the appropriate place to begin such considerations, and so we move to that stage now.

2.4 DESIGN

The design step of our development method is when we begin to consider the requirements which the computer, as opposed to the real world, puts upon us. Traditionally this would be when we designed the data structures and algorithms which the computer system would use to realize our system. We would record these design decisions in a mixture of diagrams and pseudocode. We would develop a strategy for eventually implementing our design which allowed us to test each of our design decisions in some reasonably efficient way as we assembled the actual implementation.

Our method is a little different. We shall capture our design decisions in the form of a working model. Our conjecture, stated in the first chapter, and returned to repeatedly throughout this book, is that this is a cost-effective thing to do even if the working model is eventually thrown away. The assumption is that the cost of building the working model is small in comparison with building the eventual system and that, as a consequence, iterative refinement of the model can be achieved where it may be too expensive to be contemplated after implementation has been committed.

The language for our working model is Enact. It combines some of the strengths of object-oriented programming in the style of Smalltalk with some of the strengths of functional programming. This latter aspect may not be evident until later in the book. Its inclusion greatly facilitates experimentation, and consequently iterative refinement of the architecture of the model.

A version of Enact is supplied free with this book. It will run on a minimally configured PC. The disk includes the examples developed here (and in later chapters) and as a consequence the reader can repeat and expand upon the experiments described in these pages. Appendix 1 describes how to load and execute the distributed version of Enact. It is also a manual for the language. A tutorial introduction to Enact is included in Chapter 3. Here we shall describe only what we need of the language to capture our design.

In fact, we have already gone too far in the analysis step and have begun to design the representation of our objects. This is not wrong, but neither is it necessary. The step too far was to presume that we would record the books held by a person as some sort of collection. It would have been sufficient to record that we know that a person may borrow more than one book without worrying how we were going to represent that.

Of course, the representation we chose is an obvious one and so we will not go back on it. Let us show how that is captured in Enact.

Enact allows us to build a model of the real world by having one Enact object for each real world object. Thus we need to be able to bring new objects into existence and to manipulate these objects as we would the corresponding real world entities.

Enact has classes and objects. Each object will belong to a particular class. Each object comes into existence by evaluating a constructor for the class to which it will belong. Consider the class *Book*. Its constructor is the function *book*. We can construct an object to represent the 'Stroustrup' book and assign the object to the variable *Stroustrup* by executing

```
Stroustrup :- book()
```

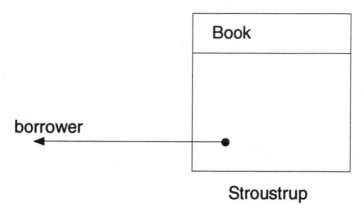

Figure 2.6 The book object in Enact.

The constructor *book* takes no arguments. The object which is constructed is shown in Fig. 2.6.

The only attribute of a *Book* which is of interest in this model is the identity of the *Person* who borrowed it. This we denote by

> `aBook.borrower`

where *aBook* is an object of type *Book*. This expression denotes a *Person*. In addition we shall have some operations on objects of class *Book* which are accessed by similar means. First we may allocate the book *aBook* to the person *aPerson* as follows

> `aBook.borrow(aPerson)`

When the book is returned, we use the operation

> `aBook.return()`

Both of these operations are evaluated for the effect they have, updating the objects *aBook* and *aPerson*. We have one more operation, evaluated for the value it returns. We can test whether or not a book is in the library (in my room, available to be borrowed) by the call

> `aBook.inlibrary()`

This returns a logical or boolean value which can be tested and acted upon.

For example, suppose we evaluate

> `aBook.borrow(aPerson) if aBook.inlibrary()`

Then the allocation of *aBook* to *aPerson* only takes place if *aBook* is not already allocated to someone.

```
class Book < Object.

book():= new Book with borrower=nil.

Book.borrow(aPerson):=
    (self.borrower:=aPerson; aPerson.allocate(self)).

Book.return():=
    (self.borrower.deallocate(self); self.borrower:=nil).

Book.inlibrary():=
    self.borrower=nil.
```

Figure 2.7 Enact specification for *Book*.

This combination of one constructor, one attribute and three operations constitute the *protocol* for the class *Book*. This protocol is established by evaluating the Enact specification shown in Fig. 2.7. This requires some explanation. The class *Book* is introduced by the first statement. This ensures that it is a subclass of the (predefined) class *Object*. (More about subclasses later.)

The constructor *book* is defined by the function definition which occurs second in Fig. 2.7. This function has no arguments and it returns an object like that shown in Fig. 2.6 by constructing a new object with its fields set accordingly. The expression

```
new Book with borrower = nil
```

constructs the said object. Here *borrower* is the attribute and its corresponding value is obtained by evaluating the expression after the = sign.

Finally, the three operations are introduced by *method* definitions. These are exactly like function definitions except that the class of object to which they apply is made apparent. Thus the call

```
Stroustrup.borrow(David)
```

invokes the first method in Fig. 2.7 since *Stroustrup* is a *Book*. In evaluating the body of this method the parameter *aPerson* is bound to *David* and the parameter *self* is bound to *Stroustrup*. In other words, within the body of a method, *self* is a way of referring to the object to which the operation was applied. In this case, the body *self.borrower := aPerson* evaluates as *Stroustrup.borrower := David*, which is of course the effect we want to have.

The remaining two methods should be obvious. We have borrowed an idiom from Smalltalk for naming parameters in a way which suggests their type. Enact is a particular mixture of concepts, both object-oriented and functional, designed to be powerful yet simple to learn. The implementation provides support for testing and experimentation (as we shall see) and we recommend various idiomatic practices to make the model both readable and testable. This way of naming parameters is one of those.

So we have made a big jump from analysis to design. Some readers may be concerned that it is almost as if we are implementing here already. This is not something to be ashamed of. We are trying to achieve a balance between effort put into design and eventually producing a working product. In practice, the cost of producing a specification of the sort shown in Fig. 2.7, if we have done sufficient work at the analysis stage, is relatively low: sufficiently low that we can afford to experiment with it, refine it, throw it away and start again if necessary. In fact, the working model often shows up inadequacies in the analysis which *require* us to go back and repeat some of that and then to bring the analysis and design into line with each other. Our exercise is too simple to illustrate that iteration. We shall see examples later in the book.

Let us move on to design the class *Person*. The *protocol* for a person is similar to that for a book. We have a constructor *person* used as follows:

$$David := person()$$

The collection of books borrowed by a person is going to be held in a collection object of class *Set* . This is a predeclared class in Enact which has constructor *set ()* and a *protocol* which includes the ability to insert and remove elements from *Set* and to determine whether or not some object is a member of the set. In our case *aPerson.books* is such a set and this is all the set protocol we shall require.

The remainder of the *Person* protocol is just two operations:

$$aPerson.allocate(aBook)$$
$$aPerson.deallocate(aBook)$$

These have the obvious meaning. If the book *aBook* is available, *aPerson* is recorded as having it by the first operation. If person *aPerson* has book *aBook* , then this record is removed by the second operation.

The specification of *Person* is shown in Fig. 2.8. The structure of this specification is more or less the same as the specification for *Book*.

```
class Person < Object.

person():= new Person with books=set().

Person.allocate(aBook):=
    self.books.insert(aBook).

Person.deallocate(aBook):=
    self.books.remove(aBook).
```

Figure 2.8 Enact specification for *Person*.

The relationship between the model of `Book` and the model of `Person` should now be apparent. When we use the operation `aBook.borrow(aPerson)` both the links between `aBook` and `aPerson` are established. The attribute `aBook.borrower` is set to `aPerson` and the collection `aPerson.books` is augmented to include `aBook`.

We now have what I will call an abstract system. This is a collection of classes (viewed as abstract data types, as we shall see) along with the protocol for using them. Although each class will have its own protocol, only some of that will be made visible to the user of the abstract system. In our case the operations `aPerson.allocate(aBook)` and `aPerson.deallocate(aBook)` are not to be made visible. The protocol for the abstract system is shown in Fig. 2.9.

```
aPerson := person()
aBook := book()
aPerson := aBook.borrower
aCollection := aPerson.books
aTruthValue := aBook.inlibrary()
aBook.borrow(aPerson)
aBook.return(aPerson)
```

Figure 2.9 Protocol for the library abstract system.

Here we see that we have available the two constructors so we can create new objects and we can enquire of the objects using the two visible attributes `aBook.borrower` and `aPerson.books`. The desirability of making attributes visible in this way is a matter of taste, which I shall discuss at length later. The only operations available to the user of this abstract system are those on `aBook`. There is a constraint which must be stated, that `aBook.inlibrary()` must be true before `aBook.borrow(aPerson)` is invoked, and it should be false before `aBook.return()` is invoked. In Chapter 3 we shall describe the rules for defining abstract systems and also introduce a protocol diagram which conveys the same information as a textual description, such as that in Fig. 2.9. In passing, let us say that it is possible, indeed it may even be desirable, to capture the properties of an abstract system in a formal mathematical way. We shall not do this. In Chapter 9 we shall describe what means are available for constructing a formal mathematical specification and discuss the state of the art and relative merits of so doing.

Again we may be inclined to the view that we are implementing rather than specifying. In fact we are building a low-cost working model. We would expect to improve it iteratively before proceeding to implementation. Part of that improvement involves experimentally testing it. This begins to give us some feedback on the consistency of our design decisions and on the completeness of our design. It is valuable when we find inadequacies and flaws: we correct them. It is valuable when we perform a series of tests which produce no apparent problems: it boosts our confidence.

If the text of Figs. 2.7 and 2.8 is loaded into Enact (as described in Appendix 1) then we are in a position to perform some model testing. Suppose we set up a number of books and persons by the following sequence of assignments.

```
Stroustrup := book().
Smalltalk80 := book().
ChandyMisra := book().

David := person().
Hugh := person().
```

The variables have been given the same names as the objects they represent.

Now we can interact with the model. In the following I have shown the response from the Enact implementation shifted over to the right. Suppose we check out some books and see who has them.

```
Stroustrup.borrow(David).
ChandyMisra.borrow(Hugh).
Stroustrup.borrower.
                                David
Smalltalk80.borrower.
                                ()
ChandyMisra.borrower.
                                Hugh
```

This appears to record the borrower correctly in each book object. To see what books a particular person has is more complicated. We need to know that a *Set* has an attribute *aSet.members* which we will show here and explain in the next chapter.

```
David.books.members.
                        (Stroustrup)
David.borrow(Smalltalk80)
David.books.members.
                        (Stroustrup Smalltalk80)
```

The list of books held by David in both cases is what we expect. In fact, we would go on and test that books could be returned and that in all cases the redundant recording of this information was consistent. Although we shall not do it here, much of this testing of the design can be automated, not least because of the functional nature of the Enact language.

2.5 IMPLEMENTATION

In a real development situation we would take the design much further before moving to implementation. We would expect to have more classes than our simple exercise has generated and, by iterative refinement at the analysis stage and by experimental evaluation of the working model at the design stage, to have arrived at an architecture in which we are confident.

Our purpose here however is to illustrate all three stages of the development from conception to product. While our product could be taken from the design stage to implementation in almost any programming language, we have chosen in this book to illustrate the implementation step using C++. Our choice of delivery language is based upon its current and future importance for systems programming, which in turn is based on the versatility of the support it gives for a wide range of programming styles, including the object-oriented style.

Chapter 4 is devoted to a preliminary description of C++, in particular its support for object-oriented programming. Throughout the remainder of the book we introduce advanced C++ concepts as we need them. Here we shall describe C++ only as far as necessary to support the implementation decisions we have taken in turning our working model into a product.

In introducing C++ here we are assuming some maturity of experience in programming on the part of the reader. Clearly some familiarity with C or C++ will make our descriptions easier to follow, but the reader who has little or no experience of these languages, a Pascal programmer say, will have little difficulty in understanding the implementation issues which have been addressed. The C++ books which the author has used are discussed in the bibliography. Readers wishing to apply the full method described in this book to their own C++ programming will need the support of a good C++ reference book, although the C++ topics discussed here and in later chapters will supplement that, not least because of the idiomatic way in which we use C++. Readers wishing to apply the method to software to be developed in another language, for example a 4GL, should be able to devise rules for coding in that language based on the rules for C++ which we introduce here. Indeed we discuss such ventures briefly in Chapter 10.

```
class Book{
public:
    Person* borrower;
    Book();
    void borrow(Person*);
    void _return();
    int inlibrary();
};
```

Figure 2.10 C++ implementation of class **Book**.

Support for object-oriented programming in C++ is centred on the class construct. A class introduces a new type, defines the storage used to represent values of that type and determines the operations which are applicable to objects of that type. Figure 2.10 shows the C++ class definition for our implementation of **Book**. In C++ such a definition introduces **Book** as a new type so that we can now declare objects of this type, such as

```
Book* b
```

The class **Book** has five members: **borrower, Book, borrow, _return** and **inlibrary**. The first of these is a data-valued member recording the borrower of the book. The remaining four are member functions corresponding to the constructor and the three methods our design required for **Book**.

C++ uses the same name for the class and for its constructor. The constructor is used whenever we allocate a new object, which we can do by means of a call such as

```
b = new Book();
```

Here, because of the way we declared it, **b** is a pointer to an object of type **Book** which has been newly constructed in space allocated (usually) in the heap. The C++ memory model is very important; we shall describe it fully in Chapter 4.

We don't know what the constructor does, because we haven't defined it yet. Before doing that, consider the decision we have made that each object will be referred to in our program by a pointer. This is not necessary in C++ in general, but fits best with the intended implementation of our design. Recall that books refer to persons and persons refer to books, so somewhere we are going to require a pointer. Experience has led us to conclude that symmetric use of pointers throughout leads to an elegant implementation, so it is that rule we shall follow throughout this particular implementation. We shall discuss this decision later in the book.

In C++, the declaration of a pointer is heralded by the use of an asterisk ***** *before* the name of the variable whose type is to be a pointer. Thus the above declaration states that **b** is a pointer to a **Book**. Similarly the class member **borrower** is a pointer to **Person** (yet to be defined). We will discuss this use of pointers fully in Chapter 4. There are two ways of writing a declaration of a pointer according to where the spacing is placed. Most authors write **Book *b** for the declaration of **b** as a pointer. I shall write **Book* b**, since I think it looks more elegant. To avoid a common pitfall I shall always declare each variable separately.

The constructor **Book** has no parameter, which is denoted by the fact that we write **()** as its parameter list. Similarly the operation (C++ calls it a member function) **borrow** has a single argument of type pointer to **Person**. This function is called for its effect only, so it has no result, denoted in C++ by the return type **void**. Similarly, **_return** has no result. Neither does it have any arguments. The logical valued operation **inlibrary** is implemented as returning **int**. This is idiomatic in C++, which represents false and true as **0** and non-**0** respectively.

Each of the members of a class defines an attribute of an object of that class, which can be accessed in various ways. We have made all the members of **Book** public, although this is a decision we shall wish to revise later. It does mean, for example, that we can refer to the data member of **b** as

```
b->borrower
```

Similary, we can invoke the (non-constructor) member functions using the same notation.

```
b->borrow(David);
b->_return();
b->inlibrary()
```

The first two of these are evaluated for their effect, the last is a logical (**int**) valued expression. We shall see them in use later in this section. We have had to modify the name of the second operator by including a leading underline to avoid the name clash with the C++ **return** operator.

```
Book::Book() {
   borrower=0;
}

void Book::borrow(Person* aPerson) {
   borrower=aPerson;
   borrower->allocate(this);
}

void Book::_return() {
   borrower->deallocate(this);
   borrower=0;
}

int Book::inlibrary() {
   return(borrower==0);
}
```

Figure 2.11 C++ implementation of member functions of class **Book**.

Now we can turn to the definition of the member functions. Consider first the constructor. This we write as shown in the first definition in Fig. 2.11. All member functions are prefixed with the name of the class to which they belong. In this case **Book::** is the prefix, so **Book::Book** is the way we refer to the constructor function at definition time. The constructor, being a member function can refer to the data members directly by name. It assigns initial values to the data member, setting the **borrower** field of the new object to **0**. We use **0** as the null pointer. C++ conventionally uses **0** for this purpose. So the call

   b = Book();

creates an object, initialized as shown in Fig. 2.12. The details of C++ syntax, for example that **=** means assignment and **==** means 'equal to', are left until Chapter 4. The reader should be able to understand the implementation without worrying about that detail at this time.

The remaining member functions shown in Fig. 2.11 should be fairly obvious. The only unusual feature is that once again we have had to prefix the name of the member function with the name of the class to which it belongs. So **Book::borrow**, in the place normally reserved for the function name, indicates that we are defining the member function **borrow** of the class **Book**.

A few minutes study of the definitions in Fig. 2.11 will convince the reader that we have

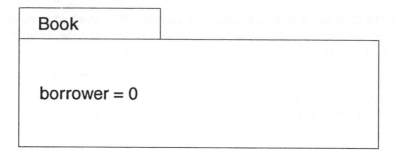

Figure 2.12 A C++ implementation object for Book.

implemented the book object just as we designed it. The operation **borrow** assigns (a pointer to) the **Person** who is to be recorded as its borrower. Conversely, the operation **_return** resets the borrower to **0**, which we are using to record that no one has the book. The **int** valued operation **inlibrary** simply returns the (logical) indication, **1** or **0**, that the book is or is not in the library (my room). Note that C++ uses **this** where Enact uses *self*.

The implementation of **Book** has been very straightforward. The major implementation decision has been that design objects will be implemented by implementation objects on the heap and referred to via pointers. So far, this implementation decision has apparently been a sensible one, giving simple and obvious implementations of our operations. This is a good sign.

The implementation of **Person** is going to require that we make use of a predefined C++ class **Set**. This corresponds to our use of the same object in the design. It is in fact *normal* practice when developing large C++ programs to depend upon a wide range of predefined classes, for collection types such as **Set**, for screen and disk management and specifically for the application domain. Reuse will be a major theme of later chapters of this book. That we encounter it from the beginning gives us the opportunity to discuss implementation in a realistic way from the outset.

To reuse an existing class we need to know its *protocol*, how to construct objects and how to access them. The protocols for our existing classes constitute our domain knowledge, on the basis of which we make our implementation decisions. As engineers of software, when we are designing, we anticipate the platform on which we are going to build by designing *for* the collection of existing classes which we plan to use. This is true whether or not our development is object-oriented, or our delivery language is object-oriented. However, when our development is object-oriented this particular method of viewing our target becomes not only simpler but the most natural of methods to adopt.

Our recollection of a protocol for a class will almost certainly be in the form of the way we will use objects of that class. This recollection will be based on our experience of using those objects in earlier implementations. So it is for **Set**. I remember its protocol as follows. I can create a new, empty set by using the constructor as follows:

```
x = new Set();
```

Having done so I can insert and remove items from the set using the following calls:

```
x->insert(p);
x->remove(p);
```

For this to work, **p** must be a pointer. I can interrogate the **Set** using various other operations. The only one I will need immediately is

```
x->member(p)
```

which is a logical (**int**) valued expression, true only if the pointer **p** is a member of the set **x**; that is, has been inserted and not removed. I shall not insert the same pointer twice. Consequently, I shall avoid the problems of not remembering whether or not that is allowed, and if it is, what it means. We will return later to an extensive discussion of the reuse of generic classes such as **Set** and so leave further discussion until then.

Having remembered how to use **Set** , our (correct) belief is that it will serve for the role we have for collections in implementing **Person**. This choice is confirmed by the class definition shown in Fig. 2.13. Once again we have made all members public. This is not in general a good decision. Indeed, it is one we shall rescind in later development of this example. It serves a minor purpose which we shall illustrate in a moment.

```
class Person{
public:
    Set* books;
    Person();
    void allocate(Book*);
    void deallocate(Book*);
};
```

Figure 2.13 C++ class definition for **Book**.

The members of class **Person** are obvious. A set for **books** is the data member. There is a single constructor which creates a new person and two other member functions, implementing **allocate** and **deallocate**, respectively.

```
Person::Person(){
    books=new Set();
}

void Person::allocate(Book* aBook){
    books->insert(aBook);
}

void Person::deallocate(Book* aBook){
    books->remove(aBook);
}
```

Figure 2.14 C++ member functions for **Person**.

The implementation of each of these member functions is straightforward. It is shown in Fig. 2.14. This is a straightforward transliteration of the design of each of these operations into C++ using the conventions we have adopted in the earlier part of this section. In particular, the decision to refer to everything through a pointer has survived this further implementation step. The constructor **Person::Person** is called, for example, by

```
p = new Person();
```

which constructs an object such as that shown in Fig. 2.15.

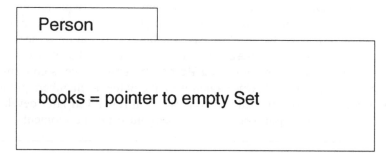

Figure 2.15 C++ implementation object for **Person**.

On calling the member function

```
p->allocate(b)
```

for example, then a pointer to the book borrowed is stored in the list attached to the member **books**. The implementation of our abstract system is now complete. We should always access the system through the operations on **Book** as our protocol determined. Thus we can call **b->borrow(p)** to add book **b** to the set of those currently borrowed by person **p**. This arrangement is shown in Fig. 2.16. We can add repeatedly to the books borrowed by **p** using **Book::borrow** and remove them from the list using **Book::_return**. Our conjecture is that this correctly implements our design.

Figure 2.17 shows the definition of five variables to hold books and persons. Each object is created by the appropriate constructor and a pointer to it is stored in the corresponding variable. This means that, for example, we can invoke an operation on one of these objects by

```
Stroustrup->borrow(David)
```

In order to test that such an allocation has worked, we could now execute a test such as the following:

```
if(Stroustrup->borrower == David)
        cout << "Stroustrup points to David\n";
```

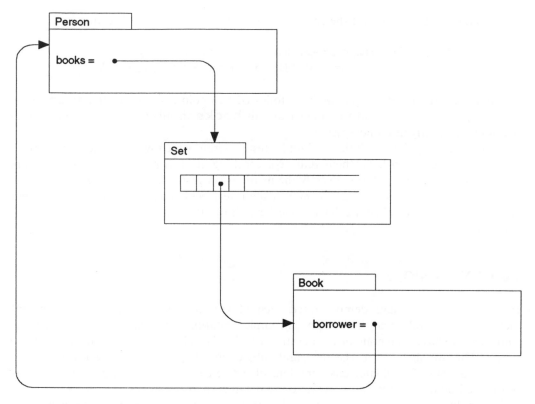

Figure 2.16 Storage structure for library.

In fact, we can test that conjecture even with just this little C++. It is the reason we left the data members of our two classes public. So let us do that now.

```
Book* Stroustrup=new Book();
Book* ChandyMisra=new Book();
Book* Smalltalk80=new Book();

Person* David=new Person();
Person* Hugh=new Person();
```

Figure 2.17 Setting up a test in C++.

Because we can access the data members of the classes directly (they are not hidden) we can access **Stroustrup->borrower** in this way. If the test succeeds, then we print an appropriate message. C++ uses streams for output (and indeed, for input). They have advantages over the normal input–output subroutine calls which we shall be discussing eventually. Meanwhile, suffice it to say that **cout<<"string"** prints the string on the principal output device (normally a screen).

In a similar way we can test the correctness of the link in the other direction:

```
if(David->books->member(Stroustrup))
        cout << "David has Stroustrup\n";
```

The only new thing here is that we have followed two pointers, one from **David** to the object representing him, and the other from his **books** member to the set representing the books currently in his possession.

We could, using these techniques, build a test program which would allocate the books to various people and have them returned, checking at each stage that these links are being properly recorded. Using exactly the methods suggested here could be quite tedious and in practice we would invest in more elaborate mechanisms of printing the current state of each object. What we have done here shows that such testing is achievable in principle.

2.6 CONCLUSIONS

In this chapter we have demonstrated each of the three stages of our development method, respectively analysis, design and implementation. The example has been fairly simple, so we have seen none of the iteration which takes place in practice in each of these stages. This we shall see in the next and subsequent chapters. Many issues have been raised and delayed until later chapters. Our objective has been to show how all the parts of the method fit together before we go on to detail each of the stages.

The analysis stage is based on the development of a conceptual model and is supported by rules about what information is to be collected about each object and by diagramming techniques which act as a visual reference for this information. We shall, in the very next chapter, enunciate these rules and diagramming techniques. The design stage is based on the idea of building a working model. The justification for doing this has yet to be explained. This is also covered in the next chapter. The Enact language is, we believe, comparatively trivial to learn. Models are very cheap to build. Consequently, we can afford to investigate various alternative proposed designs, before committing ourselves to implementation. This gives us the opportunity to explore the application domain, to understand the design options and to develop architectures for our products which will be both robust and flexible.

Design in the abstract is all very well. It is important to the well-being of our product. But it must be based on reality. The implementation stage of our methodology admits that some design decisions are influenced by the properties of the target platform. In this book we use C++ to illustrate the realities of implementation. Whilst the book is not a C++ primer, it is intended to be read by those familiar with programming but not with C++. Chapter 4 is devoted to a conversion course for those requiring a quick tour of the principal concepts of C++. Elsewhere in the book, new C++ concepts are described in a way which should be accessible to such a reader.

The material on C++ should also be of interest to the experienced C++ programmer, because I attempt to use C++ in the way that I believe its designers intended. C++ is much more than just an object-oriented language, although it is that aspect we shall concentrate on. It is a language which, like C, can be used in a very expressive way by the adoption of appropriate idioms. This idiomatic use is discussed and justified, or rather readers are asked to consider my justification and form their own opinions.

Throughout the book we work on examples. The example we have used here will be developed further. We shall enhance its functionality, we shall solve the problem of its user interface, and we shall solve the problem of the persistence of its data over time, that is, saving the data on disk. We shall also deal with the issues of the suitability of C++ as an implementation language for this application. We have already suggested that a database package would be a more economical solution (in development time), which it would. We shall show how the generic application, of which our mini-library is a specific example, is identified by exploring the application domain with our working model, and we shall show how ideally C++ is suited to the implementation of this generic product.

3

OBJECT-ORIENTED METHODS

3.1 INTRODUCTION

As we have seen in Chapter 2, object-oriented methods are central to our approach. In the last ten years, such methods have gained ascendancy over other methods of software design, primarily because they lend themselves well to the development of flexible software; software which is reasonably open to change throughout its lifetime. This is a key property of contemporary software. In this chapter we shall define the principal concepts of object-oriented methods and introduce tools, specifically diagramming techniques and a pseudocode, which enable these methods to be deployed at the analysis and design stages of software development.

The methods we shall describe are ones which we have found particularly useful. We shall not, however, be pedantic about their application. A good method, a good tool, should be a pleasure to use and should be adaptable to the way of working with which its user feels most comfortable. So you are expected to take the methods described here as examples and to adapt them to suit your own way of working. The diagramming techniques in particular are adapted to my own way of working. The diagrams are simple enough to scribble quickly with paper and pencil, which I find essential. Users of modern CASE tools will perhaps expect more decorative diagrams than those which I recommend, but they can easily extend the diagrams I will present. My diagrams have been stripped to the essential minimum. I find diagrams much the best way of quickly capturing a design idea and seeing the *whole* of a proposed system development. The iterative approach which I follow would have me discard many early alternatives, after the consideration which is possible when having them on paper in front of me.

Our method of software development will be to define an *abstract system* best suited to the application area in which we are working. An abstract system will be nothing more than a collection of abstract data types or, to use the object-oriented terminology, a collection of classes which are designed to have a sufficiently high level of abstraction that coding up the application is comparatively straightforward, but which have sufficient generality that the resulting application is open to future change in an economic way. To make our notion of abstract system more precise we must first define the principal concepts of object-oriented methods.

3.2 OBJECTS AS STATE HOLDERS

In the initial design of the simple library, described in Chapter 2, we introduced the notion of an object as being a record with attributes each of which has an associated value. As such, an object has state. We expect it to be represented in the computer by a chunk of memory. We expect to be able to change the state. Our method of modelling is guided by identifying, in the real world, entities whose state and whose relationships, each with the other, we wish to track, and to create in the computer exactly one object to represent each corresponding entity in the real world.

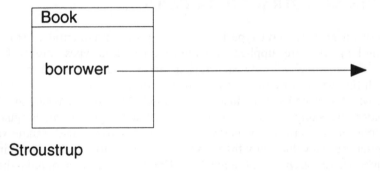

Figure 3.1 An object representing a book.

For example, the library keeps track of books. Each book is represented by an object such as that shown in Fig. 3.1. We only gave the book a single attribute, *borrower*, which was a pointer to the object representing the person who has borrowed the book. This was all that was required for the design, to the extent that we wanted to take it, to

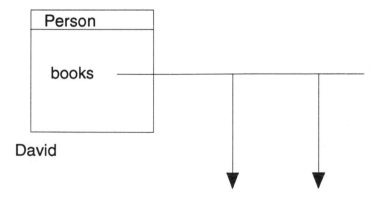

Figure 3.2 An object representing a person.

enable us to check the logic of borrowing and returning books. In a real application we would have to give the book object many more attributes, including probably title, author, publisher, acquistion number and so on. Once assigned, some of these attributes would remain unchanged. Others would change frequently to reflect the corresponding changes in the real world. The borrower attribute is a frequently changing one.

Similarly, the *Person* object shown in Fig. 3.2 may have many attributes. The one we focused on was the *books* attribute, which has a value which is a collection. In fact, a collection, as we shall see shortly, is itself an object. But collections are so ubiquitous in software design that we deal with them specially in our notations. So the collection valued attribute is shown in the diagram of Fig. 3.2 by a multi-headed arrow. The *books* attribute of a *Person* object records the books currently borrowed by that person. The collection contains (pointers to) exactly those book objects which represent the books he or she has borrowed.

3.3 OBJECTS AS ABSTRACT DATA TYPES

The notion of an abstract data type has become quite fundamental to software design. Programming languages are supplied with a few built-in data types, integer, float, boolean etc., and a few methods of data structuring, array, record etc. Many are now also provided with the means for constructing new data types. C++, for example, has the class mechanism, which can be used for just this purpose. What do we mean by abstract data type? Consider the sample, built-in data types of a programming language. Each is supplied with a set of operations which we are allowed to use to manipulate values of this type. Manipulating the values only through this set of operations, the user is indifferent to how the values are represented in the machine. For example, integers have the operations +, * etc. When adding two integers we neither know, nor care, whether their machine representation is binary, decimal or even some more esoteric form.

```
aBook := book()
aBook.borrow(aPerson)
aPerson:=aBook.borrower
aTruthValue:=aBook.inlibrary()
aBook.return()
```

Figure 3.3 Protocol for class *Book*.

We extend this notion to user defined types when we make use of abstract data types. We can say that our book object, for example, is an instance of an abstract data type because it is invested with operations, *borrow* and *return*, which enable us to manipulate it without knowing how it is represented. The very fact that we were able to define a *protocol* for use of the book object as shown in Fig. 3.3 is evidence of the nature of book as an abstract data type. The protocol gives us the ability to create new objects and to manipulate them in restricted ways.

In fact, we have allowed a little of the representation of the book object to show through to its user. This is because we have given the user knowledge of the *borrower* attribute. To be truly abstract we should have hidden this by defining an operation to return the person who has (currently) borrowed the book. I shall not be so pedantic in the early stages of analysis and design. The case for being more or less abstract has arguments on both sides. These we will expand in Chapter 9, after we have the more substantial developments of the book behind us.

3.4 OBJECTS AND CLASSES

The mechanism in object-oriented methods for introducing abstract data types is the *class*. Every object will be an instance of a class. We may say that the object belongs to the class. We may say that the class comprises the set of all objects (of that class). The class defines the operations which can be performed on objects of that class. So far, in our developing example, we have introduced two classes, *Book* and *Person*. Instances of the class *Book* are created by its constructor, which is the function *book ()* in Fig. 3.3. Once created, objects carry along with them an explicit indication of the class to which they belong. Thus, when an operation is applied to an object, it is the operation defined in the corresponding class which is actually invoked. Suppose our library were also to lend videos. Part of a suitable protocol is shown in Fig. 3.4. Suppose we have made the assignments

```
b := book().
v := video().
p := person().
```

Then the operations

```
b.borrow(p)
v.borrow(p)
```

are both equally valid, but they invoke different operations. The first borrow has been defined in the class book, while the second has been defined in the class video.

```
aVideo:=video()
aVideo.borrow(aPerson)
```

Figure 3.4 Part of protocol for class *Video*.

Traditionally the concept of class has been a difficult one to understand fully. Sometimes even the distinction between class and object is found to be difficult to understand. There are good reasons for this. Firstly, the concepts are not trivial. Secondly, they have been used somewhat interchangeably in the literature. Thirdly, they are very closely interrelated in all object-oriented languages and not always in the same ways. I find the easiest way to recall the distinction is to remember that the object is the record which has state and represents the real world entity being modelled. The class is the means for generating many instances of similar objects: it is the *type* that makes these instances similar and distinguishes them from objects of other types.

In the next chapter we shall study C++. For this language we shall see that class is very closely related to the type checking capabilities of the language and is very much a compile-time concept. That is, class names are carefully cross-checked by the compiler to ensure that all operations are applied to objects of the appropriate type (i.e. class). This checking having been performed means that C++ compilers can generate very efficient code which is safe, without having to have many run-time tests to determine object type.

Smalltalk, on the other hand, has no such distinction. Classes are themselves represented at run-time by special objects. This much more generous concept has many advantages and some disadvantages. It is not appropriate to discuss these here, since our objective is to develop a method targeted on C++. We shall, however, return to discuss the relative merits of Smalltalk in Chapter 10.

3.5 THE AUGMENTED ENTITY RELATIONSHIP DIAGRAM

When doing the analysis step of an iterative process of software development I have found the augmented entity relationship (ER) diagrams of Coad and Yourdon (see bibliography) to be particularly useful. In these diagrams, the key idea is to capture the relationships which will be established and maintained between the objects in an application. The diagram involves the classes rather than the objects, but is to be read as defining relationships between objects, as we shall see. This form of diagram has been popular for almost twenty years now in the database community and is one of the core constituents of contemporary CASE tools. The augmentation referred to is the extension to include inheritance, which we shall deal with in the next section.

Figure 3.5 ER diagram for *Book* and *Person*.

The simplest example of ER diagrams is that shown in Fig. 3.5. The diagram shows the class *Book* and the class *Person* as small rectangles, not as high as they are long. The relationship depicted by the line with crow's feet at one end is intended to represent the relationship between books and persons, which is that a certain book is with a certain person or that a certain person has a collection of certain books in his or her possession. The use of the word entity in the name of the diagram is traditional. I restrict myself to using the term entity to refer to the thing in the real world which is being modelled. Thus I would consider my copy of Stroustrup's book on C++ to be an entity in the real world. The corresponding object, depicted in Fig. 3.1, is the machine-resident representative used to model the real world entity in the developing application. The ER diagram shows the class *Book* in order to capture the notion that every book has the denoted relationship with a person.

We may or may not write the name of the relationship on the diagram. If it is not on the diagram, then it will be in the accompanying text (in the documentation). When I

Figure 3.6 ER diagram with functions named.

write the name of the relationship I anticipate how I am going to represent it in my model and in my eventual C++ implementation. The relationship of Fig. 3.5 will be represented by two attributes. The book has a *borrower* attribute whose value is a (single) person. The person has a *books* attribute whose value is a collection of persons. The relationship is one to many or many to one, depending on how you look at it, in that it relates one person to many books. We shall, eventually, record this information redundantly in the two attributes *aBook.borrower* and *aPerson.books*. This fact is recorded by writing the names of the attributes on the diagram in the positions indicated in Fig. 3.6. As I have repeatedly said, I am not pedantic about the use of diagrammatic notations. This particular form has been designed to have the least fuss and the least to remember for the recording of analysis and design information which I find most useful. So the labels may appear above or below the line; however, the end of the line at which they appear is relevant.

Relationships can also be one to one and many to many. For example, had the relationship in Fig. 3.5 been 'has at some time or another borrowed' rather than 'is currently borrowing', then it would have been many to many and had crow's feet at both ends. The other extreme must also be considered. In a relationship we take the oneness of the single-ended line to actually mean zero or one. And we take the manyness of the crow's feet to mean any number including zero. So the relationship depicted in Fig. 3.5 means that a book may or may not be on loan and that a person may have zero, one or more books. There are many different conventions in ER modelling for dealing with special cases, in particular for insisting that a relationship must be established and cannot be null. But in programming these seem less useful, and so I have not adopted any special notation to deal with them.

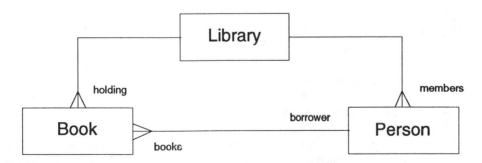

Figure 3.7 Personal library, ER diagram.

Let us develop the library example a little further to demonstrate a little more elaborate ER diagram. In Fig. 3.7 we have introduced a new class *Library*. We propose to have an object of this type to denote the library and to have this object related to books and persons in a particular way. The relationship between a library and some books is that the library currently holds those books, that is, has acquired them, whether or not they are on loan. The relationship between a library and some persons is that the library has those persons as its members, that is, they have at some time in the past joined the library. Note that both relationships are one to many, indicating our intention that a book can only be held by a single library and that a person can only be a member of a single library. The first assumption seems entirely reasonable while the second is not. However, since the intention of the application we will develop here is to model only a single library (i.e. there will be exactly one object of type *Library*) we need not deal with that issue here (but see Exercise 2).

So far what we have seen is a simple version of traditional ER diagrams. For object-oriented methods these diagrams have been augmented to cover inheritance, or subclasses, as we shall now see.

3.6 SIMPLE INHERITANCE

Consider again the extension to our library which records information about videos as well as books. We could make this extension by having a separate relationship between a person and the videos which that person has borrowed. This solution is sketched in Fig. 3.8.

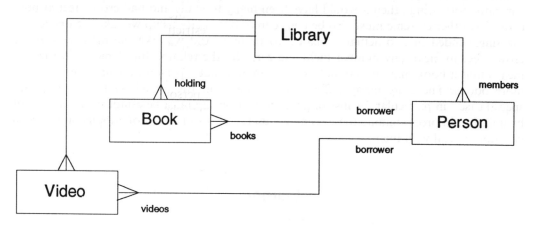

Figure 3.8 One possible extension, to include *Video*.

A rather neater solution however, which embodies better our objective of flexible, extensible software, is to make use of the notion of inheritance. Note that the solution of Fig. 3.8 would require us to design operations (*borrow, return*) etc. on videos not at all different from the operations we have already designed for books. This is trivial of course. We just copy them. But then their equivalence is no longer explicitly recorded. Future change is compromised in that changes will have to be made twice and that will not only mean extra work, but will probably eventually lead to error when changes are made inconsistently.

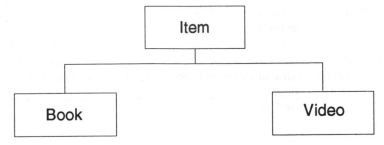

Figure 3.9 Inheritance: superclass with two subclasses.

Instead we introduce the notion of a subclass (or, alternatively, of a superclass). We recognize that books and videos are very similar. We introduce a class of items which are either books or videos. We call this class *Item*. We say *Item* is a superclass of *Book* and also a superclass of *Video*. Alternatively, we say *Book* and *Video* are both subclasses of *Item*. A book will have all the characteristics of an item and some unique ones of its own. Similarly, a video will have all the characteristics of an item and some unique ones of its own. An item is something which can be borrowed and returned, so the borrow and return operations clearly belong to *Item*. We say that the subclasses *Book* and *Video* inherit the operations *borrow* and *return* from *Item*. Figure 3.9 shows the diagrammatic means which we use to depict inheritance. The subclasses are arranged into a tree-like structure below the superclass. We would never intend to have objects of class *Item*, only objects of class *Book* and *Video*. This restriction is not one which it is necessary to obey, but it is one we have found to be useful. When the inheritance structure is included in the full ER model we arrive at the structure shown in Fig. 3.10. Note that the relationships are with the superclass *Item*. That is, the library has many items in its holding and each item may be borrowed by a person. As far as borrowing and returning are concerned, items do not have to be distinguished into books and videos. Part of the protocol which would now be established for this extended model is shown in Fig. 3.11. Note that all operations are on items. Only the constructors are specific to the

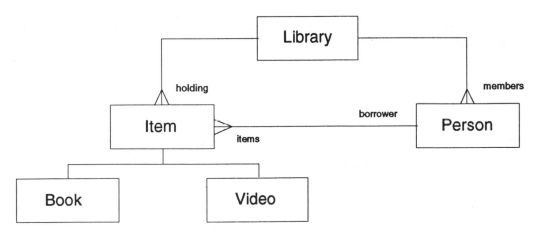

Figure 3.10 Alternative extension (better).

subclasses. When it is necessary to have distinct operations for book and video, these operations are defined differently in each subclass. However, it is normal for all subclasses of a given superclass to have exactly the same interface and for the behaviour of each operation to be different for each subclass. The fact that the behaviour of *borrow* and *return* is identical for both kinds of item is perhaps a little unusual. It is a bonus.

```
aBook:=book()
aVideo:=video()
anItem.borrow(aPerson)
anItem.return()
aPerson.items
anItem.borrower
anItem.inlibrary()
```

Figure 3.11 Protocol for *Book* and *Video*.

As a trivial example of different behaviours, consider how we might implement an operation on a person which gives us the number of books currently on loan to him or her. In our model we have only recorded the collection of items, so the size of this collection is not the answer, since it will also include the videos on loan. A simple way to calculate the value that we want is first to construct the collection of books held by the person and then to calculate the size of that collection. To construct the collection of books from the collection of items we will have to work our way through the larger collection, choosing those items which are books. So we would require for this purpose an operation such as *anItem.isaBook()* which returns *true* when *anItem* is a book and returns false when it is a video. This effect can be achieved by giving separate definitions for each subclass:

```
Book.isaBook() := true.
Video.isaBook() := false.
```

Note that the protocol is still *anItem.isaBook()*, but that this is realized by two separate definitions.

Actually, while this is an adequate solution, it is not the best one. With an operation like *isaBook* it is a good idea to define

```
Item.isaBook() := false.
```

and then to override this definition in the case of *Book* by the addition of

```
Book.isaBook() := true.
```

Now when we call *anItem.isaBook()*, if *anItem* is a book then the definition attached to *Book* is invoked and we get true. If *anItem* is a video, since there is *no* definition of *Video.isaBook()* then the operation in the superclass is invoked and we get *false*. This is a classic example of inheritance in action. The reason this solution is better is that it states explicitly that only *Book* will respond *true* to *isaBook*; everything else will respond *false*. So in future, when we extend the library yet again by adding a new subclass to *Item*, say *CD*, we do not need to define *CD.isaBook()*, but simply inherit the operation from *Item*.

We have only described simple inheritance, where each subclass has exactly one superclass. Later we shall encounter multiple inheritance, where each subclass has more than one superclass. In this case it inherits attributes, and in particular operations, from all its superclasses. There are naturally occurring situations when multiple inheritance seems the appropriate mechanism to use. Rather than contrive an example here, we shall leave it until Chapter 5, when one such natural occurrence appears, and deal with the relevant properties there.

3.7 COLLECTIONS

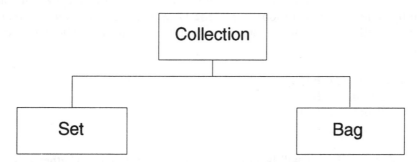

Figure 3.12 Class hierarchy for collections.

We shall make much use of collections in this book. Indeed, all major software applications need to make use of different kinds of collection. The classification of collections has been one of the major successes of object-oriented methods. The Smalltalk collection classes, described in Goldberg and Robson, have been extremely influential. There are many libraries which can be purchased which supply collection types based on the Smalltalk classification. C++ compilers usually come equipped with equivalent libraries; see, for example, Borland and Zortech offerings in this respect. The NIII library has been publicly available for a long time now. Details of these references are given in the bibliography. It is important to a programmer's productivity that he or she has access to a suitable library of collections. The above sources are among the many that a programmer might go to for such support. It would be impractical for us to try to introduce any of those substantial libraries in this book, but we do want to give the flavour of them. Accordingly we will introduce a trivial library which serves the purpose of the applications developed here. The entire library is presented fully in Appendix 2. Here we make a start on its definition and use it as an example when we describe Enact later in this chapter and when we describe C++ in the next.

We shall have only two types of collection, a set and a bag. The difference is that a set only records the first insertion of an object, whereas a bag records every insertion. If an object is already a member of a set, inserting the object again will not change the set. Figure 3.12 shows the classes involved here. Every *Collection* is either a *Bag* or a *Set*.

```
aBag:=bag()
aSet:=set()
aCollection.insert(anObject)
aCollection.remove(anObject)
aTruthValue:=aCollection.member(anObject)
aNumber:=aCollection.size()
```

Figure 3.13 Protocol for `Collection`.

We can insert and remove objects from collections of either type and we can enquire whether or not an object is currently a member of either type of collection. We can also enquire of the size of either type of collection. A summary of the protocol for this subset of the operations on collections is shown in Fig. 3.13. This means that we can construct a collection by either of the operations $c := set()$ or $c := bag()$, and in either case we get an empty collection. Now we can, for example, execute the following sequence of operations

```
c.insert(ob1).
c.insert(ob2).
c.insert(ob1).
c.size().
```

The response to `c.size()` will be either *2* or *3* depending upon whether *c* is a set or a bag.

Appendix 2 shows that there are many more operations than just these few on collections. We shall introduce them throughout the remainder of the book as we need them.

3.8 PROTOCOL DESCRIPTION

We have made quite a lot of informal use of the notion of protocols in this and the previous chapter. In many respects this is the central notion behind the object-oriented methods we are describing and the basis for the definition of abstract systems. We shall see in Chapter 9 how the concept of a protocol is related to theoretical advances in software engineering. In this section I just want to be a little more precise and lay down some ground rules for describing protocols. I shall give two forms: the textual form we are already used to and an alternative diagrammatic form. The textual form tends to be the more appropriate for capturing the evolving design and recording a concise definition of the protocols. The diagrammatic form gives a better view of the *whole* of the abstract system and the relationship between the various operations within it. Each has its merits. Each is complete in its own right. It is possible to derive one form from the other, if all the relevant information has been recorded. We have not always been so careful in the past, a problem which we shall put right here.

```
aBook := book()
aBook.borrow(aPerson)
aPerson:=aBook.borrower
aTruthValue:=aBook.inlibrary()
aBook.return()
```

Figure 3.14 Protocol for *Book*.

First let us look at the textual form. The protocol is the interface which a user has to an abstract system. The abstract system is a collection of classes along with their operations. The protocol is therefore specified by writing typical invocations of the operations. We adopt the convention for naming variables (which comes from the Smalltalk literature) that the class name prefixed with 'a' or 'an' is a variable of the class type. Thus, in the protocol specification shown in Fig. 3.14 the variables *aBook* and *aPerson* are considered to be of type *Book* and *Person* respectively. Next we distinguish between operations which are functions and operations which are procedures, called for the side-effect they have of updating objects to which they have access. Functions return a value and have no side-effect, a convention which we adopt uniformly because we believe it leads to good design. In the protocol they are always shown in assignment statements so that the type of their result can be denoted. Operations called for the effect they have are, of course, not shown as having a result. In Fig. 3.14 only *borrow* and *return* have a side-effect.

Another distinction which we have to make is whether an operation is a *method* of one of the classes or simply a global subroutine. Here *borrow, return* and *inlibrary* are methods of the class *Book*. They are invoked using the dot notation and it is this notation which makes it clear in the protocol that these are indeed methods. The only global subroutine in Fig. 3.14 is the constructor function *book()*.

Of course, the protocol is not just syntax, as in Fig. 3.14. We need to accompany this with narrative describing to the user how to understand the relationship between the operations. The narrative for this protocol may run something like the following.

An object of class *Book* is used to represent a book. A book records the identity of a person to whom it is on loan. A book is created by the constructor *aBook := book()*. Subsequently we can record that it is on loan to *aPerson* by the call *aBook.borrow(aPerson)*. When the book is returned to the library, its allocation to a person can be removed by the call *aBook.return()*. The truth-valued function *aBook.inlibrary()* is *true* only when the book is currently in the library and *false* otherwise. When it is *false*, the identity of the person who has borrowed it can be determined by accessing the attribute *aBook.borrower*.

There is no merit at all in making the attribute *borrower* explicitly available to the user. We should better have hidden it behind an operation. Recognizing this we shall defend our decision at this stage by saying that during analysis and early design we do not always distinguish between these two concepts. In fact we think of the attribute *borrower* (as seen by the user) as if it were an operation, a function. We certainly do not intend that users be allowed to assign to the attribute. They must restrict themselves to the usages shown in the protocol.

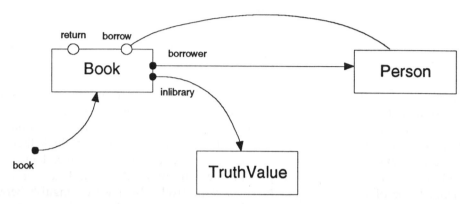

Figure 3.15 Protocol diagram for *Book*.

When we come to capture the protocol information in diagrammatic form, then we adopt drawing conventions which make these distinctions clear. Figure 3.15 shows a protocol diagram for the interface to *Book*. It has exactly the same information in it as the textual form in Fig. 3.14. A function is shown by a small black dot, its result class is at the head of an arrow and its arguments, if any, are connected to the dot by lines. An operation with a side-effect is shown by a larger, open circle. Its arguments are connected to the circle by lines. When an operation is a method (what C++ will call a member function) the operation symbol (dot or circle) is shown embedded in the edge of the box denoting the class of which it is a method. Apart from the order in which arguments appear in a call, all the information in the textual form of the protocol is recoverable from that in the diagrammatic form. The elements which comprise a protocol diagram are shown in summary in Fig. 3.16. Figure 3.17 gives a diagram for the protocol of collections as introduced in the previous section. We have shown the result of the two constructor operations as if they create collections. It would be more correct to have shown the targets of these operations as the appropriate subclasses, as in Fig. 3.18. I regard this as rather a matter of taste and prefer the less cluttered diagram (Fig. 3.17) that results from leaving the subclasses implicit.

In practice, as we develop an abstract system, we define operations on classes which eventually get hidden from the user of the abstract system as higher level operations subsume them. Thus the diagram we might use to document a part of the system for subsequent maintenance will include operations which we do not propose should be available to the user. It is only necessary to note that more or less detailed protocols will be required for each purpose.

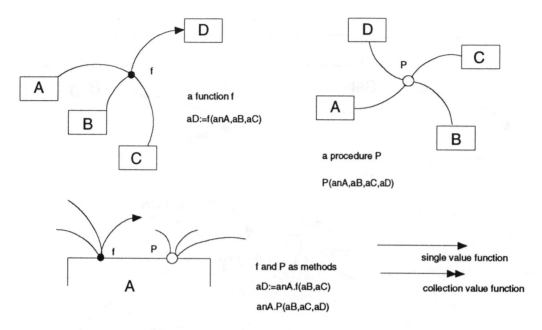

Figure 3.16 Elements of protocol diagrams.

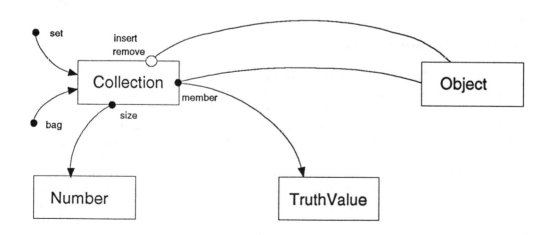

Figure 3.17 Protocol for *Collection*.

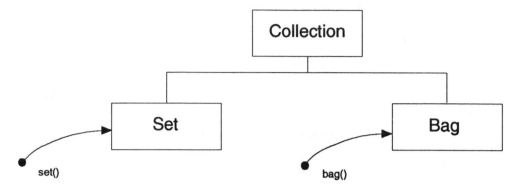

Figure 3.18 More accurate protocol for constructors.

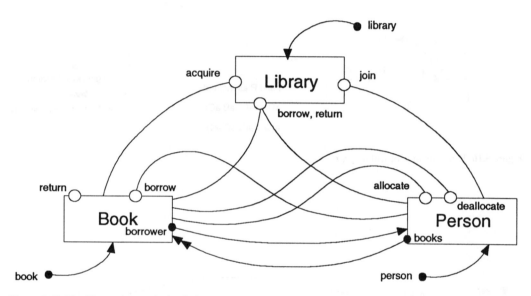

Figure 3.19 The library as seen by its designer.

In this respect, let us give both forms of the protocol for the extended library of Fig. 3.7. If we include all of the operations, the entire protocol for all three classes, on a single diagram then we get the designer's view in Fig. 3.19. This diagram is so cluttered that in practice it would be separated into three diagrams, one centred on each of the classes. The user's view is much simpler. It is shown in Fig. 3.20. Both these diagrams include some new operations on *Library* which we have not yet defined (see Fig. 3.36 and accompanying text). The operations of borrowing and returning are now operations on the library object (presumably invoking the operations on *Book*). Who is the user? In our case, later in the book we shall write a complete application including a menu-driven front-end for recording borrowings. So the user of this abstract system is that application. The abstract system depicted in Fig. 3.20 is the part of the eventual system which records the current library status in a form in which it can be interrogated and updated. Actually, there are still a couple of operations missing from both these diagrams. Eventually we

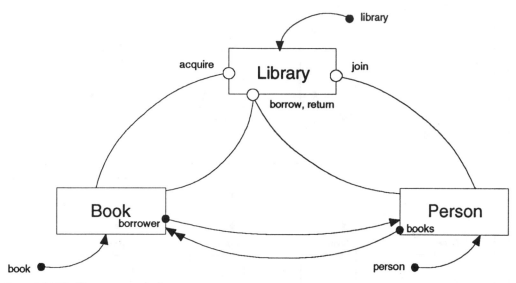

Figure 3.20 The library as seen by its user.

shall reveal them. You might like to consider for yourself what they are before we encounter them in Chapter 7.

3.9 THE OBJECT DIAGRAM

In Chapter 2 we saw a third kind of diagram which I have found particularly useful. This is a diagram which displays the actual objects rather than the classes. I call it, I trust appropriately, the object diagram. I actually find it useful at two quite distinct stages of development. The first stage is at the very beginning of design, or even part way through the analysis stage, when I am trying to convince myself and perhaps colleagues that the proposed model is in fact complete and consistent. Then a sketch of the abstract layout of objects and their pointers to each other can be accompanied by a verbal description of how the major operations are going to be carried out. The fact that the object diagram contains no more information than the ER model is not relevant here. The argument can be made more convincingly using the object diagram.

The second occasion on which I find the object diagram most useful is much later when considering the obligations C++ places upon its users for memory management. We need to be able to determine when storage for objects can be recovered, and this requires that we know which objects have access to which. This is a topic we shall leave until much later in the book, when we have studied sufficient of C++.

The object diagram is quite straightforward. Figure 3.21 shows the object diagram for part of the library. There are two diagramming conventions, one for boxes and one for arrows. Each object is a box, this time taller than it is wide, with its class name clearly marked in a section at the top of the box. The remainder of the box is used to record the value of attributes. Where we want to be able to refer to the object in the accompanying narrative we write the name of the object below (or alongside) the box which represents it.

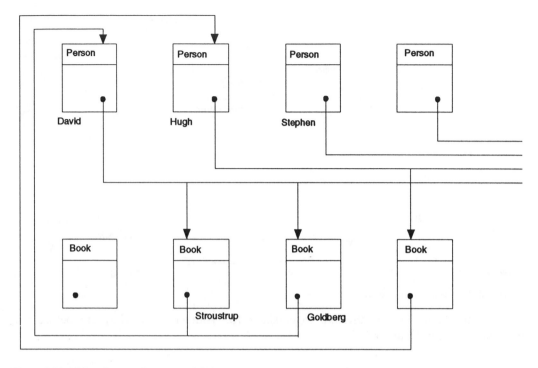

Figure 3.21 Object diagram for personal library.

Next, we use arrows to denote object-valued or collection-valued attributes of an object. A single-headed arrow serves for an object-valued attribute. In Fig. 3.21 each book has a single-valued attribute *borrower* which is shown by the arrow pointing to a person. When many books point at the same person we gather their arrows into a single arrow with many tails, as we have done with the arrows from *Stroustrup* to *David* and from *Goldberg* to *David*.

A collection-valued attribute is shown by an arrow which has many heads and disappears off the diagram as if going on for ever. Each person in Fig. 3.21 has a collection-valued attribute *books* shown by such an arrow. The empty collection is shown by a disappearing line with no heads. In the diagram, *Stephen* has no books.

We may or may not include the name of the attribute on the diagram. Where it is obvious from the accompanying narrative which attribute is meant we shall usually leave it off the diagram.

The object diagram complements the ER diagram by presenting the same information in a different way. The ER diagram corresponding to Fig. 3.21 is the very simple diagram in Fig. 3.5. In a sense, Fig. 3.21 could be automatically derived from Fig. 3.5. It is not always the case. In going from Fig. 3.5 to Fig. 3.21 we have made it clear that we have decided to store the relationship between *Book* and *Person* *in both directions*. We could have decided differently, and almost certainly will in larger systems. An alternative object diagram for Fig. 3.5 is shown in Fig. 3.22. Here we see that we have have only stored the information about who has which book in one direction, from *Person* to collection of *Book*. We have, however, access to the collection of all persons. To determine who has a

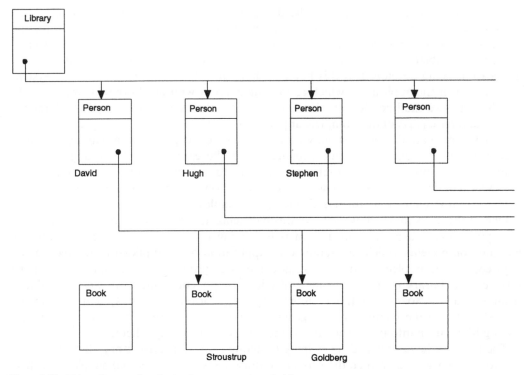

Figure 3.22 Object diagram for alternative arrangement of objects.

particular book we must search each person in turn. This is a much poorer way to record the relationship, but it does illustrate our point. The existence of alternative object models for the same ER model is what makes the object diagram so valuable. Using it we can clearly argue the merits of one organization over another.

The organization of these diagrams on the page is quite important. You will see that I have adopted a policy of drawing arrows in regular arrangements reminiscent of buses on hardware diagrams. The arrangement of arrows into bundles running parallel to each other is used to suggest that they have the same meaning or purpose. The arrangement of objects into regular groupings has a similar effect. It is worth experimenting with various different organizations on the page; since the purpose of the diagram is to communicate to your colleagues (or to yourself at some future date) you want to make the diagram as evocative as possible. This diagram is the closest I have been able to come to acquiring the benefits which a hardware design acquires from a circuit diagram.

3.10 ABSTRACT SYSTEMS

Now we have introduced all the elements which constitute the notion of an abstract system, the notion which underpins the methods described here. Basically, we are advocating object-oriented methods. The notion of an abstract system is a way of organizing the elements which constitute an object-oriented method into a reasonably coherent methodology. An abstract system is what we aim for. It is the product of the analysis stage and the beginning of the design stage. It comprises a set of interrelated classes each implementing an abstract data type. Ultimately we define a protocol for the entire abstract system in terms of the protocol for each class which comprises it. Usually we define an abstract system for each important part of our eventual product. For the application being developed in this book we have already developed an abstract system for the part of the application which records data about who has borrowed which book. In Chapter 5 we shall develop an abstract system for the user interface and in Chapter 7 for the database parts of our complete application.

In developing an abstract system, we try to develop concepts which are at a sufficiently high level of abstraction that the explanation of the expression of the application is relatively straightforward, so that our attempts to reason about its correctness are relatively painless. But we also want the abstractions to be sufficiently close to the machine that implementing them is also relatively painless.

One of the ways in which we achieve this balancing act between the respective needs of the application and its implementation is by aiming for reusability of components. By making components which are reusable in application after application we reduce the high cost of the implementation constraint upon our productivity. In our case we have targeted our library on reusing some collection components which we expect to obtain from a library. Also, anticipating a lifetime of change for our abstract system will encourage us to make the components as generic as possible, so that we are not constantly having to dig deep into them when it becomes necessary to change them.

The tools we have provided for helping to iterate toward a satisfactory abstract system are to be seen as aids rather than as mandatory steps in a development plan. Each is complementary to the other. The ER diagram helps the analyst focus on the classes and the relationships between the real-world entitities, which will be mirrored in the objects of those classes. The protocol description, probably initially textual, helps the analyst focus on the behaviour of the sytem being analysed and, as he or she becomes a designer, helps to design a suitable interface to the eventual computer-based solution. Once a protocol has begun to settle down I find that the protocol diagram helps me to recognize gaps in the interface and shows up complexities which are best removed by another iteration.

The object diagram provides a third view of the system under development. We have said that it is useful closer to implementation, a situation we won't encounter in this book until a little later. But it is also useful very early on when trying first to get a handle on the classes. Don't be afraid to postulate an object diagram and then throw it away. It will help you to understand some of the entities involved in the eventual solution.

Of course the objective of the analysis stage is to end up, after a few iterations, with a consistent set of diagrams and protocols constituting an abstract system which can convincingly be defended as an adequate understanding of the problem in hand and a realizable solution to it. When that stage is reached we very definitely move on to design.

3.11 THE DESIGN STAGE

Clearly there is no firm dividing line between analysis and design. Once we have arrived at an abstract system with protocols informally specified we have reached the point in design, however, where we must get down to the details. For this purpose many methods advocate the use of a *pseudocode* which is either textual or graphical. So shall we, but with the added possibility that, with a little extra work, this pseudocode can actually be executed with the benefit that some very definite evaluation of the design can take place. Many inconsistencies and incompletenesses which might not be detected until we are much later in the development processes (executing C++) might be detected by an executable *working model* at this stage.

Now of course the key qualification here is whether or not the additional effort involved in writing pseudocode which is executable is indeed very small. There is one reason why it might be and one reason why it might not, which we must discuss before we proceed further. The reason why it might be quite economical is that the pseudocode can be at a very high level of abstraction, requiring only very short implementations of each function because the high level abstractions which it provides are well suited to the nature of the problem. The reason why the cost might not be low is that the very nature of pseudocode is lost by making it executable. The reason that pseudocode is advocated for early detailed design is that it is partly formal and partly *informal*. Where users of pseudocode do not wish to enter too deeply into design they can simply incorporate an informal description. This possibility is lost if the pseudocode is executable (at least in the way we shall encounter it in Enact). So our proposal to build a working model hinges on the fact that the modelling language (replacing the pseudocode) is simple and cheap to use by virtue of its high-level concepts and that the benefits which accrue from early detection of inconsistencies far outweigh any additional cost which is incurred.

Whether or not you decide to use the executable form of Enact, you will find the basic concepts of Enact form a suitable pseudocode. That is to say, Enact can be used as a pseudocode, where gaps are left and where some parts are left unelaborated, left simply as an informal statement. The framework which Enact supplies for capturing the details of the design before proceeding to C++ is such that the eventual implementation step is much more economically and soundly made.

Of course, I shall proceed on the assumption that you may wish to execute the Enact working model and I will provide all the necessary information to make that possible. I shall develop the example via working models and describe the benefits of doing that as I go. I believe that this is an efficient route even to learning C++, because it will now begin to confirm our understanding of the basic ideas of object-oriented programming and equipped with these we shall be better able to make sense of the way in which they are supported within C++.

3.12 INTRODUCTION TO ENACT

We have already made some use of Enact in Chapter 2 without being specific about how the expressions in the language are constructed. Also, when writing protocol descriptions in this chapter we have been making use of Enact as a pseudocode. Now it is time to be precise about how Enact is to be written if it is to be acceptable to the interpreter. If you have access to a machine on which Enact will run it is worthwhile typing in some of the examples which we shall use to illustrate the language, just to confirm your understanding of it.

There is nothing special about Enact, except that it can be provided by the author free of charge. Appendix 1 gives details of how to use the version supplied with this book and how to obtain other versions. Indeed, other languages would be just as suitable, and in many respects more suitable to the purpose to which we are going to apply Enact. In Chapter 9 we shall discuss the relative merits of Smalltalk and ML as alternative modelling languages and describe how the methodology advocated here can be simply adapted to the use of those languages in place of Enact. We shall even discuss the use of C++ itself for modelling – it has some advantages and some, I think overwhelming, disadvantages. Again, these discussions must be left until the very end of the book.

Enact is a very simple language. It is provided with some high-level abstractions which fit well with the development of models from ER analysis, in particular, the use of collection-valued attributes to record relationships and the powerful operations which are supplied for manipulating collections. In fact, Enact is a marriage of ideas from functional programming and object-oriented programming. It is a marriage of ideas from ML and Smalltalk. The extent to which this marriage was advisable and the extent to which it has been successful is for the reader to judge. We shall be discussing it from a theoretical and a practical point of view in Chapters 9 and 10 respectively.

3.13 ENACT IS AN EXPRESSION LANGUAGE

The primary building block for programs in Enact is the expression. An expression comprises variables, constants and operators, and always has a value. The simplest example of an expression is an arithmetic expression, such as

```
a + 2 * b
```

Here we have an expression with two variables (a and b), one constant (2) and two operators (+ and *). All operators have a precedence which we define numerically, although it is really only relative precedence which is important. In fact, the numerical precedences of + and * respectively are 5 and 4. Lower numerical values for precedence means that the operator binds more tightly, so that the above expression has its usual mathematical meaning in that * binds more tightly than + .

The emphasis on precedence is important because Enact is built *exclusively* from expressions formed by operators and operands. The operators all have a precedence. There are 13 levels of precedence from 1 (highest) to 13 (lowest) and they are organized so that familiar mathematical and programming expressions acquire their usual meaning.

4	* / mod
5	+ –

Figure 3.23 Precedence of arithmetic operators.

Arithmetic expressions involve integer constants, integer-valued variables and the five arithmetic operators shown in the precedence table in Fig. 3.23. Integer arithmetic is performed with (at least) 32 bit accuracy. The division operator a/b computes the quotient and *a mod b* computes the remainder. Operator precedence can of course be overridden in the usual way using parentheses, so that the expression

    (a + 2) * b

causes the addition to take place before the multiplication, as we would expect.

Where an operator such as minus is used without parentheses, as in

    a − b − c

we need to know which minus is done first in order to know what this expression means. In Enact the left operator will be evaluated first. It is as if we had written

    (a − b) − c

which is in fact the usual interpretation of the former expression. Explicit parentheses must be used if this is not what was intended. If a complex expression is written, and there is any doubt in the author's mind as to the grouping, then the most sensible thing to do is to include extra parentheses to ensure the required evaluation. If the author has doubts then a reader certainly will. The technical term for the disambiguating grouping (of operators of the same precedence) to the left is called *left association*. We say binary operators of the same precedence are left associative. All Enact operators are left associative, which is exactly what we want in all but a few cases. We shall point out the problem cases when we encounter them.

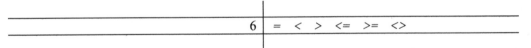

Figure 3.24 Precedence of relational operators.

The next most important form of expression is the truth-valued expressions formed by comparing arithmetic values. This is achieved using the usual relational operators shown in Fig. 3.24. They all have lower precedence than the arithmetic operators, so that an expression such as

    a + 1 < b * 2

is, as we would expect, a comparison between the two arithmetic values *a+1* and *b*2*. This expression will evaluate to one of the truth values *true* or *false*. The only unusual operator is the one we have chosen for not equal to: *<>*.

Truth values can be combined using the usual operators *and* and *or* and the function *not*, which have the precedence shown in Fig. 3.25. Consider the binary operators first. Their relative precedence means *and* binds more tightly than *or*, as is usual and their precedence relative to arithmetic and relational operators means that we can write many

3	*not*
7	*and*
8	*or*

Figure 3.25 Precedence of logical operators.

truth valued expressions without parentheses. For example

$$0 < a \quad and \quad a < n + 3$$

parses as if we had written

$$(0 < a) \quad and \quad (a < (n+3))$$

The function *not* is unary and has higher precedence than *and* and *or*, as is usual. Since its precedence is also higher than arithmetic and relational operators, its argument usually needs to be parenthesized, as in *not (a<b)*. Taking together all the operators we have introduced so far allows us to write arithmetic- and truth-valued expressions in the form with which we are familiar from mathematics and other programming languages. Variables are simple identifiers made from letters and digits and the underscore character. The only restriction is that the initial character may not be a digit. Constants are either integers or one of the truth values *true* and *false*. Negative integers are prefixed with the symbol ~ rather than the minus sign. So

$$1 - 7 = \sim 6$$

is a true statement. Enact does not have a unary minus. The best way to negate the value of an expression is to subtract it from zero, for example,

$$0 - x$$

10	*then if*
11	*else*

Figure 3.26 Precedence of conditional operators.

Now we move on to an unusual feature of Enact, the way that it defines conditional expressions. In fact, as Fig. 3.26 shows, these are built from binary operators just as any other expression. The simplest form of conditional expression is illustrated by

$$x < y \quad then \quad x \quad else \quad y$$

which means, 'return the value of x if $x < y$, otherwise return the value of y'. The two operators *then* and *else* work together as follows. The expression a *then* b evaluates a. If it is *true*, it then evaluates and returns b , otherwise it returns the special value *undefined*. The expression c *else* d first evaluates c . If this is *not* the special value *undefined* then the value of c is returned, otherwise d is evaluated and its value returned. In the example we have given above, which actually parses as

```
((x<y) then x) else y
```

the subexpression *((x < y) then x)* will evaluate either to the value of x or to *undefined*. The expression formed with the *else* operator will accordingly evaluate to either the value of x or the value of y , exactly as we have stated it would.

The relative precedence of *then* and *else* , to each other and to the arithmetic relational and logical operators, means that most conditional expressions can be written with minimal parentheses. For example,

```
x = 0  then  0  else
y = 0  then  0  else  a/(x*y)
```

needs no extra parenthesization. The evaluation order guarantees that the division by $x*y$ will only be performed if both x and y are non-zero.

The omission of *if* from the above forms is unusual, but not difficult to get used to. In fact, Enact uses *if* as an alternative to *then* so that b *if* a means the same as a *then* b , so the above expression could have been written

```
0 if x = 0
else  0 if y = 0
else  a/(x*y)
```

and has exactly the same meaning.

In addition to the operators defined in this section, Enact provides list processing primitives and various other operators which we do not require in the remaining chapters of the book. A complete list of the Enact operators is included in Appendix 1.

3.14 FUNCTION DEFINITION

The principal means of computing with Enact is by means of function definition. When interacting with the implementation one normally constructs a number of function definitions in a file, loads that file into the Enact system and then interacts with the system by calling various of the functions with actual arguments. The Enact interpreter then prints the computed value on the screen. Let us look at some simple function definitions.

```
f(x,y) := x + y.
```

This defines a function f which has two arguments, assumed to be numbers, and returns their sum. Once defined in this way we can invoke the function with calls such as:

```
f(99,273).
f(99,f(99,99)).
f(x+1, y*99).
```

The number and type of arguments must match exactly. Consider now a more useful definition:

```
min(x,y) := x < y then x else y.
```

which computes the minimum of two numbers. We can use this to compute the minimum of four numbers by a call such as

```
min(min(a,b), min(c,d)).
```

Usually in Enact we build more powerful functions by combining lesser functions, as for example,

```
min3(a,b,c) := min(a, min(b,c)).
min4(a,b,c,d) := min(a, min3(b,c,d)).
min5(a,b,c,d,e) := min(a, min4(b,c,d,e)).
```

The expression after the := is called the function body. For a function to be called from inside another function body, it is necessary that that function has been previously defined. This means that the interpreter must see it first. The above sequence of definitions obeys this rule. We could not have presented them to the interpreter in another order (but see Appendix 1 for chapter and verse on this restriction).

We can, however, make recursive definitions, such as:

```
fac(n) := n = 0 then 1 else n * fac(n-1).
```

where the recursive call is correctly interpreted. This, you should recognize, is the familiar factorial function. We shall not have a lot of need of recursion in Enact used as a modelling language for our methodology. Rather, we make use of the common iterations over collections which are captured in special library functions.

	3	function application
		arithmetic,
		relational,
		logical,
		conditional operators
	12	:=

Figure 3.27 Function definition, precedences involved.

The way in which the interpreter parses function calls and function definitions depends on the precedences of the two operators involved. These are shown in Fig. 3.27. There is an operator involved in function application. Uniquely it is represented by no symbol at all. The call $f(x,y)$ is considered to be an occurrence of the function application operator between the function f and the argument list (x,y) . This 'invisible' operator has precedence 3, higher than any of the operators introduced so far. This means, for example, that

```
f(1,2) * f(3,4)
```

applies both functions before multiplying their results.

When we make a function definition we do so using the assignment operator $:=$, which has precedence 12, lower than any operator introduced so far. A definition is of the form

```
Expression := Expression
```

where the expression on the left of the assignment is a function application with variables as its arguments and where the expression in the right of the assignment is any form of expression at all, usually involving all the arguments from the left.

We shall actually only need to make use of the simplest of the facilities which Enact provides for function definition and application. Nevertheless, it is important for the reader to note that these facilities are defined with the meanings that have come to be conventionally accepted, in particular with respect to binding, which is described in the appendix and will be described a little later in this chapter when we encounter what are called lambda expressions.

3.15 ASSIGNMENT STATEMENTS AND STATEMENT SEQUENCING

The assignment operator can be used to assign directly to variables (and, as we shall see later, to the attributes of objects). At the topmost level, when interacting with Enact, this can be most useful; for example,

```
a := min(43,47).
b := min(72,103).
c := min(a,b).
```

returns the values of the three computed minima for us to inspect (assuming that we are checking that our definition of min is working). The value of an assignment statement is the value assigned, but this is seldom useful.

12	:=
13	;

Figure 3.28 Relative precedence of sequencing and assignment.

We can also use assignments in the body of function definitions. We must also make use of the sequencing operator *;*, whose precedence is the lowest possible (13), as Fig. 3.28 shows. Semicolon is just a binary operator which evaluates its two arguments in order from left to right. Now look at the following alternative definition:

```
min4(a,b,c,d) :=
    (x := min(a,b);
    y := min(c,d);
    min(x,y)).
```

The body of the function consists of a sequence with assignment statements. The relative priority of *;* and *:=* ensure this is interpreted correctly. The assignments to x and y are performed first and then the value of *min(x,y)* is computed and returned as the result of the function. So x and y are behaving as temporary variables. Now for the unusual part. Neither x nor y, mentioned in the body of this function, are global variables. In fact the occurrences of x and y in the body of the function behave as locally declared temporary variables. If we had had global variables x and y, they would be unchanged by a call to this version of *min4*. All variables in an Enact function body are taken to be local to the body. This is to discourage the building of models with a dependence on many global variables. We shall see that this is not too big a restriction. Again, the binding rules in Enact are fully explained in Appendix 1.

One last imperative feature of Enact is used to construct iterations: the loop operator. In fact, the Enact user is discouraged from using this low level feature. It is used to define some basic operations over lists, as you can see in Appendix 2, section 4, and its meaning is described fully in Appendix 1. The use of Enact for modelling requires that we remain at a high level of abstraction and low level iteration using loop or recursive function definitions is discouraged. Finding yourself doing it should be taken as a sign that the design you have developed may not be adequate. You may not have fully understood the domain. Look for a model which avoids these concepts.

3.16 CLASSES AND OBJECTS

Now for the important part. In Enact an object is always created as belonging to a particular class. So before we can create an object we must establish the class it is to belong to. Let us take the simple example of a point in space represented by two coordinates x and y, such as might be found in a simple graphical package. Let us introduce a class *Point* to be the type of such an object. In Enact we would write

```
class Point < Object.
```

Here class is a binary operator with the lowest priority (see Fig. 3.29). It collaborates with the < operator to recognize the names of the two classes which are the arguments of < . The right-hand argument must be a class which already exists and the left-hand argument is then created as a subclass of this existing class. To get things started, Enact provides the class *Object*, which then becomes the root of all classes. This is the simplest mechanism

1	new
3	. same as application
6	<
7	with
13	class

Figure 3.29 Precedence of operators for objects and classes.

for introducing new classes. When we study multiple inheritance we will see a more general solution.

Now that we have a new class, we can create objects which belong to it by using the operator *new*, as follows:

```
aPoint := new Point.
```

The precedence of *new* is very high, as can be seen from the table of object and class operators in Fig. 3.29. The above assignment creates an object, but one with no attributes. Another binary operator `with` allows us to create an object with some initialized attributes, as follows:

```
aPoint := new Point with x = 7 with y = 12.
```

You should now be an expert at seeing how the relative precedence of these operators works. Because `with` is of lower precedence than either *new* or = (see Fig. 3.29) the evaluation of the above expression creates first a new `Point`, then gives it attribute x initialized to 7, then gives it attribute y initialized to 12.

Since creating points is going to be a common thing, and since this is a rather long expression, it is recommended that you use a constructor function to create them. An Enact convention for classes is that their names shall have an initial capital letter. Then the same identifier, but with an initial lower-case letter can be used for the constructor, so

```
point(x0, y0) :=
        new Point with x = x0 with y = y0.
```

Now we can use this repeatedly, for example,

```
aPoint1 := point(7,12).
aPoint2 := point(~7,~12).
```

Next we need to be able to access the attributes of an object. This is where the dot operator is used. This is an operator with the same priority as function application, for reasons which will become apparent. So we can write, for example,

```
aPoint1.x + aPoint2.x
```

selecting the *x* attribute of the two points and then adding them. We can also assign to attributes

```
aPoint1.x := 8
```

which overwrites the value in the attribute *aPoint1.x*.

Next, let us look at the definition of methods. In Enact, no new machinery is needed. This is achieved in Enact by a function definition, where the function is given a special form of name. For example:

```
Point.shift(x0,y0) :-
        (self.x := self.x + x0 ;
        self.y := self.y + y0).
```

This is the definition of a method which has a side-effect on the point to which it is applied, adding values to both its *x* and *y* attributes, with the effect of shifting it in space. This method would be invoked, for example, by the call

```
aPoint1.shift(10,17)
```

after which the value of *aPoint1.x* will have been increased by *10* and the value of *aPoint1.y* will have been increased by *17*.

Going back to the definition we see that the function name has the class name prefixed to it. This is the way we indicate which class the method belongs to. Inside the body of the method, as well as accessing the explicit parameters *x0* and *y0* we have access to an implicit parameter *self* which is initialized to the value of the object to which the method was applied. Suppose we make the call *aPoint1.shift(10,17)*. When evaluating the body of *Point.shift* the variable *self* has the value *aPoint1*.

An alternative definition might have been

```
Point.shift(aPoint) :=
        (self.x := self.x + aPoint.x ;
        self.y := self.y + aPoint.y).
```

which would be called, for example, as

```
aPoint1.shift(aPoint2)
```

or, even

```
aPoint1.shift(point(10,17))
```

Note how in the body of this new definition the attributes of the point being shifted are distinguished from the attributes of the point being used to measure how far to shift by.

It is important to distinguish between methods such as *shift*, which have a side-effect on the object to which they are applied, and methods which have no effect. Consider the following method:

```
Point.shifted(aPoint) :=
        (x := self.x + aPoint.x ;
        y := self.y + aPoint.y ;
        point(x,y)).
```

This is a pure function. It has no effect upon the object to which it is applied (or any other object); rather it creates a new object which has a shifted value. It would be called, for example, by

```
aPoint3 := aPoint1.shifted(aPoint2)
```

Neither *aPoint1* nor *aPoint2* would be altered by this call. The definition could have been written more neatly as

```
Point.shifted(aPoint) :=
        point(self.x + aPoint.x ,
              self.y + aPoint.y).
```

but although this is shorter it is in no way different in effect from the earlier definition. Recall that the variables x and y in the earlier definition are local to its body.

3.17 SIMPLE INHERITANCE

```
class GeometricObject < Object.

class Point < GeometricObject.

class Circle < GeometricObject.
```

Figure 3.30 Classes for geometric objects.

Suppose now that we decide to elaborate our geometric objects to include, as well as *Point*, such objects as *Circle, Rectangle, Polygon* etc. How might we organize these classes into an appropriate hierarchy with *Point*? The things they have in common we would put into a superclass and put only the unique features into the relevant subclass. Then objects of the subclass will inherit the common properties of the superclass. A simple illustration will suffice to make this point clear. Consider only the classes *Point* and *Circle*. The property they have in common is the fact that both will have an x, y position in space. A *Circle* will in addition have a *radius*. We could simply make *Point* the superclass and *Circle* the subclass, but a slightly more elaborate solution is to be preferred. We introduce a new class *GeometricObject*, which is to be the superclass. It will have no objects, other than objects of its subclasses. We will make *Point* and *Circle* subclasses of *GeometricObject*, as shown in Fig. 3.30.

```
point(x0,y0)  := new Point with x=x0
                            with y=y0.

circle(x0,y0,r) := new Circle with x=x0
                              with y=y0
                              with radius=r.
```

Figure 3.31 Constructors for geometric objects.

The constructors for these new objects are shown in Fig. 3.31. We do not provide a constructor for *GeometricObject* because we do not intend to use objects of the superclass type. This convention is referred to as making *GeometricObject* an abstract class, a concept we shall explain fully when we study C++. An operation such as *shift*, which is equally applicable to *Point* and *Circle*, can be implemented as an operation of *GeometricObject* as follows:

```
GeometricObject.shift(x0,y0) :=
      (self.x := self.x + x0 ;
       self.y := self.y + y0)
```

Now if we define

```
aPoint := point(7,12) .
aCircle := circle(15,33,50) .
```

the operations

```
aPoint.shift(10,17)
aCircle.shift(10,17)
```

both invoke the inherited function defined for *GeometricObject*.

Some operations will have identical definitions for each subclass and can then be put in the superclass, as we have done for *shift*. Of course, this is not true of all operations. For example, suppose we define on operation *size* which returns a measure of the sizes of each *GeometricObject*. Its definition will be different in each subclass.

```
Point.size() := 0 .
Circle.size() := self.radius .
```

Now if we have a variable which has been initialized to contain a *GeometricObject*, but we don't know of which subtype, the call

```
aGeometricObject.size()
```

will invoke one or other of the above methods as appropriate. At design time, we don't know which. In either case we will get the correct number as result.

Now we are in a position to illustrate one of the strengths of object-oriented design: its ability to define generic methods which call more specific methods. Suppose we require a function which compares the sizes of two *GeometricObjects*. We can define

```
GeometricObject.biggerthan(aGeometricObject) :=
    self.size() > aGeometricObject.size() .
```

This is a generic method which is defined in the superclass, so we can call it with any of the following forms:

```
aPoint.biggerthan(aPoint)
aPoint.biggerthan(aCircle)
aCircle.biggerthan(aPoint)
aCircle.biggerthan(aCircle)
```

In all cases the calls to the subclass method *size* will be to the method determined by the type of object to which it is applied. The great strength of object-oriented programming is its ability to define generic methods of this sort. When we come to extend the classification of *GeometricObjects* to include *Rectangle*, *Polygon* etc. we will need to define size operations on them, but we will not need to redefine *biggerthan*. The extensibility of the design is considerably enhanced by this property. We shall see it occurring again and again in subsequent pages.

3.18 COLLECTIONS

In Enact there are certain predefined functions and predefined classes. They are all listed in Appendix 1. Fundamental to the use of Enact as a modelling tool for software development is the nature of the very simple, yet adequately powerful, *Collection* classes.

```
class Collection < Object.

class Bag < Collection.

class Set < Collection.
```

Figure 3.32 Declaration of classes for collections.

We have two different kinds of collection, respectively a bag and a set. The classes for these have been declared as shown in Fig. 3.32, which should be compared with the diagram in Fig. 3.18. Each of the subclasses *Bag* and *Set* has its own constructor; for example, we call

```
aBag := bag() .
aSet := set() .
```

```
Set.insert(anObject) := ...
Bag.insert(anObject) := ...
Collection.member(anObject) := ...
Collection.remove(anObject) := ...
Collection.size() := ...
```

Figure 3.33 Some methods for collections.

to create empty collections of each type. The various simple operations and objects of this type have been described. Their definitions have the form shown in Fig. 3.33. We can use these operations, for example, to build up a collection of points, using assignments such as

```
aBag.insert(aPoint1) .
aBag.insert(aPoint2) .
```

We can determine whether or not a particular point is in the collection by a call such as

```
aBag.member(aPoint)then ...
```

```
class Person < Object.

person():= new Person with books=set().

Person.allocate(aBook):=
    self.books.insert(aBook).

Person.deallocate(aBook):=
    self.books.remove(aBook).
```

Figure 3.34 Enact model of *Person* (cf. Fig. 2.8).

We make use of collections to model multi-valued relationships. For example, in our library, we intend that a *Person* shall have a collection of books, those currently on loan to that individual. This has been modelled in Enact, as shown in Fig. 3.34. When a person is constructed with the call

```
aPerson := person() .
```

then an object of class *Person* is created, with an attribute *books* which is a collection, a set, initially empty. Subsequently, when we call

```
aPerson.allocate(aBook)
```

then this in turn invokes

```
aPerson.books.insert(aBook)
```

which adds *aBook* to the collection. Since this collection is a set, the book will only actually be added if it is not already in the set.

In the expression *aPerson.books.insert(aBook)* the dot operator associates to the left so that the first subexpression to be evaluated is *aPerson.books* which, as we know, is a set. The insert method is then applied to this set, so it is the method *Set.insert* which is invoked. When we make the call

```
aPerson.deallocate(aBook)
```

however, this in turn calls

```
aPerson.books.remove(aBook)
```

Once again, *aPerson.books* is a *Set*, but there is no operation *Set.remove*, so the operation invoked this time is *Collection.remove* (see Fig. 3.33). This is the simplest form of inheritance in action.

```
class Book < Object.

book() := new Book with borrower=nil.

Book.borrow(aPerson) :=
    (self.borrower:=aPerson; aPerson.allocate(self)).

Book.return() :=
    (self.borrower.deallocate(self); self.borrower:=nil).

Book.inlibrary() :-
    self.borrower=nil.
```
ß

Figure 3.35 Enact model of class *Book* (cf. Fig. 2.27).

When we developed our library a little further, we included a class *Library*, which was to have two collection-valued attributes, *members* for the people who joined the library

```
class Library < Object.

library():=new Library with members=set()
                        with holding=set().


Library.acquire(aBook):=
  self.holding.insert(aBook).

Library.join(aPerson):=
  self.members.insert(aPerson).

Library.borrow(aPerson,aBook):=
  aBook.borrow(aPerson).

Library.return(aPerson,aBook):=
  aBook.return().
```

Figure 3.36 Enact model of class *Library*.

and *holding* for the books acquired by the Library. Figure 3.7 gives the ER model for this elaboration and Figs. 3.34, 3.35 and 3.36 together give the Enact model of this elaboration. The model of the Library class is particularly relevant here. We see the use of sets again to record books acquired by the library and people who join as members. We also standardize on a (abstract system) user interface by redefining the operations *borrow* and *return* in a uniform way on the *Library* object. Even though we do not need to know who has returned a book, our model requires that we supply a person as returner. This might afford some opportunity for checking that the person does indeed have the book, but we do not take this opportunity. You may be worried by this, and you should be. But everything will be OK in the eventual application, because the surrounding application code, as we shall see, will guarantee that when a book is borrowed it is indeed available for loan and when it is returned, it is indeed returned by the 'correct' person.

If we have defined

```
    aLibrary := library()
```

then we can refer to *aLibrary.members* and *aLibrary.holding*. This will afford us the opportunity to illustrate some of the more powerful operations on collections which make modelling in Enact an economical thing to do. There is nothing original about these 'higher level' operations. They are available in Smalltalk and common in functional programming languages. We adopt the naming convention of Smalltalk in order to clarify the relationship for readers who know that language or who go on to study it as an alternative to Enact.

Figure 3.37 shows the definition of the higher order operations on collections. The operation

```
aCollection.collect(aFunction)
```

constructs a new collection by applying *aFunction* to each member of *aCollection*, and collecting the results. Suppose we define

```
numberofBooks(aPerson) := aPerson.books.size()
```

then the call

```
aLibrary.members.collect(numberofBooks)
```

will apply the function *numberofBooks* to each member of the *Library* in turn. This results in a collection of numbers. It will be a collection of the same type as *aLibrary.members*, that is a set. So we have constructed a set of numbers. If we were doing this interactively with the Enact implementation, then we might make the assignment

```
aSet := aLibrary.members.collect(numberofBooks).
```

To see the result it is necessary to ask Enact to show

```
aSet.members
```

which is a printable list, in this case a list of numbers, such as

```
(0 7 1 2 4)
```

showing that the various members of the library currently have either 0, 7, 1, 2 or 4 books on loan. Note that, since the result is a set, none of the numbers is repeated. If, as is likely, more than one individual has (say) 0 books, when 0 is collected into the result set this repetition is subsumed.

```
aCollection:=aCollection.collect(aFunction)
aCollection:=aCollection.select(aFunction)
aCollection.forEachDo(aFunction)
```

Figure 3.37 Some higher order operations on collections.

The second higher level operation on collections allows us to select those members of a collection which satisfy a certain property. The call

```
aCollection.select(aFunction)
```

again applies *aFunction* to each member of *aCollection*. This time *aFunction* is truth-valued and the effect of the above call is to construct a new collection by selecting those members of *aCollection* for which *aFunction* is true.

For example, suppose we define the function

```
inlibrary(aBook) := aBook.inlibrary()
```

then we can make the call

```
aSet := aLibrary.holding.select(inlibrary)
```

to construct in *aSet* the subset of *Books* from *aLibrary.holding* which are actually in the library.

Both the higher order operations *collect* and *select* are pure functions. They construct new collections as a result and do not alter the collection to which they are applied. One higher order operation which is called for its side-effect, however, is

```
aCollection.forEachDo(aFunction)
```

Here *aFunction* is applied to each member of *aCollection* for the effect it has. For example, if we define

```
return(aBook) := aBook.return()
```

then make the call

```
aPerson.books.forEachDo(return)
```

then we work our way through the collection *aPerson.books* and apply the function *return* to each one. This higher order operation is much to be preferred to the basic looping facilities of Enact. Models should be so defined that iteration over collections using *collect*, *select* or *forEachDo* are capable of succinctly defining the meaning of all application-level operations.

There are other higher level operations, which are summarized in Appendix 1. Where we make use of them in the more advanced stages of the book, we shall introduce them at that time.

3.19 LAMBDA EXPRESSIONS

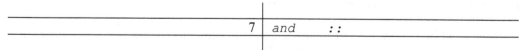

Figure 3.38 Operator for constructing lambda expressions.

You will have noticed the need to define explicit functions for use with the higher order operations of the previous section. There is a shorthand that can be used instead, a means for defining a function without having to give it a name. This is a so-called *lambda expression*, a name acquired from functional programming. A similar facility in Smalltalk is the block construct. C++ has no equivalent, so when applying higher order operations in C++ we shall be forced to define named functions. But for modelling, it is often simpler to use the lambda expression.

As an example, the lambda expression

```
aPerson::aPerson.books.size()
```

has the same meaning as the function *numberofBooks*. The lambda expression is constructed using the operator *::* (which has precedence 7; see Fig. 3.38). The left-hand operand of *::* is a variable or a list of variables, the arguments of the function. The right-hand operand of *::* is an expression forming the body of the function. Care has to be taken with the relative precedence of operators in the body of the function. If their precedence is higher than 7 that is OK, but if any operator in the body has precedence lower than 7, the body must be enclosed in parentheses. A lambda expression denotes a function. Just as

```
numberofBooks(aPerson) := aPerson.books.size()
```

defines a function, which we can refer to as *numberofBooks*, so the above lambda expression defines the same function. We use the lambda expression itself to denote the function. So the call

```
aLibrary.members.collect(aPerson::aPerson.books.size())
```

constructs a set of numbers, being the numbers of the books on loan to various members of the library. Similarly,

```
aLibrary.holding.select(aBook::aBook.inlibrary())
```

constructs a set of books, those members of *aLibrary.holding* which are not currently on loan. Finally,

```
aPerson.books.forEachDo(aBook::aBook.return())
```

will apply the *return* operation to each member of the set *aPerson.books*.

Consider the two statements

```
newSet := set()
aSet.forEachDo(anObject::newSet.insert(aFunction(anObject))).
```

This has the effect of constructing *newSet* from *aSet* by applying *aFunction* to each member of *aSet* and collecting the result. In other words, it means the same as

```
newSet := aSet.collect(aFunction).
```

A glance at Appendix 2 will show you that this is not how *collect* is implemented. It is presented here to convince you that *forEachDo* is quite general purpose. Where the higher order operation which you require is not already provided by Enact, it can usually be defined using *forEachDo*. The recommended method of modelling is to encapsulate appropriate iterations over collections in higher order operations like *collect* and *select*. By and large, *collect* and *select* will be adequate for our purposes here.

3.20 CONCLUSIONS

This chapter has run through all of the elements of our analysis and design tools. These comprise the means for developing an object-oriented abstract system and capturing it in diagrammatic and textual form using entity relationship diagrams, protocol specifications and a diagram of the arrangement of objects which we call the object diagram. We have seen the pseudocode which we use to capture a protocol textually develop into an executable modelling language, Enact, which has the abstractions within it necessary to build a working model of our evolving design. In particular we have seen how collections can be used to model many-valued relationships, and this will form the basis of the modelling method we shall apply in subsequent chapters. The theoretical basis for the development steps we advocate will be discussed, but not until Chapter 9. And we leave until Chapter 10 a discussion of alternative approaches to the one we advocate here.

The target for our developments is C++. Before we proceed to the implementation of our application we need to study C++. This we shall begin in the next chapter. After a concise introduction to C++, intended to be accessible to programmers unfamiliar with the language and of interest to those who already know it, the remainder of the book is devoted to developing sufficiently elaborate examples that the reader may be convinced that there is some substance to the methods which we advocate. So, without further ado, let us begin with C++.

3.21 EXERCISES

1. Devise a protocol for communicating with a simple vending machine. The machine will accept a coin and dispense a chocolate. No chocolates will be dispensed unless they have been paid for. What restriction does that place on the possible order of operations in your protocol?

2. The ER diagram of Fig. 3.7 allows us to have more than one library coexisting. Extend the model so that a person can be a member of more than one library and show how the protocol can be extended to distinguish between the books that he or she has on loan from each.

3. Fully develop the Enact model of the extension to the library which allows members to borrow books and videos (see Fig. 3.10 and accompanying text). In particular develop operations which allow the library to determine easily how many books and how many videos an individual currently has on loan.

4. Extend the library model so that the collections of books in and out of the library are held separately. Does this implementation make any difference to the operations we define as part of the protocol?

5. A system for filing documents is required. Documents may be stored in folders, which in turn may be stored in cabinets. Develop an abstract system for this problem and create an Enact model of it.

6. Large assemblies of mechanical and electrical components are organized hierarchically. The depth of the hierarchy is not usually fixed. For example, a PC consists of a motherboard, disk drive etc. The motherboard in turn consists of memory banks, processing chips, peripheral chips etc. Develop an abstract system which allows information about such assemblies to be recorded and queried.

7. Using the description of systems built from assemblies of components developed in answer to Exercise 6, it is possible to do simple fault analysis as follows. Basic components are marked as faulty or non-faulty. Assemblies which contain at least one faulty component are deduced to be faulty. Develop a protocol for adding this fault information to the objects representing components.

8. Given a set s and a set t, using only the operations $collect$ and $select$, show how to construct the set which contains all the members of s which are also members of t. Show how to construct the set whose members are in either s or t but not in both. What do your operations do if s and t are bags?

9. An alternative way of modelling relationships, rather than having each object in the relationship have a (possibly collection-valued) attribute, is to use a special association object (see Rumbaugh). For example, the relationship that a person borrows a book introduces an association object to record the borrowing. The object refers to the person and the book. The library contains a set of such associations to record all current borrowings. Develop a model of this sort for our simple library and compare its complexity with the model developed in the chapter.

10. The fact that a book is borrowed by a particular person is recorded redundantly in our simple library. We have the constraint

```
aBook.borrower=nil or
    aBook.borrower.books.member(aBook)
```

A similar constraint can be defined for each person as follows:

```
aPerson.books.all(aBook::aBook.borrower=aPerson)
```

See Appendix 1 for a definition of `aCollection.all`. Define similar constraints for the relationship between a library and its holding and a library and its members. When is it ever necessary to test that such constraints are indeed satisfied?

4

INTRODUCING C++

4.1 INTRODUCTION

C++ is an important language. It has become the standard language for much of system programming activity and increasingly the language of choice for application programming. Many of the suppliers of C compilers now supply C++ as their standard offering, where their compiler can be used to compile either language; for example, see the Borland and Zortech documentation, referred to in the bibliography. There are many reasons why C++ has achieved this ascendancy. Primary among these reasons is that it is an extension of C, which had already gained great importance because of its role as the programming language for UNIX and for many of the major PC applications. Another reason for C++'s ascendancy, which we should not ignore, has been the availability of good compilers. The combination of a language which provides support for the facilities programmers want, in this case object-oriented methods in an extension of C, with the availability of good compilers from major suppliers, has ensured a rapid growth in the market for C++.

The language is, to my way of thinking, an elegant, if rather complex, extension of C. In its turn, C was an elegant language, which established a tradition for programming basic systems software in a high-level, machine-independent way. The elegance of C hinges on its ability to balance the needs of the machine language programmer (for efficiency, in particular) with the productivity of the high-level language programmer who operates at a higher level of abstraction. The earliest version of C to gain widespread use is usually referred to as Kernighan and Richie (or K&R) C, as a reference to their seminal book *The C Programming Language* (see bibliography). Many compilers for C used to be advertised as conformant to the K&R 'standard'. The next version of C to gain acceptance was the eventual official standard ANSI-C, now documented in the later version of Kernighan and Richie's book. ANSI-C cleaned up some of the problems which had developed with respect to interpretations of K&R C and, significantly, added stronger type checking to the language. The development of C++, by Stroustrup, began before this standardization was completed, but was clearly aware of the ANSI work.

Consequently, to the maximum extent that it is possible, ANSI-C is a subset of C++. This has significant commercial advantages for the users of both C and C++. Much code which companies own was written long enough ago to have been written in K&R C. New code which they write will almost certainly be written in ANSI-C or C++. Old code will, when economically viable, be rewritten in one of the more modern dialects. That C++ can be adopted by a company still needing to use C (old or new) for commerical reasons is a consequence of the decisions made by the language's designers, for which we must give them much credit. C++ is assured of a long life because of this link with the past.

It has a link with the future too, for there have been many (evolving) versions of C++. Version 1 has been available for many years. It has been superseded by Version 2, which is the version we shall describe here. Forthcoming extensions, available in Version 3 of the language, will be discussed later in the book as we encounter the need for them. And perhaps its most abiding link with the future is its openness as a language. C++ is a language which is a good platform for many different styles of programming. It is a particularly good platform for the object-oriented style and it is that aspect of C++ which we shall emphasize here.

This chapter has been written for someone who already has experience of programming but not necessarily of C or C++. We shall introduce, rapidly to begin with but with increasing gentleness, those concepts which we will need later in the book as the foundation of our programming. This chapter is self-contained. It can be read on its own. It is a primer for the subset of C++, and the style of usage of C++, which we adopt throughout the remainder of the book. Advanced C++ topics are delayed, either to be introduced as needed or to be discussed in Chapter 9.

4.2 EXPRESSIONS IN C++

Highest precedence

				!	logical not
		*	/	%	multiplying
			+	-	adding
<	>	<=	=>		comparison, inequality
			==	!=	comparison, equality
				&&	logical and
				||	logical or
				=	assignment

Lowest precedence

Figure 4.1 Relative precedence of some C++ operators.

Expressions in C++ always have a value. Statements which are executed for their effect only are distinguished from expressions. They are introduced later. The simplest form of expression is an arithmetic expression, such as

```
a + 2 * b
```

This is an expression with two variables, one constant and two operators. The variables will have been declared to be of some numeric type. Let us assume for the moment that they are integers and have been declared:

```
int a,b ;
```

Then in the original expression we are doubling the integer valued **b** and adding **a** to it. The arithmetic operators have their usual relative precedence. The relative precedence of each of the arithmetic, relational and logical operators is shown in Fig. 4.1. We see that multiply and divide have the same precedence and both have higher precedence than addition and subtraction. This is the relative precedence we have always learned to expect for these operators, both in mathematics and in programming. Of course, the precedence can always be defeated by the use of parentheses. Thus

```
(a+2) * b
```

does the addition before the multiplication.

char	a single byte, big enough to hold a single character
int	an integer, usually 16 or 32 bit, whatever is natural for machine
long	an integer, with at least 32 bit precision
float	a floating point number, natural size for machine, usually 32 bits
double	a double precision floating point number, usually 64 bits

Figure 4.2 Some arithmetic types in C++.

C++ expects all variables to be declared and to have a type. The declaration given earlier introduces two variables of type **int**. This is the most common type for simple variables to have in C++ programs, as we shall see. Figure 4.2 lists some of the arithmetic types available in C++ with an explanation of their differences. C++ tries to give the programmer the ability to write portable code while still having reasonable control over the performance of the code generated by the compiler. For example, if a variable is being used to store a return code which is a small integer in the range (say) 1 to 1000, then the programmer will probably declare that variable to be of type **int**. The space allocated for it will then be guaranteed to be big enough (2 bytes) and the actual space allocated will be an amount which is natural for the machine for which the code is generated. This guarantees that the generated code will be simple and efficient. If, however, the variable to be declared is known to take on values in excess of those which can be represented in 2 bytes, then the programmer will declare the variable to be **long**, ensuring at least 32 bit accuracy. The source code of the C++ program thus records the programmer's design decisions in a portable way, whereby the compiler can take advantage of architectural properties of the machine for which it is compiling. This is a degree of control still much needed by systems programmers but wrapped up in a way which makes it tolerable for those who don't need it. It very much demonstrates the way in which the spirit of C has been retained in C++.

Returning now to the operators listed in Fig. 4.1, a little explanation of the C++ idiosyncrasies is warranted. Most arithmetic operators will group to the left, when this matters. So, for example,

a - b - c

means the same as **(a-b) - c** and had we intended differently we would have had to insert parentheses explicitly to achieve it.

Highest precedence

	&&	logical and
	||	logical or
	?:	conditional
	=	assignment

Lowest precedence

Figure 4.3 Relative precedence of **?:**, (cf. Fig 4.1).

The relational operators **<**, **>**, **<=** and **>=** are as we would expect. Comparison for equality and inequality uses unusual forms of the operators, respectively **==** and **!=**, pronounced 'equals' and 'not equals', respectively. Numerical values can be compared using these six operators in expressions such as

a + 1 < b * 2

An unusual feature of C++ is that it uses numerical values to represent truth and falsity. True is represented by **1** and false is represented by **0**. So the value of the above expression will be **0** or **1**.

The choice of operators for logical and and logical or is **&&** and **||** respectively. Thus

0 < a && a < n + 3

is a well-formed logical expression. If **0 < a** evaluates to **0** (false) then the whole expression is false, **a < n + 3** not being evaluated. If **0 < a** evaluates to **1** (true) then **a < n + 3** is evaluated and its value becomes the value of the whole expression. The meaning of **||** has a similar property of only evaluating its second argument if necessary. These operators are sometimes referred to as conditional logical operators, to distinguish them from operators which evaluate both arguments (**&** and **|** in C++). We shall always make use of the conditional operators.

The remaining operators in Fig. 4.1 which we have not explained, respectively have the highest and lowest precedence. The logical negation is written

! (a<b)

where the parentheses are essential because **!** has higher precedence than **<**. The assignment operator will be dealt with later. It is included in the table largely to explain the C++ convention, inherited from C, that assignment is **=** and equality comparison is **==**.

The reader may be intrigued that the comparison operators have not all been given the same precedence. The reason, I believe, is so that **==** can be used as logical equivalence as well as numerical equality. Thus an expression such as

$$\textbf{a < b == c < d}$$

can be written without parentheses to mean **a < b** and **c < d** are either both true, or both false (not, I suspect, a very useful feature).

Another unusual form of expression in C++ is the conditional expression. We describe it here, mostly for completeness. We shall introduce a conditional statement later which is commonly used in preference to the conditional expression. The expression

$$\textbf{x < y ? x : y}$$

is a conditional expression which has the value **x** if **x < y**; otherwise it has the value **y**. The operator here is a combination of the two symbols **?** and **:** (which can be read as *then* and *else*, respectively). In terms of its relative precedence, as Fig. 4.3 shows, it is slightly less binding than the logical operators and slightly more binding than assignment. However, despite knowing this, my experience with this expression is such that I often guard against misinterpretation by enclosing both the subexpressions and the entire expression in extra parentheses, unless they are entirely trivial, thus making it clear what my intentions are.

Use of the conditional expression can be cascaded; thus

$$\textbf{x == 0 ? 0 :}$$
$$\textbf{y == 0 ? 0 : a/(x*y)}$$

can be written without extra parentheses. Since subexpressions are evaluated only if necessary, **a/(x*y)** will only be evaluated here if both **x** and **y** are non-zero. Note that, the conditional expression can be used to define conditional logical operators. For example, **(a&&b)** means the same as **(a?b:0)**, while **(a||b)** means the same as **(a?1:b)**. Conditional expressions are very versatile, but I seldom see them used. It seems that in practice, conditional statements are both adequate and more tolerable. We shall meet them soon.

4.3 FUNCTION DEFINITIONS

Programs in C++ are built as collections of function definitions. In C++ functions may or may not return a value. Functions may or may not have a side-effect. In general, the way of using C++ is to put a collection of function definitions into a file and then to compile that file. Figure 4.4 shows a trivial, but complete, C++ program comprising two function definitions. Let us study how that program has been built.

```
#include <iostream.h>

int f(int x, int y){
  return x+y;
}

int main(){
  cout << f(99,273) << " " << f(99,f(99,99)) << "\n";
  return 0;
}
```

Figure 4.4 A trivial, but complete, C++ program.

The first function definition is

```
int f(int x, int y){
    return x + y ;
}
```

which defines the function **f** to have two arguments, respectively **x** and **y**. Both arguments are of type **int**, and the result of the function is of type **int**. The body of the function is the bit in braces. It is in fact a compound statement (as we shall discuss later) but the salient feature is that it contains a **return** statement which includes an expression to be evaluated to determine the result of the function on each call. All of the syntactic elements shown here are essential, including the declaration of types for arguments and results, the braces around the body of the function and the semicolon which comprises part of the return statement.

In C++ a single function such as **f** is not a complete program. We need an infrastructure around it to present a standard structure to the compiler. The compiler expects to find a definition of a function **main** (which may or may not have parameters, about which more later). From **main** we arrange to call the functions, such as **f**, that we have defined and arrange to print out values computed by these functions. In Fig. 4.4 we show a conventional definition of **main**, with no arguments but with a result type **int** , which will be a return code used by the operating system to determine whether or not the program has been successful. Deep in the body of **main** we see some calls of the function **f**. In particular, we see

f(99,273)

which invokes **f** giving **x** the value **99** and **y** the value **273**. Since both actual arguments are already of type **int**, this process of initializing the arguments of the function is straightforward. In general, as we shall see later, this can involve quite subtle type conversion, a task which C++ undertakes on our behalf, normally with great success. The function returns the value **372** to the site of the call. The call

```
f(99, f(99,99))
```

will invoke **f** twice, first with **x=99**, **y=99** to return **198**, then with **x=99**, **y=198** to return **297**. Thus the consequence of all this evaluation is to return the two integers **372** and **297** to the function main.

It will be as if we had simply evaluation

```
cout << 372 << " " << 297
```

This is a particular form of the C++ stream output expression. The operator **<<** means output to. It expects a stream as its left operand and a printable value as its right argument. It returns a stream. Thus the value of **cout << 372** is a stream; in fact, it is the stream **cout** with **372** appended to it. The stream **cout** is special. Whenever something is appended to it, it appears (eventually) on the screen. Since **cout << 372** returns a stream, **cout << 372 << " "** appends a space to that stream, with the obvious effect. This in turn returns a stream, and then **cout << 372 << " " << 297** finally appends **297** to the original output stream.

C programmers would write something different to achieve the same effect. They would write

```
printf("%d %d" , 372, 297)
```

which calls a standard function **printf** to print on the screen. The C++ method has significant advantages. In particular, the format to be used for printing is determined by the operator **<<** from the type of the expression being printed (in our case **int**). This is quite an advanced feature of C++, so we won't describe it further until we are better equipped. Figure 4.5 shows that the operators **<<** (for stream output) and **>>** (for stream input, used later) have a precedence slightly lower than addition but higher than comparison. If in doubt, as always, use parentheses to achieve the precedence you need.

Highest precedence

+ -	adding
<< >>	stream operators
< > <= >=	comparison, inequality

Lowest precedence

Figure 4.5 Relative precedence of stream operators.

One final remark needs to be made about the program in Fig. 4.4. The first line,

```
#include <iostream.h>
```

is necessary because the definitions of the input–output operations on streams are not part of the C++ language but are included (as we shall see) in one of its standard libraries. Usually this library is called **iostream** and its user description is in the standard header file **iostream.h**. We shall encounter header files and separate compilation later in the chapter. For the time being suffice it to say that the **#include** directive is a mandatory requirement. The effect is to include in your program file, at this position, all of the text in the file **iostream.h**. This text contains all the declarations of types, functions, operators and global variables that are required to input and output simple streams. In particular, the variables **cout** and **cin** are declared there.

```
long min(long x, long y){
   return x<y?x:y;
}
```

Figure 4.6 Function to compute minimum of two longs.

Consider now the function definition in Fig. 4.6. This function computes the minimum of two **long** (i.e. **long int**) arguments. The fact that we have specified that the arguments are of type **long** means that the actual arguments in a call such as **min(a,b)** will be converted to **long**, if possible, as part of the initialization of **x** and **y**, upon entry to **min**. For example, if **a** is **int** and **b** is **long**, then this call will first convert **a** to **long** and then carry out the comparison, returning a **long** result. Most arithmetic types can be converted to any other arithmetic type, which may involve loss of information. For example, the call **min(5.4, 4.5)** will return **4**, because both **float** arguments were converted by truncation to **long**.

```
long min(long x, long y, long z){
   return min(x,min(y,z));
}
```

Figure 4.7 Function to compute minimum of three longs.

```
double min(double x, double y){
   return x<y?x:y;
}
```

Figure 4.8 Function to compute minimum of two doubles.

Consider now the definition of a function to compute the minimum of three arguments, shown in Fig. 4.7. In C++ we can give this function the same name **min** as the function with two arguments, even when using them both in the same program. This is referred to as overloading of the function name. C++ uses the number and type of arguments to determine which function to call. The calls of **min** from within the body of the function defined in Fig. 4.7 are calls to the version which expects two **long** arguments. Figure 4.8

shows a third definition of **min**, this time to determine the minimum of two double floating point numbers. All three of these definitions can coexist in the same program, the compiler deciding for each call which definition to use. If all three are indeed available then the call **min(4.5,5.4)** will use the floating point version and return the double **4.5**.

The order of function definitions in a file is not important, except that functions may only call ones which have been declared earlier. Thus since **min(long, long, long)** calls **min(long, long)**, the two-argument function must be declared before the three- argument function.

Recursive function definitions are allowed. The simplest form of the factorial function is shown in Fig. 4.9. The embedded recursive call causes no confusion for the compiler. The arguments of C++ functions behave as initialized local variables, where the initialization is taken from the actual argument in the call. Each recursive invocation has its own local variable **n**.

```
long fac(int n){
   return n==0?1:n*fac(n-1);
}
```

Figure 4.9 Recursive factorial function.

Syntactically, function application is like an invisible operator. That is, in the call **f(x)** it is as if there were an operator between the function name and the opening parentheses, but an operator which requires no symbol to represent it. This is a most binding operator. Its precedence is higher than any operator we have yet encountered, including the unary operators, such as logical negation (**!**). This means that expressions such as

f(x) + f(y)

Highest precedence

f(...)	function application
!	logical not
* / %	multiplying
+ -	adding

Lowest precedence

Figure 4.10 Relative precedence of function application.

parse just as we could expect them to. Figure 4.10 shows the relative precedence of function application.

4.4 ASSIGNMENT AND STATEMENTS

In C++ the assignment operator is a simple **=** sign. Thus the expression

```
a = min(43, 47)
```

assigns the value **43** to the variable **a**. The assignment expression, like any other expression, has a value. Its value is that of the assigned value, in this case **43**. Thus we can write, for example,

```
a = b = min(43, 47)
```

and assign the value **43** to both **a** and **b**. This works because, unlike all the operators we have met so far, assignment associates to the right. In other words, the above expression is equivalent to

```
a = (b = min(43, 47))
```

The relative precedence of the assignment operator is very low. As we showed in Fig. 4.1, in fact it has the lowest precedence of all the operators we will use.

Although it is quite a common idiom in C to make use of the fact that an assignment has a value, we shall not use that property ourselves. Rather, we shall use assignment simply for the side-effect which it has. In C++, when an expression is evaluated only for the effect it has, such an expression is taking the role of what is called a statement. A statement is an instruction to the machine to change state in some way, or carry out some action. A statement has no value, only an effect.

The assignment expression can be converted to a statement by appending a semicolon. So, for example,

```
a = min(43, 47);
```

is an assignment statement. Effectively, the semicolon means 'discard the value of the expression, I am not interested in it'. A sequence of statements can be made into a single, compound statement by enclosing them in braces. So, for example,

```
{x = min(a,b);
 y = min(c,d);
 z = min(x,y);}
```

is a compound statement. Note how each constituent statement has its own semicolon, including the last statement. This is mandatory syntax in C++. The whole construction including the braces has the status of a single statement, which means it can occur anywhere a single statement is allowed or expected, as we shall see.

Other forms of statement are important to us. A declaration is a statement. For example,

```
long x, y;
```

is a declaration. It is also a statement. In C++ declarations can occur anywhere that statements can occur. However, as we read the text of a program left to right it is necessary for declarations to occur before any use of the variables which they declare. It is also common in C++ to initialize variables when they are declared, effectively exploiting the fact that declarations can be delayed until the last moment before they are needed. Hence the following is also a valid (if unusual) compound statement.

```
{long x = min(a,b);
long y = min(c,d);
long z = min(x,y);}
```

These are not assignment statements, but initialized declarations, a distinction which will become important when we study classes.

Another important aspect of declarations is the scope of the variables which they introduce. Effectively, C++ has three distinct scopes, respectively block, class and file. A compound statement with at least one declaration is a block. A block forms a scope. If the above compound statement occurs as the body of a function, then the scope of the three new variables it introduces is the body of that function. This means that storage for them is allocated on entry to the function and discarded on exit. We shall discuss the other scopes later.

```
long min(long a, long b, long c, long d){
  long x=min(a,b);
  long y=min(c,d);
  return min(x,y);
}
```

Figure 4.11 A four argument **min** using local variables.

Figure 4.11 shows a definition of a four-argument version of **min** which uses local variables to hold intermediate values. The body of the function is a compound statement, as it must be. All function definitions must have a compound statement as a body. The positioning (on the page) of the braces for the function body is a widely used convention in C++ which, when a file has many function definitions, leads to a familiar and elegant layout for the text in that file. The compound statement encloses three constituent statements, respectively two initialized declarations followed by a return statement. In C++ the return statement is constructed from the **return** operator, followed by the expression whose value is to be returned, followed by a semicolon.

Another important statement is the conditional statement. Examples of its use are the following:

```
if(x < 0) x = 0 ;
if(y < 0) z = -y; else z = y;
```

A conditional statement is heralded by the use of the keyword **if**. There follows a test, enclosed in parentheses (mandatory) which is an expression evaluated to determine whether or not its value is **0** (false). The statement immediately following the test is executed only if the test evaluates to non-**0** (true).

If the conditional statement has an else part, then that is chosen if the test is false. Consequently, the above conditional statements respectively set **x** to zero if it is less than zero and set **z** to the absolute value of **y** . Note the positions of the semicolons. They are part of the assignment statements included in the conditional statement, not part of the conditional.

```
long fac(int n){
  if(n==0) return 1; else return n*fac(n-1);
}
```

Figure 4.12 Recursive factorial (cf. Fig. 4.9).

Figure 4.12 shows the recursive factorial written using the conditional statement, rather than the conditional expression. I find it more elegant. Comparing Figs. 4.9 and 4.12 should fix the syntax for expressions, statements and for function definitions in the reader's mind.

```
for (int i=1;i<=10;i=i+1){
  cout<<i;
  cout<<" ";
  cout<<i*i;
  cout<<"\n";
}

i=1;
while(i<=10){
  cout<<i<<" "<<i*i<<"\n";
  i=i+1;
}
```

Figure 4.13 Alternative forms of loop, same effect.

C++ has various statements for constructing loops. Figure 4.13 shows the for statement and the while statement. Each of these loops counts to 10 and prints a list of 10 squares. We shall not go into the details of the syntax here, except to remark that, as we have written them, all the parentheses and semicolons are mandatory. Also, we ought to remark that experienced C and C++ programmers would find one thing odd about Fig. 4.13. That is the assignment **i=i+1** . This can be, and usually is, written **i++** . C++ has many extra operators of this sort which combine the benefits of brevity, succinctness and efficiency. We shall use such operators without defining them here. Rather, we shall define those we need, as we need them.

4.5 OBJECTS AND CLASSES

Now for the important bit. C++ provides exactly the mechanisms we require to implement our object-oriented designs. It provides the means for us to create objects on which we can define operations which behave according to the type of the object. The means for bringing objects into existence is to define a new type by means of a class declaration. A class declaration determines how storage is to be used to represent an object and which operations are to be available to manipulate that storage. A class gives us the means to define an abstract data type.

A simple class for objects used to represent points in a two-dimensional space is shown in Fig. 4.14. A class declaration is heralded by the keyword **class**, followed by the name of the type being introduced, followed by a list of members enclosed in braces. This is in turn followed by an important semicolon.

```
class Point{
public:
  int x,y;
  Point(int,int);
  void shift(int,int);
};
```

Figure 4.14 A class declaration.

This is one of the few places in C++ where a semicolon follows a closing brace. It is because C++ would allow the declaration to include the names of some objects to be declared along with the class. These names would occur between the closing brace and the semicolon. It is a rarely used device, but accidentally omitting the semicolon is a common error.

The part of the class declaration in braces is called the member list. It introduces the names of the members of the class. These are the attributes which all objects of this class will have. In our case, an object of class **Point** will have attributes **x**, **y**, **Point** and **shift**. These are respectively referred to as data members (**x** and **y**), a constructor which is a special member function (**Point**) and an ordinary member function (**shift**). The data members are the attributes which every object of type **Point** will have, in this case two integers, the **x** and **y** coordinates respectively. We can in fact expect any object of class **Point** to occupy sufficient storage to store two integers. In most C++ implementations, this is all it will occupy. The member functions define the operations which can be applied to objects of this type.

With a class declared as in Fig. 4.14 we can declare a variable of type **Point** by the declaration

```
Point aPoint1(7,12);
```

This will allocate storage on the stack for a single object of type **Point** and allow us to refer to that object as **aPoint.** This declaration will call the constructor **Point::Point(int, int)** to initialize the **x** and **y** attributes of **aPoint1** to **7** and **12** respectively. Similarly, we can create a second object by the declaration

```
Point aPoint2(-7,-12);
```

Now that we have these two objects we can access their data members directly in expressions such as

```
aPoint1.x + aPoint2.x
```

This is because we have made the data members public. By default all members of a class are private unless we declare otherwise. The use of the access specifier **public:** at the beginning of the list of members overrides this default. We shall see later how the access specifiers can be used to control the interface to an object to be exactly what we require.

The operator dot (**.**) used in expressions of the form **aPoint1.x** has exactly the same precedence as function application. That is, its precedence is very high. In expressions of the form **a.b.c.d**, the operator associates to the left (as in fact do most operators) so this means the same as **((a.b).c).d**. However, we will have restricted use for such cascading, since we never (or very seldom) make data members public. The fact that dot and function application have the same precedence is important. They both associate to the left, so an expression of the form **a.b().c()** means call the member function **b** of the object **a**; when it returns an object which has member function **c**, call that member function, that is, it means **(a.b()).c()**.

If a data member is public, as **x** and **y** are here, it is possible to assign directly to it. For example,

```
aPoint1.x = 8;
```

overwrites the value of the attribute **aPoint1.x**. It is not normally desirable to allow assignment to data members and this can be prevented by making data members private, which is what we shall eventually do in this example.

```
Point::Point(int x0, int y0){
  x=x0; y=y0;
}
```

Figure 4.15 Constructor for class **Point** (cf. Fig. 4.18).

```
void Point::shift(int x0, int y0){
  x=x+x0; y=y+y0;
}
```

Figure 4.16 Member function for class **Point**.

Figures 4.15 and 4.16 show how the two member functions are defined. Observe how similar they are. Each is a function definition which introduces a new function. The C++ convention for constructor functions is that they have exactly the same name as the class. The constructor function is therefore, necessarily given the name **Point**. We are free to determine how many arguments the constructor function has. Indeed, we may have many constructor functions for a single class, all with the same overloaded name, distinguished by the types of their arguments. Sometimes it is important to have a parameterless constructor. If no constructor is supplied by the programmer, the compiler will supply a default, parameterless one.

In defining functions which are members of classes we must use the compound name built by prepending the class name to the function name. Thus **Point::Point** and **Point::shift** are the full names (the qualified names) of the member functions of the class **Point**. As we shall see, this naming convention, allows reuse of member names without ambiguity. The effect is as if the definitions of the member functions were local to the class whose name they carry. Hence the definitions in Figs. 4.15 and 4.16, where they refer to the variables **x** and **y**, are referring to the data members of the class **Point**. Consider the calls

```
Point aPoint1(7,12);
aPoint1.shift(10,17);
```

The declaration calls the constructor which creates a new object of type **Point** with data members **x** and **y** set to 7 and 12 respectively, as shown in Fig. 4.17.

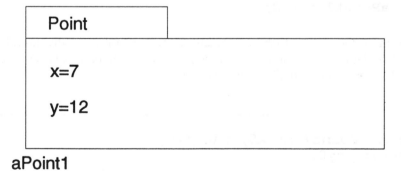

Figure 4.17 Point aPoint1 (7,12).

Effectively, the declaration allocates sufficient storage on the stack (we shall discuss stack and heap shortly) to store a **Point**, then calls **Point::Point(int,int)** to initialize it. This call has **x0=7** and **y0=12**, so the assignments in the body of the constructor serve to initialize the data members correctly.

There are other aspects of the declaration of class **Point** and the definition of its two member functions on which we should remark. First, the fact that in the member list the arguments of the member functions can be specified by giving only their type. There is no need to name the arguments. Second, that the return type of the ordinary member function **shift** is **void**. Thus the specification **void Point::shift(int,int);** means we expect to define a member function which takes two **int** arguments and returns a **void**. Returning **void** is C++ for returning nothing. The default return type, if we had omitted the word **void**, is in fact **int** (a hangover from C). We do not want this, so we must explicitly state the return type. A constructor has no return type. The appearance of the specification in the class declaration means that a corresponding definition will be required elsewhere before our program is complete.

While the definition of the constructor shown in Fig. 4.15 is correct, it is not in the best style. There is a special mechanism for initializing data members and we should use it, even though in this simple case it makes no difference. Its proper use will be important when our class definitions get to be more elaborate. Figure 4.18 shows a definition of the constructor when the function heading is followed by a member initialization list, heralded by the use of the single colon. This initialization list, which precedes the function body, contains initializations of the form data member followed by initialization in parentheses. Since this particularly simple constructor has no more to do than initialize its data members, its function body is empty.

```
Point::Point(int x0, int y0):x(x0),y(y0){
}
```

Figure 4.18 Alternative (better) definition of constructor for **Point**.

The member function **Point::shift** in Fig. 4.16 alters the values of the data members according to the values of its arguments. Notionally it shifts the point by the amount **x0, y0**. Since the data members of class **Point** are public, we could have had the same effect as **aPoint1.shift(7,12)** by assigning directly to them:

```
aPoint1.x = aPoint1.x + 7;
aPoint1.y = aPoint1.y + 12;
```

It is not usually a good idea to leave data members public. It may be appropriate while testing a program to have direct access to data members, but not when the program has been completed. Rather, we want the class **Point** to be an abstract data type with a simple well-specified interface. It is better to make access to that interface exclusively through member functions.

```
class Point{
  int x,y;
public:
  Point(int,int);
  int xval();
  int yval();
  void shift(Point);
};
```

Figure 4.19 Class **Point** with hidden data members.

```
Point::Point(int x0, int y0):x(x0),y(y0){
}

int Point::xval(){return x;}

int Point::yval(){return y;}

void Point::shift(Point p){
  x=x+p.x; y=y+p.y;
}
```

Figure 4.20 Definitions of new member functions.

This is what we have done in Fig. 4.19. Here the class **Point** is declared with its two data members taking the the default access rights, that is, they are private to the class. This new class has six members: the two hidden data members, a constructor, two new function members for accessing the data members and a revised shift function which takes a **Point** as argument. The definitions of the public members are shown in Fig. 4.20. The use of an argument of type **Point** for the member function **shift** changes the interface a little. It means that we can now make calls such as

```
aPoint1.shift(aPoint2)
```

where **aPoint1** and **aPoint2** have been declared appropriately. It also means that a call such as

```
aPoint1.shift(Point(-7,-12))
```

is allowed. The argument here is a call on the constructor to create a temporary object which is used to initialize the parameter **p** in the call to **shift**.

The new member functions allow us to access the coordinates of a point, as for example in

```
aPoint1.xval() + aPoint2.xval()
```

but do not allow us to update the data members directly. Thus the only way to alter the values of the data members is through calls on the member function **shift**. Consequently it is essential that the data members are initialized by the constructor. The provision of this single constructor guarantees the initialization.

Take a closer look at the definition of **Point::shift** in Fig. 4.20. In it the assignment statement

x = x + p.x

occurs. Since this function is a member of the class **Point**, which will be invoked for example by the call **aPoint1.shift(aPoint2)**, then the uses of the data member **x** in this assignment refer to **aPoint1.x** while the uses of **p.x** refer to **aPoint2.x**. Even though the data members are private, both these usages are valid within a member function. That is what private means. Member functions have privileged access to data members. Nowhere else may such usage be made. Actually, this last remark is not strictly true, because C++ provides mechanisms for granting access to other so-called friend functions and friend classes. This is not a mechanism we shall exploit.

```
class Point{
  int x,y;
public:
  Point(int,int);
  int xval();
  int yval();
  Point shifted(Point);
};
```

Figure 4.21 A version of class **Point** with no side-effect.

C++ provides support for many paradigms and has many mechanisms which allow programmers to tailor their usage to match just the paradigm they wish to employ. As an example of how we can get close to a functional or declarative paradigm, observe the revised definition of class **Point** in Fig. 4.21. The only change is to replace the member function **shift** by a member function **shifted** which has no side-effect (see Fig. 4.22). The call **aPoint1.shifted(aPoint2)** changes neither **aPoint1** nor **aPoint2**. Rather, it returns a new **Point**, whose coordinates are those of **aPoint1** shifted by an amount equal to the coordinates of **aPoint2**. It would be used as follows, by declaring a new **Point** and initializing it:

Point aPoint3 = aPoint1.shifted(aPoint2);

or by the explicit overwriting of an existing **Point**:

aPoint1 = aPoint1.shifted(aPoint2);

The effect of the first usage, the initialized declaration, is to leave **aPoint1** and **aPoint2** unchanged and to bring a third point **aPoint3** into existence. The effect of the second usage, the overwriting assignment, is to change the coordinates of **aPoint1** by copying the coordinates of the temporary containing the result of the call **aPoint1. shifted(aPoint2)**. While all this looks fairly obvious, C++ is employing some subtle, elegant and important semantics here.

The initialized declaration appears to have allowed us to create a new **Point** without the benefit of a constructor; it has not. We have made implicit use of what C++ calls a copy constructor to construct **aPoint3**. This copy constructor is something we can either supply ourselves when defining the class or allow the C++ compiler to supply on our behalf. We have taken the default, in which case the copy constructor supplied by the compiler will have copied the data members from the result of **aPoint1.shifted (aPoint2)** to the new object **aPoint3** on our behalf. The ability to redefine the copy constructor, combined with the fact that in C++ there are established places where it will be used (such as initializing arguments on function calls, and returning results of functions) provides a powerful means for the programmer to control such important aspects of the program as memory management. This is too advanced a topic for this chapter and not one we shall need in the immediately following chapters. It is one we shall return to in Chapter 9.

A similarly subtle behind-the-scenes activity is taking place in the assignment

```
aPoint1 = aPoint1.shifted(aPoint2);
```

```
Point Point::shifted(Point p){
  return Point(x+p.x,y+p.y);
}
```

Figure 4.22 Definition of pure function **shifted**.

This time it is the assignment operator which is invoked. But again we could have supplied our own definition of what it means to assign one **Point** to another. Because we have not done so, C++ has supplied the default, which is to do member by member copy from the temporary variable used to store the result of the function call. Again, because we can redefine this operator, it gives us a sometimes necessary degree of control over the way that this is accomplished for our own types. We shall discuss how this is exploited in Chapter 9.

We have much more to learn about objects and classes, and in particular how C++ provides support for inheritance. However, we have delayed too long a proper discussion of memory management in C++ and so we must turn first to that.

4.6 POINTERS AND MEMORY

When we make a declaration such as

```
Point aPoint(7,12);
```

sufficient memory is allocated to store the data members of **aPoint**. A simple declaration of this kind is either static or automatic, depending upon whether it occurs at the top level, outside all function and class declarations (a rare thing), or nested within one. Take the simplest case, where this declaration occurs inside the function **main**. It is making use of what is called automatic allocation or stack memory. The memory for the created object is automatically allocated on the evaluation stack. This memory will be discarded on exit from the function **main**.

```
void f(){
  Point aPoint2(-2,2);
        . . .
}

main(){
  Point aPoint1(7,12);
  f();
        . . .
}
```

Figure 4.23 Example of memory allocation.

Consider the more elaborate case in Fig. 4.23. On entry to function **main**, space is allocated on the stack for the object **aPoint1**. On entry to function **f**, additional space is allocated on the stack for object **aPoint2**. When function **f** is exited, the space allocated for **aPoint2** is discarded. Should another function be called by **main**, this discarded space will be automatically reused for any objects which that function needs. Ultimately, when we exit **main**, the space for **aPoint1** is also discarded. That all seems fairly obvious and useful.

```
void f(Point aPoint){
  Point aPoint2(-2,2);
  aPoint.shift(aPoint2);
        . . .
}

main(){
  Point aPoint1(7,12);
  f(aPoint1);
        . . .
}
```

Figure 4.24 Memory allocation for function with parameter.

Consider now a slightly more elaborate example, shown in Fig. 4.24. This time we have given **f** a parameter. Now on entry to **f** sufficient space is allocated on the stack for two objects **aPoint** and **aPoint2**. The argument is allocated space which is initialized by copying (using the default copy constructor) from **aPoint1**. The object **aPoint2** is initialized conventionally. Both of these objects are destroyed on exit from **f**. This definition of what it means to pass an object as an argument to a function has some important consequences. Since it is a copy of the object which is being worked on in **f**, none of the changes to the argument will be transmitted to the object **aPoint1** in **main**.

```
void f(Point& aPoint){
  Point aPoint2(-2,2);
  aPoint.shift(aPoint2);
       . . .
}
```

Figure 4.25 Use of a reference argument.

One way to overcome this is to make the argument of **f** into a reference. The revised definition of **f** is shown in Fig. 4.25. The type **Point&** means reference to **Point**, so **aPoint** is now of that type. This means that operations in **f** are actually operations on the corresponding actual argument **aPoint1** (which is probably what we intended in the first place). As far as memory allocation is concerned, we have reverted to the situation where, on entry, space is allocated on the stack for one object only, that is for **aPoint2**. There is no additional storage requirement for the argument. Reference types are an important C++ extension to C. Any type can have an associated reference type, and, used in the way we have illustrated here, means we can implement the passing of parameters by reference both to avoid the expense of copying and to provide the means for changing objects by side-effect in subroutines.

Reference types, however, are not as general as pointers and there are necessary parts of the C++ memory model which require as to use the more general notion of pointer. Suppose I declare

```
Point* p;
```

Then **p** will be a variable of type pointer, restricted to point to an object of type **Point**. If we have already declared, for example,

```
Point aPoint1(7,12);
Point aPoint2(2,-2);
```

then we can make **p** point at the first of these objects by the assignment

```
p = &aPoint1;
```

and to the second by the assignment

```
p = &aPoint2;
```

This use of **&** is quite separate from the earlier use of making a reference type. This use of **&** is a unary operator, meaning, 'take the address of'. Once we have established **p** to point to an object of type **Point**, we can access the attributes of the object pointed to using the operator **->**, as, for example,

```
p -> xval()
```

```
void f(Point* aPoint){
  Point aPoint2(-2,2);
  aPoint->shift(aPoint2);
     ...
}

main(){
  Point aPoint1(7,12);
  f(&aPoint1);
     ...
}
```

Figure 4.26 Use of a pointer as argument.

which will return the **int** which is the current value of the **x**-coordinate of the object pointed to by **p**. The operator **->** has exactly the same precedence as the dot used for de-referencing objects. We use **->** when the left operand is a pointer and we use dot when the left operand is an object. Figure 4.26 shows how a pointer as a parameter can achieve the same result as a reference type, but somewhat less elegantly.

A pointer is, however, a very versatile tool. It is a concept which current computer architectures are organized to support efficiently. Consequently, by the nature of the mission which has been established for C++, pointers are a necessary mechanism for us to learn. We can hand around pointers to objects much more economically than we can hand around the objects themselves. Typically, the assignment of a pointer is a single machine instruction. The memory allocated to a pointer is typically a single machine word. But there are pitfalls. We must ensure that the memory to which our pointer refers remains valid as along as we continue to use the pointer. Given the story at the beginning of this section about automatic storage we can see how it would be an easy mistake to make. All we need to do is to set a pointer to point to memory allocated in a function used as a subroutine. After exit from that subroutine, the allocated memory will be recovered (by reusing that part of the stack) and so the pointer will point dangerously at some memory which is either not in use or has been reused for some other purpose. Thus, always be extremely cautious when setting up pointers to point to automatic storage. It is best avoided.

But the need to be able to create objects in subroutines and to return pointers (to them) to the caller is a real one which remains to be solved. What we need is storage whose allocation and deallocation is not automatically tied to the entry to and exit from functions. Such storage does exist in the C++ memory model. It is usally referred to as the free store, or the heap, and allocation and deallocation are controlled explicitly by the programmer.

The heap is a separate area of storage from the stack. The compiler will allocate memory for the compiled code, for the static data whose allocation can be determined at compile time, for the stack used for automatic data and for the heap in some way which ensures that sufficient is available for each purpose. The heap is organized as a free store in such a way that memory for objects can be allocated from it, explicitly returned to it and subsequently reallocated for reuse.

Allocation is achieved by the operator **new** which returns a pointer to the allocated storage. For example,

```
Point* p;
p = new Point(7,12);
```

allocates memory on the heap for a new object of class **Point**, initialized using the constructor for that class, and assigns a pointer to that newly allocated memory to the (correctly declared) variable **p**. This object will persist for the lifetime of the program, or until explicitly deleted. Responsibility for hanging on to the pointer is, however, entirely left with the programmer. To return the memory allocated by **new** to the heap, the operator **delete** must be used, as in

```
delete p;
```

If **p** still points to the object allocated earlier, then this memory will be returned to the heap for eventual reuse. If large objects are used for temporary storage, or if many objects are used temporarily, it is good housekeeping to return them to the heap after use. Failure to do so could cause premature exhaustion of memory.

```
class Point{
  int x,y;
public:
  Point(int,int);
  int xval();
  int yval();
  Point* shifted(Point*);
};
```

Figure 4.27 **Shifted** using pointers (cf. Fig. 4.22).

In general, memory management is an issue which requires consideration on a global rather than local level. Some applications require that quite stringent regimes of memory allocation and deallocation are adhered to in order to survive over long periods of time, while other applications have simpler memory requirements, seeing their occupancy grow slowly and seldom shrink. C++ provides the means for the programmer to control either regime. In subsequent chapters we shall need to consider memory management for our evolving application. We shall deal with its specific requirements as we encounter them. In Chapter 9 we will return to a general discussion of this important topic for C++ programmers.

```
Point* Point::shifted(Point* p){
   return new Point(x+p->x,y+p->y);
}
```

Figure 4.28 **Shifted** using pointers (cf. Fig. 4.22).

To conclude our study of pointers and memory, consider the revised definition of the class **Point** shown in Figs. 4.27 and 4.28. Now, if we declare

```
Point* p = new Point(7,12);
Point* q = new Point(-2,2);
```

where we have initialized the pointers **p** and **q** to point to new objects on the heap, then we can call, for example,

```
p = p -> shifted(q);
```

where all copying of objects has been avoided. But we have committed the sin of losing a pointer to an object on the heap (the one originally allocated to **p**) with now no chance of recovering its memory. This simple example clearly illustrates how much care we must take when using heap storage. It contrasts with the abandon with which we were able to use the automatic storage in the example in Figs. 4.21 and 4.22. But, ultimately, automatic storage is not sufficient and we must face the engineering task of using heap storage properly. This is a major part of the coming chapters.

4.7 INHERITANCE

There are many facets to the mechanisms which C++ provides for supporting object-oriented programming. Inheritance is one of them. There are many aspects of inheritance, some of which can be resolved at compile-time and some which must be left until run-time. The mechanisms which require run-time support are nevertheless economically provided by C++. They also provide apparently essential functionality, the run-time determination of which method to apply to an object. This late binding is one of the important building blocks of object-oriented programming. It is only deployed in C++ when use is made of the virtual mechanism described later in this section. First we deal with the kind of inheritance which is resolved at compile-time.

```
class GeometricObject{
  int x,y;
public:
  GeometricObject(int,int);
  int xval();
  int yval();
  void shift(int,int);
};
```

Figure 4.29 New base class (same interface as **Point**).

We expand our geometric example to include, as well as the class **Point**, a class to represent circles. A circle will have a centre point and a radius. The fact that both **Point** and **Circle** share the property that they have an **x, y** location (in the case of the circle, its centre) can be factored out of their representation. Accordingly, we define a new class **GeometricObject** which has in fact exactly the same interface as the class **Point** of the earlier sections. This is shown in Fig. 4.29. Now we use this as what is called a base class, for two derived classes **Point** and **Circle**. Their definitions are shown in Fig. 4.30.

```
class Point : public GeometricObject {
public:
  Point(int,int);
};

class Circle : public GeometricObject {
int radius;
public:
  Circle(int,int,int);
};
```

Figure 4.30 Two derived classes with same base class.

The hierarchy of classes which is then established is shown in Fig. 4.31. Look first at the definition of class **Point**. It explicitly names a base class **GeometricObject**. In fact, the heading

```
class Point : public GeometricObject
```

states that **Point** is a derived class of the base class **GeometricObject** and that it inherits the public members of **GeometricObject** in order to make them public to its users (the keyword **public** ensures this onward transmission). Apart from the inherited public members, the class **Point** defines one new member, a constructor for creating instances. Similarly the class **Circle** inherits from **GeometricObject** and provides one new private data member and a public constructor.

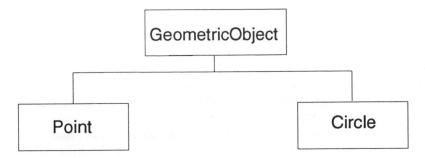

Figure 4.31 Inheritance relationship between base and derived classes.

We do not intend to create objects of type **GeometricObject**, although we have not excluded that. We do intend to build objects of type **Point** and **Circle**. A **Point** will have two data members (**x** and **y**) and a **Circle** will have three (**x**, **y** and **r**). In both cases the **x** and **y** attributes have been inherited from **GeometricObject**. So when we allocate memory for a **Circle** we would expect it to occupy more space than that required for a **Point**.

```
GeometricObject::GeometricObject(int x0, int y0):
   x (x0),y(y0){
}

Point::Point(int x0,int y0):GeometricObject(x0,y0){
}

Circle::Circle(int x0,int y0,int r):
   GeometricObject(x0,y0), radius(r){
}
```

Figure 4.32 Constructor functions for all three classes.

The definition of the corresponding constructors is shown in Fig. 4.32. The constructor for **GeometricObject** is as we have had it earlier for **Point**. The constructor for **Point** is in the standard form for initializing the part of the object which represents the base class. It is rather as if we were initializing a data member: the constructor **Point** hands its arguments on to the constructor **GeometricObject**, and does no more. The constructor for **Circle** has to do a little more work. It must of course initialize the part of the object inherited from the base class, so it calls the **GeometricObject** constructor to do that. Then it initializes a private data member **radius** in the conventional way.

So we can construct a point and a circle as follows:

```
Point aPoint(7,12);
Circle aCircle(12,-2,10);
```

and we can shift both of these objects by the calls

```
aPoint.shift(2,2);
aCircle.shift(-2,-2);
```

They both inherit the operation from their base class. Both execute the same code. Both experience the same effect of a change to their **x** and **y** coordinates. Which method to invoke is resolved at compile-time. The variables **aPoint** and **aCircle** are both of type **GeometricObject** so they inherit **shift** from that. We could have redefined **shift** in either or both of the derived classes, in which case the method in the derived class would have been used if available and the method in the base class only if no redefinition takes place in the derived class.

```
class GeometricObject{
  int x,y;
protected:
  GeometricObject(int,int);
public:
  int xval();
  int yval();
  void shift(int,int);
  virtual int size();
};
```

Figure 4.33 Base class with protected constructor and virtual function.

We do not intend to build objects of type **GeometricObject**, but only of the derived classes **Point** and **Circle**, so we should not have made its constructor public. But we cannot make it private, because private is what it says: even derived classes cannot access private members. There is an intermediate level of access which is appropriate. We make members protected by the keyword **protected**, which means they are inaccessible to the users of the class except for the derived classes. We will make **GeometricObject**'s constructor protected from now on. This you can see in Fig. 4.33, which we will come to discuss shortly.

Apart from the obvious benefits of sharing of common parts of their definitions, dividing classes into a hierarchy of types in this way has the benefit that we have a type which we can use to refer to objects which are either points or circles. If we declare a pointer to be of type **GeometricObject***, as follows,

```
GeometricObject* g;
```

then we can assign pointers to either points or circles to **g**. Both of the following assignments are valid:

```
g = &aPoint;
g = &aCircle;
```

Now if we call

```
g -> shift(2,2);
```

depending on which of the assignments took place, the corresponding object will be correctly shifted. This is rather fortunate, for had we overidden the definition of **shift** in one of the derived classes, the call **g -> shift** would not have invoked it. This is because the type of **g** is **GeometricObject*** and the resolution of which method to use has been carried out at compile-time. The choice of **GeometricObject::shift** is the answer the compiler determines, regardless of our attempt to override it. To achieve the effect we undoubtedly want, we must make use of the virtual mechanism.

```
class Circle : public GeometricObject {
int radius;
public:
  Circle(int,int,int);
  int size();
};
```

Figure 4.34 Derived class with virtual function (virtual is inherited).

```
int GeometricObject::size(){
  return 0;
}

Circle::size(){
  return radius;
}
```

Figure 4.35 Definition of virtual functions.

To illustrate the virtual mechanism we will use a slightly different example. Consider the revised definition of our base class, shown in Fig. 4.33. We have added a new public member function **size** which takes no arguments and returns an **int**. We have also specified that this new member function is **virtual**. This means that it may (probably will) be redefined in one or more of the derived classes and that, when invoked through a generic pointer, it is the method most suited to the type of object pointed at which must be invoked. This is quite a complex meaning. It means that at compile time we only need know that the object pointed at will be an instance of one of the classes derived from **GeometricObject**. If the derived class has a redefinition of **size()** then that definition will be invoked in preference to the base class definition. In Figs. 4.34 and 4.35 we have presumed that we do redefine **size()** for **Circle** but not for **Point**. So we give definitions for just two version, **GeometricObject::size()** returns **0** and

Circle::size() returns **radius**. Now, suppose **g** is of type **GeometricObject***, then the call

```
g -> size()
```

will invoke one or other of the methods in Fig. 4.35 according to the actual type of the object pointed to by **g**. Effectively, it does this by determining the type of the object and calling the corresponding function; in case the object is a **Circle** then **Circle::size** will be called. In case the object is a **Point** then **GeometricObject::size()** will be called, since **Point** does not override that definition.

```
class GeometricObject{
  int x,y;
protected:
  GeometricObject(int,int);
public:
  int xval();
  int yval();
  void shift(int,int);
  virtual int size();
  int biggerthan(GeometricObject*);
};
```

Figure 4.36 Function **biggerthan** will be inherited.

As currently organized, the only types of object which **g** can point to are either **Point** or **Circle**. We have excluded the creation of objects of type **GeometricObject**. If we were to add a new derived class, with base **GeometricObject**, it would automatically inherit **size** until we were to override it. More significantly, we can write code which will not change even if we add new derived classes. A typical example of this versatility is shown in the definition of **GeometricObject::biggerthan** which is defined in Figs. 4.36 and 4.37. This is a new member function **GeometricObject::biggerthan** which would be invoked, for example by a call

```
g1 -> biggerthan(g2)
```

allowing us to compare the sizes of two **GeometricObjects** without knowing their types at compile-time.

```
int GeometricObject::biggerthan(GeometricObject* g){
  return size()>g->size();
}
```

Figure 4.37 Both calls to size will invoke virtual functions in derived classes.

If we were to extend our program to include a third derived class, it would not require any change to the code of the base class. In fact, C++ compilers even support the fact that if the base class has been separately compiled it need not be recompiled for this type of change, an important separation of concerns when it comes to distributing software.

4.8 COLLECTIONS

Of course, C++ provides facilities for arrays, as we shall show, but by far the more common means of using collections is to obtain a library of classes which provides a wider range of collection types. Most compilers now come with a library which supports singly and doubly linked lists and perhaps more elaborate table mechanisms. These libraries can be far from trivial, but their use saves a great deal of labour on the programmer's part. Rather than try to introduce any particular commercial library here, we shall describe the altogether more trivial library which is listed in Appendix 2. This is similar in spirit to many of the commercial libraries and so serves as an introduction. It will also serve our purposes throughout this book, where arrays as supplied in the base language prove to be insufficient.

But first let us look at arrays. A declaration such as

```
Point p[100];
```

allocates (automatic) storage for 100 **Point**s. The array elements are subscripted with the integers 0 to 99. C and C++ both start their array indexing at 0. The storage for array **p** is allocated on the stack. It is possible also to allocate storage on the heap, as we shall see.

For the declaration to work, because we are creating an array of objects, it is necessary that the class **Point** has a parameterless constructor. Since whenever we have defined this class (such as in Fig. 4.30) we have only given it a constructor with two parameters, we would need to extend this definition accordingly. A suitable parameterless constructor might set both coordinates of the point to zero.

Reference to each of the array elements is made using the indexing operator (square brackets) which has exactly the same relative precedence as function application (which in turn is the same as dot and **->**). So **p[13]** is the 14th element of **p**. We can use it in any way we would use a **Point**, including

```
p[13].shift(p[12])
p[i] = p[i+1].shifted(delta)
```

The storage for **p** persists as long as we are in the function which declared it

By declaring an array at the outermost level, outside all functions, its storage will be static lasting the duration of the program. But its size would be determined at compile-time. An alternative way to have storage persists longer than the lifetime of an individual function application is to allocate that storage on the heap. For example,

```
Point* p = new Point[100];
```

allocates storage for 100 **Point**s on the heap. The array is referred to as before, **p[13]** and so on. The only difference is that the storage persists after exit from the function in which it is allocated. The declaration perhaps deserves some explanation. The intitializing expression **new   Point[100]** allocates the storage on the heap, calling the parameterless constructor for each element. It returns a pointer to the first element of the array. The form of the declaration **Point* p = ...** ensures that this pointer is allocated to **p** but does not very clearly document the fact that we intend to refer to elements of **p** by subscripting.

Since the storage has been allocated on the heap we can discard it using **delete**, but we must indicate that it is an array which is being discarded by the usage

```
delete[] p ;
```

Finally, it is possible to declare two-or more-dimensional arrays in C++ by the device of declaring an array of arrays, as follows:

```
Point q[100][10] ;
```

which gives us 10 one-dimensional arrays, each of 100 elements, referred to for example by expressions such as **q[13][3]**, which yields the 14th member of the 4th array. Structures of this sort are a lot less common in C++ than they would be in other languages, for the reason that we have suggested earlier, that more powerful collection types than arrays are normally provided via libraries of collection classes.

The library we shall use is listed in Appendix 2. Here we shall describe part of it in order to introduce the reader to the basic ideas behind its design and, in particular, how to make use of it. There are many problems which the designer of a library such as this one has had to face and, as you will see as you inspect other libraries, many different solutions. One major problem, to which there are a number of established solutions of varying degree of complexity and versatility, is that of how much the collection knows about the types of its members. The solution we have chosen is probably the simplest, but the least safe, of all the alternatives. We shall assume that the object placed in a collection is represented by a pointer and we shall *not* record in the collection the type of the object pointed at. This will mean that when we remove an object from a collection we shall not be able to determine from the pointer what type that object is, unless we provide the means for doing that ourselves. C++ does provide the means to develop collection classes which are more type-safe than those which we shall present. The methods of doing this are summarized in Chapter 9. However, we shall be concerned with the correctness of the code we develop and our design methods will protect us from the pitfalls which our collection classes might engender. The benefit of this typeless pointer is a powerful set of basic operations which are comparatively straightforward to explain.

The mechanism in C++ for having typeless pointers is to use the type **void*** which means pointer to anything. Thus, if we have the declarations

```
void* v; Point* p; Circle* c;
```

then we can make the assignments **v = p** and **v = c** freely. We say we are casting a

Point* to a **void***, and casting a **Circle*** to a **void***, respectively. This casting is implicit. When we carry out the assignment the other way, however, we must explicitly cast the **void*** to the appropriate type before assignment using either **p = (Point*)v** or **c = (Circle*)v** as appropriate. The potential for disaster here should be obvious to the reader. We shall take extreme care.

```
class Collection{
private:
  ...
protected:
  Collection();
public:
  ~Collection();
  virtual void insert(void*)=0;
  void remove(void*);
  int size();
  int member(void*);
  void forEachDo(void(*)(void*));
  Collection* select(int(*)(void*));
  Collection* collect(void*(*)(void*));
  ...
};
```

Figure 4.38 Base class for collections (simplified).

```
class Set : public Collection {
public:
  Set();
  void insert(void*);
};

class Bag : public Collection {
public:
  Bag();
  void insert(void*);
};
```

Figure 4.39 Derived classes for **Set** and **Bag**.

Figures 4.38 and 4.39 show simplified versions of the C++ collection classes, which are completely listed in Appendix 2. There is a base class, **Collection**, which is abstract in the sense that its constructor is hidden. We have two derived classes, **Set** and **Bag** which inherit the protocol for collections, each giving a slightly different interpretation.

Sets do not allow repetition, so inserting the same element into a **Set** for a second or subsequent time has no effect. **Bags** do allow repetition. The operation **Collection::insert** is pure virtual, thus ensuring that the class **Collection** is abstract. By adding the annotation **=0** to the public virtual function **insert** we are stating that no implementation of this function will be provided for the base class, so its implementation in every derived class is mandatory. A class with such a *pure virtual* function is called abstract and the compiler will ensure that no objects of that class are created. Thus the only use of a class with a pure virtual function is as a base class. The implementation of the pure virtual operation is divided between **Set::insert** and **Bag::insert** in the familiar way. Apart from this, the only other operations which **Set** and **Bag** implement themselves are the constructors. Figure 4.40 shows the subclass relationship between these new classes. Let us look at how a user would make use of these classes before we study how to implement them.

The declarations

```
Bag* aBag = new Bag();
Set* aSet = new Set();
```

create two new collections, respectively a **Bag** and a **Set**. We have chosen to access these objects through pointers. This is an idiom we shall adopt uniformly from now on. When we look at the implementation of **Collections** we shall see that, whatever we had done here, the actual elements of the collection would be allocated in the heap. Once we have created the two objects we can begin inserting and removing elements from them. They are initially empty. We could for example insert two **Points** into the **Bag** as follows:

```
aBag -> insert(aPoint1);
aBag -> insert(aPoint2);
```

The other simple operations shown in Fig. 4.38 allow us to determine the size of a collection **aBag -> size()** and to determine if some object is or is not a member of a collection **aBag -> member(aPoint)**.

If we believe that a particular object is a member of a collection, we can remove it by the call **aBag -> remove(aPoint)**. If **aPoint** is not a member of **aBag** then this operation has no effect, otherwise **aBag** is changed to exclude **aPoint**. All these operations have been illustrated using **Bag**. They are all available for **Set**, with the difference that an object never appears in a **Set** more than once.

There are means whereby the members of a collection can be retrieved from that collection one at a time. These operations will be described as they are needed later in the book. They are included in Appendix 2, of course. Rather than retrieve elements one at a time, Fig. 4.38 shows operations which allow us to act on all the members of a collection in the same way. These are the operations **Collection::forEachDo**, **Collection::collect** and **Collection::select**. Each of them is unusual in that they require a function as a parameter.

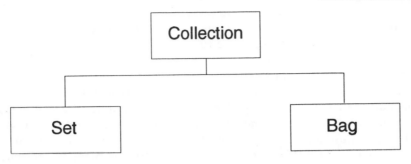

```
void shiftPoint (void* aPoint) {
  ((Point*)aPoint)->shift(-2,-2);
}


aBag->forEachDo(shiftPoint);
```

Figure 4.41 A call of `Collection::forEachDo`.

Consider the specification of **Collection::forEachDo**. The type of its argument is **void(*) (void*)**, which means (pointer to) function taking **void*** as argument and returning **void** (i.e. nothing). Thus, if we define the function **shiftPoint**, as shown in Fig. 4.41, the call **aBag->forEachDo (shiftPoint)** applies the function **shiftPoint** to each element in **aBag**. Thus, every **Point** in that collection will be shifted two places left and down. In the definition of **shiftPoint** the cast of **aPoint** to type **Point*** is necessary and the extra set of parentheses around the cast is also necessary because the **->** binds more tightly than the cast. In fact, the relative precedence of casting in this form is higher than any of the binary arithmetic operators, but below that of the unary operators.

```
int shiftx, shifty;

void shiftPoint (void* aPoint) {
  ((Point*)aPoint)->shift(shiftx,shifty);
}


shiftx=-2; shifty=-2; aBag->forEachDo(shiftPoint);
```

Figure 4.42 Use of globals to simulate free variables.

The use of functions as arguments to other functions will become ubiquitous in our style of programming in C++. Some of the rules need therefore to be explained, not least of all because this seems to be an area of C++ usage where authors differ in the idioms they adopt. First, the only kind of function which can be passed as an argument is a top-level definition. Consequently, the only variables which may be referred to in the body of such a function are parameters and global (i.e. static) variables. We shall need to pass functions which refer to static variables as a means of getting round this restriction. Figure 4.42 shows this awkward (and weak) device in use, where we are able to shift each point by an amount specified just before the call of **forEachDo**. Its meaning, and its weaknesses, should be obvious from inspection.

```
void f(void g(int)){          void f(void (*g)(int)){
  g(3);                          (*g)(3);
}                             }

void h(int x){ ... }          void h(int x){ ... }

f(h)                          f(&h)
```

Figure 4.43 Implicit and explicit type conversion for functions used as parameters.

Other rules with respect to functions as parameters of functions are rather less restrictive and more a matter of taste. In fact, what C++ passes as an argument is a pointer to a function. However, conversion in both directions from function to pointer-to-function and vice versa are automatic (and unambiguous) in C++, so we need not explicitly take addresses, or de-reference addresses or specify that the argument is in fact a pointer type. The compiler takes care of all that. But because of the opportunity which C++ provides for explicitly stating all of this type of information you will discover when you read other C++ books that there is little in the way of conventional usage in this area. Also, many authors use **typedef** to simplify the use of function types, which is important when they get complex, so again the number of degrees of freedom for differences in usage increases. Figure 4.43 captures the difference between the implicit and explicit use of types in this area. Both examples are interpreted identically by the C++ compiler. The left-hand usage is simpler.

```
int firstQuadrant(void* aPoint){
  return ((Point*)aPoint)->xval()>0 &&
         ((Point*)aPoint)->yval()>0;
}

Collection* aBag1=aBag->select(firstQuadrant);
```

Figure 4.44 Constructing a subcollection using **select**.

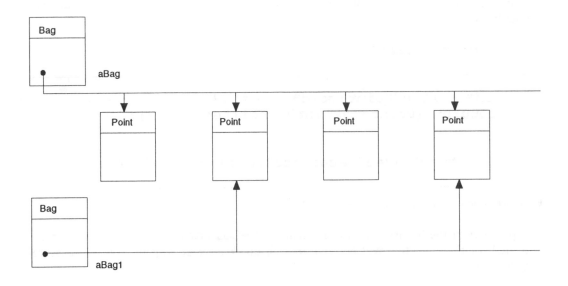

Figure 4.45 The subcollection contains the same objects.

Similar to **forEachDo**, in the sense that it has a function as argument, is **Collection::select**. This time, the argument function takes a **void*** and returns an **int**. It is used as a test, so the **int** it returns is considered to be a logical value. Figure 4.44 shows an example of its use. The function **firstQuadrant(p)** returns **1** (true) if the point **p** is in the first quadrant (both **x** and **y** coordinates positive). The call **aBag -> select(firstQuadrant)** then returns a completely new collection, of the same type as **aBag**, in which are just those objects which satisfy the predicate **firstQuadrant**. There are two important ideas here: it is a completely new collection, but the objects in the collection are the same objects as those in the original collection. We think of each object as having an identity (its address, the value of our pointer to it). The collections are collections of these identities. Figure 4.45 shows the sharing which takes place. So, the sequence of statements

```
Bag* aBag1 = aBag -> select(firstQuadrant);
aBag1 -> forEachDo(ShiftPoint);
```

has the effect of first determining those points which are actually in the first quadrant and then of shifting only those points by a certain amount.

This all looks very elegant. But something unpleasant is happening to storage. We are filling it up and may soon run out. This is something we need to take care of. When we constructed **aBag1** above we allocated space for the new collection, which of course we needed, but, having then used the **Point**s in that new collection, presumably we were finished with it. Again, C++ provides the mechanism. The programmer must make appropriate use of it. The mechanism is a destructor, the opposite of a constructor. The destructor for collections is **~Collection**. This is a conventional way of naming the destructor, class name prefixed with **~** . It is called (sometimes implicitly, but in our case explicitly) when we say

```
delete aBag1;
```

```
void* shiftedPoint(void* aPoint){
  return ((Point*)aPoint)->shifted(-2,-2);
}

Collection* aBag2=aBag->collect(shiftedPoint);
```

Figure 4.46 Constructing a collection of shifted points.

The provider of the library will have implemented **~Collection** so that any storage allocated for the collection will be recovered. A quick look at Appendix 2 will reassure you that this happens.

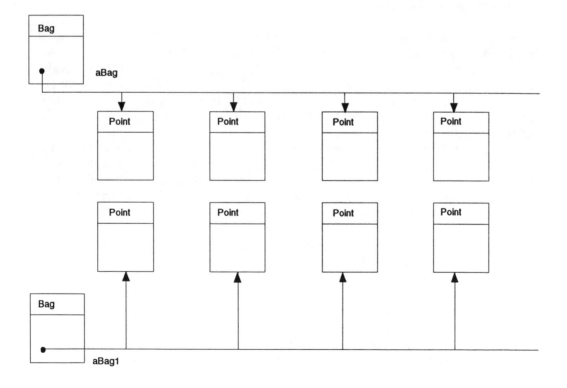

Figure 4.47 The shifted points are all new.

We have one remaining operation on collections shown in Fig. 4.38. This is **Collection::collect**. This is very similar to **select**, in that it constructs a completely new collection. This time however, the members of the new collection will (almost certainly) be different objects from those in the original collection. The function argument to collect expects a **void*** as argument and returns a **void*** as result. An example is shown in Fig. 4.46. Here we have a function **shiftedPoint**, which, given a **Point** as argument, returns a new (shifted) **Point** as result. Calling **aBag -> collect(shiftedPoint)** applies **shiftedPoint** to each object in the collection **aBag**. It collects the result of applying this function into a new collection. The consequences are shown in Fig. 4.47. Each original **Point** object in **aBag** begets a new **Point** object in **aBag1**, constructed from the original by shifting it the given amount. The type of the new collection is the same as the type of the original, so only if it is a **Bag** are we certain that it will have the same numbers of members as the original.

There is little more to the collections in Appendix 2 than we have shown here, but their implementation is interesting and perhaps worth studying before serious use is made of collections in later chapters. In particular, the requirement on the user to use **delete** explicitly and the restrictions which that imposes will be better understood once the implementation has been studied. Details are in Appendix 2, along with a discussion of alternative methods of implementation.

4.9 THE LIBRARY REDONE

In Chapter 2 we introduced the Library example and made a start on coding that design in C++. At that time we said the coding was not as we would eventually require it. In particular, we had allowed public data members, which was useful for debugging purposes, but generally not an advisable use of C++ freedoms. In Chapter 3 we extended the design a little, so that as well as classes **Book** and **Person** we had a new class **Library**. An object of type **Library** would be used, for example, to hold the list of members of the library and the list of acquisitions. The ER diagram which we proposed to describe the relationships to be maintained is shown in Fig. 3.7. The eventual designs of the operations on these three classes (the abstract system) are shown in Figs. 3.34, 3.35 and 3.36, respectively. Our implementation task is to convert this design into C++.

```
class Person{
  char* _name;
  Set* _books;
public:
  char* name();
  Set* books();
  Person(char*);
  void allocate(Book*);
  void deallocate(Book*);
};
```

Figure 4.48 Revised class **Person**.

The implementation is shown in the sequence of Figs. 4.48–4.53. It is reasonably unremarkable except for the conventions we have adopted. Firstly, every object is allocated on the heap and referred to via a pointer. Thus one always sees the types in the code in their pointer-to form, viz **Book***. Since all variables are of the pointer-to variety, the de-referencing will always be by the **->** operator, for example **aBook   -> borrow(aPerson)**. We have made data members private, to prevent assignment to them, and defined a function with the 'same' name to access their values. To avoid name clashes, the data member has been given a leading underscore in its name. You can see all these conventions applied already in the class **Person** specified in Fig. 4.48.

```
Person::Person(char* n):_name(n),_books(new Set()){
}

char* Person::name(){return _name;}

Set* Person::books(){return _books;}

void Person::allocate(Book* aBook){
  _books->insert(aBook);
}

void Person::deallocate(Book* aBook){
  _books->remove(aBook);
}
```

Figure 4.49 Member functions for class **Person**.

There is an implementation extension which has been applied in Fig. 4.48 beyond what was designed in Chapter 3. We have added a new data member **_name** of type **char***. This is the C++ convention for referring to a string, which is going to be needed to be able to store an externally usable name for each **Person**. This is the string which will appear on the screen when queries result in computation of an object of type **Person**. We will print **aPerson -> name()**. This extension of the data members involves a corresponding extension of the constructor, as Fig. 4.49 shows. The space for the string is not allocated in the object **Person**, only space for a pointer to the string. This is something we must remember. When we create a new **Person** we have to allocate space for his or her name.

So a **Person**, as implemented in Figs. 4.48 and 4.49, has a name and a collection of books (a **Set**). Having created a **Person** we can determine the individual's name and the collection of books he or she currently holds. We can allocate a **Book** to the individual or remove a **Book** from him or her, in which case it will be inserted into and removed from (respectively) that person's collection.

```
class Book{
  char* _name;
  Person* _borrower;
public:
  char* name();
  Person* borrower();
  Book(char*);
  void borrow(Person*);
  void _return();
  int inlibrary();
};
```

Figure 4.50 Revised class **Book**.

```
Book::Book(char* n):_name(n),_borrower(0){
}

char* Book::name(){return _name;}

Person* Book::borrower(){return _borrower;}

void Book::borrow(Person* aPerson){
  _borrower=aPerson;
  _borrower->allocate(this);
}

void Book::_return(){
  _borrower->deallocate(this);
  _borrower=0;
}

int Book::inlibrary(){
  return(_borrower==0);
}
```

Figure 4.51 Member functions for class **Book**.

A very similar description serves for our implementation of **Book** as shown in Figs. 4.50 and 4.51. Again, we have an additional data member, **_name**. The other data member points to the **Person** (if any) who currently has borrowed the **Book**. Having created a **Book**, it is possible to read the two data members using the corresponding member functions. It is also possible to determine whether the **Book** is in the library and to borrow and return the **Book**. The implementation of these last two functions, shown in Fig. 4.51 deserves a little explanation. They are symmetric. **Book::borrow** assigns **aPerson** to the borrower attribute. Then it updates the corresponding entry in **aPerson** by the call **borrower -> allocate(this)**, which is equivalent to **aPerson -> allocate(this)**. C++ uses the keyword **this** to denote the object upon which the operation was invoked, in this case a certain **Book**. The statement **borrower -> allocate(this)** therefore ensures that the **Person** borrowing the book has recorded it in their collection.

The reader may worry that we have done no checking to see that, for example a **Book** when borrowed, is indeed in the library. Responsibility for ensuring that will be left to the functions which call **borrow**. The user interface we provide will only allow books to be selected which are in the library and only selected books can be borrowed. So eventually we shall be protected from this potential error.

```
class Library {
  Set* _members;
  Set* _holding;
public:
  Library();
  Set* members();
  Set* holding();
  void acquire(Book*);
  void join(Person*);
  void borrow(Person*, Book*);
  void _return(Person*, Book*);
};
```

Figure 4.52 Class **Library**.

The class **Library**, shown in Figs. 4.52 and 4.53, has two data members, respectively holding the collections of objects representing the **Persons** who have joined the **Library** and the **Books** which have been acquired. Two operations allow us read access to these data members and two operations (**acquire** and **join**) allow us restricted updating capability. Finally, we elevate the **borrow** and **return** operations to be operations on **Library**, largely to make the interface a little more uniform.

```
Library::Library():_members(new Set()),
  _holding(new Set()){}


Set* Library::members(){ return _members;}

Set* Library::holding(){ return _holding;}

void Library::acquire(Book* aBook){
  holding()->insert(aBook);
}
 void Library::join(Person* aPerson){
  members()->insert(aPerson);
}

void Library::borrow(Person* aPerson,Book* aBook){
  aBook->borrow(aPerson);
}

void Library::_return(Person* aPerson,Book* aBook){
  aBook->_return();
}
```

Figure 4.53 Member functions for class **Library**.

```
void printBookName(void* aBook){
  cout<<((Book*)aBook)->name();
}
```

Figure 4.54 A suitable function for **forEachDo**.

Given these definitions, we can construct a test program as follows. We declare some useful objects:

```
Library* lib = new Library();
Person* Tom = new Person("Tom");
        .
        .
        .
Book* Proust = new Book("Proust");
        .
        .
        .
```

Then we go through the process of joining the members and acquiring the books.

```
lib -> join(Tom);
        .
        .
        .
lib -> acquire(Proust);
        .
        .
        .
```

Next we can allow **Person**s to borrow **Books** by calls such as

```
lib -> borrow(Tom,Proust);
        .
        .
        .
```

Once a network of borrowings has been established, we can test some returns. At suitable intervals we can inspect the values of various objects, for example by

```
cout << Proust -> borrower() -> name();
```

To see the collection of Books held by a particular Person, we use the function defined in Fig. 4.54 along with the call

```
Tom -> books() -> forEachDo(printBookName);
```

Even though this implementation is quite simple, testing of this sort is necessary to discover minor errors and to reach a degree of confidence that the quality of the implementation is adequate.

4.10 CONCLUSIONS

In this chapter we have tried to introduce C++ in a gradual way, attending only to those concepts which we shall need later in the book. We have omitted much of advanced C++, but that will be introduced as and when we need it. We have also used C++ in a style with which the author at least is comfortable. We have pointed out places where our style differs from that of other authors. But the reader will want to study those other authors' work eventually. In the bibliography I have described the books which I have found most useful and what I believe I learned from them. This may help the reader decide in which order to read them. Most are books on C++, of course. A few are on other languages (e.g. Smalltalk) which have influenced my style to date. Programming is an engineering skill. It is a professional tool carrying responsibility along with its use. It is a foreign language needing style in its use. It is a mathematical discipline. It is a craft learned by apprenticeship. In these many dimensions it is unique among the engineering tools which we use to make modern day artefacts. It is learned by experience and by absorbing the experience of others. Read these books (and use good compilers) and judge for yourself which techniques you are comfortable with and which improve your productivity and the quality of your product. I hope by taking the view of C++ that I have taken here, that it makes your study of those other authors both more efficient and more pleasant. For further discussion of these points, see the annotated bibliography.

4.11 EXERCISES

For these exercises, you should make use of a C++ compiler, if you have access to one. At least compile your solutions even if you have not completed them to a state where they can be executed.

1. Write a C++ program to compute the nth Fibonacci number, which is given by

    ```
    f(0) = 1
    f(1) = 1
    f(n) = f(n-1) + f(n-2)  when n>1
    ```

    Ensure the program can read n and print $f(n)$. Copy the structure from Fig. 4.4 and the necessary recursion from Fig. 4.12.

2. Write a C++ program which constructs an array of 10 points, where the points are equally spaced (1 unit apart) along the x-axis. Print the array contents. Now shift each of the array members by adding to its y-coordinate an amount equal to its x-coordinate. Again print the array members. This exercise is to encourage you to learn details of the C++ syntax by copying suitable constructions from the various examples in this chapter (see for example Fig. 4.13 and the discussion of arrays).

3. Revise the definition of **Point** in Figs. 4.19 and 4.20 to include an operation **Point::expand(int)** which multiplies each of the **x**- and **y**-coordinates by a fixed value. Incorporate this revised definition in a suitable test program.

4. This exercise is a way of studying memory allocation. Modify the constructor for **Point** to print out a message, saying that it has been called with specific parameters. Now, complete and construct the programs of Figs. 4.23 to 4.26 and execute them. The allocation of memory should be as described in the text. If you also implement a printing destructor, such as

    ```
    Point::~Point(){
        cout << "destroyed Point " << x << y << "\n";
    }
    ```

    then the coming and going of space can be precisely observed.

5. Devise an experiment which, using the printing constructor and destructor of Exercise 4, demonstrates the loss of space which can occur when a pointer to heap storage is overwritten by (for example)

    ```
    p = p->shifted(q);
    ```

6. Extend the class hierarchy of Figs. 4.29 and 4.30 to include classes derived from **Circle** which represent double and triple concentric circles. A double concentric circle has two radii and a triple concentric circle has three. Construct a program which illustrates that the inherited shift operation works for all types of object.

7. Write a C++ program which uses the operation **GeometricObject::biggerthan** (Fig. 4.37) to sort three **GeometricObject**s into ascending order of size. Print their type and size. This program will illustrate the use of virtual member functions. Now add a new definition of a class derived from **GeometricObject** (say a square) and define its size (say its side length). Show that the sorting still works even when some of the objects being sorted are of the new type and even though none of the definitions of the base classes or the sorting algorithm have been altered.

8. Repeat Exercise 2, using **Collections** as specified in Fig. 4.38. It is quite interesting to run this example with the printing constructor and destructor of Exercise 4. Remembering to **delete** collections explicitly, once you have finished with them, will illustrate whether or not the members of a collection are deleted as a consequence.

9. Complete and construct the test program for the extended library (Figs. 4.48 to 4.53). Devise suitable tests. Further extend the library to include videos (see Fig. 3.10 and Exercise 3 of Chapter 2). Be certain to use inheritance. Again devise suitable tests. This is not a vacuous exercise. It brings together all you have learned in this chapter. Also it prepares you to study comprehensive testing, which we ourselves turn to at the end of Chapter 7.

10. Study the details of collections in Appendix 2. In particular, look at the C++ definition of **Collection::all**. Show how the invariants of Exercise 10 of Chapter 3 can be coded in C++ using the appropriate library functions. Add these tests to the program developed in Exercise 9.

THE METHOD APPLIED – A SECOND EXAMPLE

5.1 INTRODUCTION

The method we have outlined in Chapters 2, 3 and 4 is not prescriptive about the order in which we tackle the steps of a software development process. Rather, it provides the means whereby we can record decisions made at each step of the design. When a new problem is faced, whether it be a completely fresh start or the evolution of something which already exists, we have only a very tenuous and informal grasp of the elements of the problem. We have only a relatively vague understanding of the domain of the problem. We engage in an analysis activity which improves our understanding of the problem domain and captures this developing knowledge, usually in diagrammatic form.

In particular we use the ER diagram and object diagram to communicate our early understanding of the problem. As our understanding improves and we begin to grasp the details we will develop an abstract system, a collection of classes (or abstract data types) and their protocols within which we can express solutions to our design problem. The development of the abstract system is at the interface between analysis and design. As we begin to take account of how we are going to deploy the machine in our solution, as we begin to design programs, then we need to become more formal than our diagramming techniques allow. We make use of a formal design language, Enact, either as a pseudo-code or as a modelling or rapid prototyping medium. The idea here is that we make use of sufficiently high-level abstract concepts that the building of a detailed formal model is not expensive. We may choose not to complete this model, but simply to use its development as a framework for subsequent implementation. Or we may choose to make the Enact specification sufficiently complete that we can execute it on an Enact implementation. The advantage of doing the latter is that it helps to confirm the consistency of our design decisions at an early stage, at a stage when correcting design errors might still be reasonably economical.

Perhaps more importantly, development of a working model provides valuable feedback on the complexity of our solution and provides us with the opportunity to improve our design iteratively, in particular with respect to its openness to future change, while it is still economical to do that. We aim to develop an abstract system which is generic in the sense that it can be reused for future evolutions of this design and as a component in designs of other software products.

Thus we have a picture of iterative refinement of our understanding of the problem and of development of the solution, each step being captured informally, then semi-formally, then formally, using first diagrams, then protocols and finally a detailed working model. All this takes place before implementation.

```
class Point < GeometricObject.
```
```
class Point :
    public GenericObject{
    ...
    Point(int,int);
    void shift(Point*);
    ...
};
```

```
Point.shift(aPoint):=
  ( self.x:=self.x+aPoint.x;
    self.y:=self.y+aPoint.y ).
```
```
void Point::shift
    (Point* aPoint){
  x=x+aPoint->x;
  y=y+aPoint->y;
}
```

```
point(x0,y0):=
  new Point with x=x0
          with y=y0.
```
```
Point::Point(int x0, int y0):
    GeometricObject(x0,y0){}
```

Figure 5.1 Some correspondences between Enact and C++.

However, implementation is of course our objective. It is not in itself sufficient to have an elegant, proven design, although that makes the implementation step a surer, more certain step to take. The consequences, we trust, of our investment in good analysis and design is that we will produce high-quality code with greater economy than if we had turned to coding at an earlier stage. In this book we have chosen C++ as the language for coding. Our methods are targeted particularly on that language and our desire to use its support for object-oriented programming. Our formal design notation, Enact, encourages us to specify our classes in a way which is particularly suited to eventually being coded in C++. Figure 5.1 shows some obvious correspondences between Enact and C++. If we had a complete Enact working model we could use it as a skeleton for the C++ code, changing the syntactic details in a straightforward way following the rules implicit in Fig. 5.1.

These rules assume that our C++ objects will be on the heap and accessed via pointers. They assume that we will make extensive use of libraries of predefined classes, such as collection classes. Transliteration from Enact to C++ would only be a first step. There are important implementation issues to do with memory management and performance which can only adequately be dealt with at a very detailed level. For example, for a particular example we might determine that a particular C++ collection class (available, let us suppose, commercially) is going to give us a necessary performance improvement. Some detailed work would be required to fit this specific component neatly into our design without upsetting the integrity of the architecture which we have developed for its solution.

Thus the methods which we have developed span the whole spectrum of software development, from analysis, through design, to Implementation. There are certain qualities which we are trying to engender in our products, in particular correctness and flexibility. The first is engendered by the way in which we test design and implementation, the second by the way that object-oriented methods support the evolution of generic components. In this chapter we shall show each of the stages of development for a new problem and show how the qualities we have discussed are achieved. In so doing we shall introduce a generic component for a simple user interface which we shall then, in the next chapter, fit on to our original problem of recording the coming and going of books from my personal library.

5.2 THE THERMOMETER PROBLEM

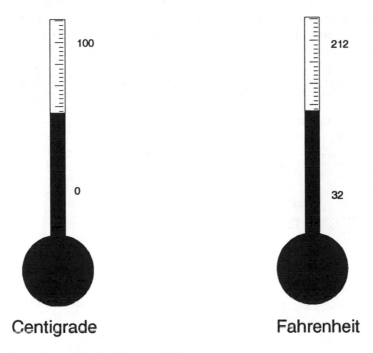

Figure 5.2 Two thermometers showing the same reading.

This is a very simple problem, but it is illustrative of a genre of problems to do with a reactive user interface, where the user edits some areas on a screen setting off a chain of events which then make changes to other areas of the screen. We imagine two thermometers, one giving readings in Fahrenheit and the other readings in Centigrade. We imagine a screen arranged as in Fig. 5.2 where the two thermometers are displayed graphically. We imagine that the user can edit (perhaps by pointing with a mouse) the reading on either thermometer. The consequence of this editing will be that both thermometers will change to show the new temperature, the appropriate conversion between scales having been done automatically, behind the scenes. Thus, for example, if we click on 32 on the Fahrenheit thermometer we expect that thermometer to change to show that reading and the Centigrade thermometer to change to read 0. Then if we click on the Centrigade thermometer at 100 we expect that thermometer to change to show that reading and the Fahrenheit to change to read 212.

In fact, the user interface components which we use in this book, which are introduced in the next section, are not powerful enough to give us this nice graphical interface. Rather, we shall construct an interface which looks something like that in Fig. 5.3. There is a menu which allows us to choose between the thermometers which one we are going to change. There is a prompter which pops up and lets us enter a numeric value for the new temperature and there is a pair of displays, one for each thermometer, which show the current readings. In the figure the two readings are consistent (as integer values) and the user is part way through entering a new Centigrade value. If we were to press ENTER at this stage, the Centigrade display would change to 78 and the Fahrenheit to 172.

What we are doing here is domain analysis. We are understanding the problem. We have begun the analysis stage for our new problem. We have an insight. Whichever user interface we were eventually to choose, there is a common design part which is the part of the solution which records temperatures and keeps them consistent with each other and

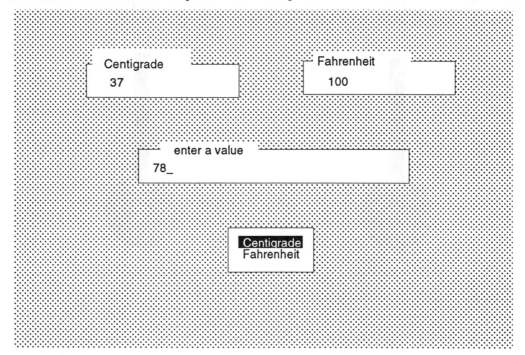

Figure 5.3 A simpler user interface.

which implements the conversion. So we realize that we can develop this part of the application independently of the user interface. We have decomposed the problem into two more manageable parts. We can postpone the development of the user interface until after we have developed support for thermometers. Note that we used a quite valid bit of lookahead here: we anticipated the user interface components we were going to use. We did this early because we need to check that the design we are about to do will be consistent with that target. We might expect to have to iterate a little to get a perfect fit but we would not expect to get an awkward mismatch. This kind of lookahead from analysis to later stages is an essential part of our activity. At the same time, we should keep the two parts as cleanly and clearly separate as economically possible, for it is that physical separation which ensures greater future flexibility. The very fact that we have anticipated two different interfaces here and a potential evolution from one to the other at a future date means that we should not become too locked in to the actual user interface objects which we anticipate using. We should make the thermometer part of our application as open as possible to accepting either interface.

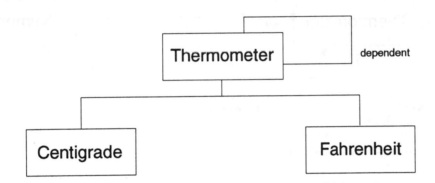

Figure 5.4 ER diagram for thermometers.

That said, our task is actually fairly trivial. There is not much to synchronizing two thermometers. Nevertheless, let us do it properly. What are the entities in the real world which we are to represent? We have two different types of thermometer, we have temperature readings and we have the fact that one thermometer may be dependent upon another. Our thermometers only differ in the scale which they use. We would expect them to have identical protocols allowing us to set and query the temperature which they record, so we would expect to use inheritance to factor out the common behaviour of a thermometer and to locate the specialized behaviour, to do with being Centigrade or Fahrenheit, in the subclasses. This is what we have done in Fig. 5.4, which shows an ER diagram introducing three classes *Thermometer*, *Centigrade* and *Fahrenheit*. *Thermometer* will be an abstract class; we shall only create instances of its subclasses *Centigrade* and *Fahrenheit*. Each thermometer will have a single dependent, which will be another thermometer. This is shown in Fig. 5.4 as the relationship link which relates *Thermometer* to itself.

```
aThermometer:=centigrade()
aThermometer:=fahrenheit()
aThermometer.addDependent(aThermometer)
aThermometer.set(aNumber)
aNumber:=aThermometer.get()
```

Figure 5.5 Abstract system for thermometers – external protocol.

The external protocol which we propose for our abstract system is shown in Figs. 5.5 and 5.6 in (respectively) textual and diagrammatic form. We have constructors for each of the two subclasses and the ability to link two thermometers together by the operation *addDependent* as follows:

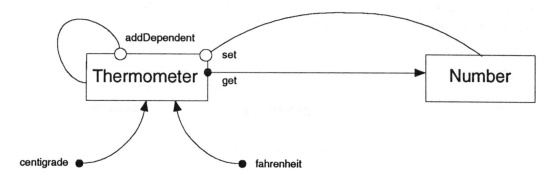

Figure 5.6 Abstract system for thermometers – external protocol.

```
C := centigrade().
F := fahrenheit().
C.addDependent(F).
F.addDependent(C).
```

This creates the situation shown in the object diagram of Fig. 5.7. Now the application making use of these two linked thermometers can set their temperature readings and retrieve these settings using the remaining operations listed in the protocol, for example,

```
F.set(78).
t := C.get().
```

Here we would expect the result in *t* to be *172*. How does this happen? The call of *F.set* must use the dependent link to change the value of *C* also. But of course, that at least seems possible, if not indeed trivial. So we have a solution. We have completed our analysis and moved into design. We have, in Fig. 5.5, an abstract system adequate to our purpose; now we need to design the mechanisms which give each of the operations the meanings which we have attributed to them.

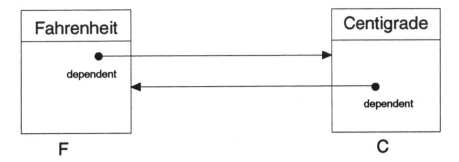

Figure 5.7 Object diagram for thermometers.

There must be many solutions to this design problem. The one we have chosen is motivated by a desire to be reasonably generic. We do not want to make different operations for *Fahrenheit* to communicate with *Centigrade* and for *Centigrade* to communicate with *Fahrenheit*, particularly since we might at a later stage link *Fahrenheit* to *Fahrenheit*, and we might at a later stage introduce a third or fourth type of *Thermometer*. We want a solution which is extensible in these ways (see the exercises for examples).

```
aThermometer.setAbs(aNumber)
aNumber:=aThermometer.getAbs()
aThermometer.reset()
```

Figure 5.8 Abstract system for thermometers – hidden (implementor's) protocol.

The solution we have chosen is as follows. Look at Fig. 5.7. When we set the temperature in F it advises its dependent C of this fact by calling $C.reset()$. This is a hidden operation, part of the implementor's protocol not available to the user of the abstract system. A call to *reset* is an instruction to the dependent thermometer that it is necessary to update its value. Now we have a problem, that we have to handle conversion in an extensible way. We do this by adding two more hidden operations, which respectively allow us to enquire of and set a thermometer's value using a standard scale for communication purposes. We could have chosen any scale for this purpose. We chose a (quasi) absolute scale. So with these additional operations, whose protocol is shown in Fig. 5.8, we can ensure C updates itself by the call

```
C.setAbs(F.getAbs())
```

What happens here is that F responds with its absolute value (having converted from Fahrenheit) and then C accepts this value and (converting to Centigrade) sets its own value to correspond. The important property of this part of the protocol is that

```
aThermometer1.setAbs(aThermometer2.getAbs())
```

works regardless of the actual type of *aThermometer1* or *aThermometer2*.

```
class Thermometer < Object.


Thermometer.get(aNumber):=self.temp.

Thermometer.addDependent(aThermometer):=
  (self.dependent:=aThermometer).

Thermometer.reset():=
  self.setAbs(self.dependent.getAbs()).

Thermometer.set(aNumber):=
  (self.temp:=aNumber;
   self.dependent.reset() if self.dependent<>nil).
```

Figure 5.9 The class *Thermometer* in Enact.

```
class Centigrade < Thermometer.

centigrade():= new Centigrade with temp=0
                          with dependent=nil.

Centigrade.getAbs():=self.temp+273.

Centigrade.setAbs(aNumber):=
        (self.temp:=aNumber-273).
```

Figure 5.10 The class *Centigrade* in Enact.

```
class Fahrenheit < Thermometer.

fahrenheit():= new Fahrenheit with temp=32
                          with dependent=nil.

Fahrenheit.getAbs():=(self.temp-32)*5/9+273.

Fahrenheit.setAbs(aNumber):=
        (self.temp:=(aNumber-273)*9/5+32).
```

Figure 5.11 The class *Fahrenheit* in Enact.

Now we are in a position to detail the design completely using Enact. This we have done in Figs. 5.9, 5.10 and 5.11, which show the three classes *Thermometer*, *Centigrade* and *Fahrenheit*. We see that each *Thermometer* has two attributes, *temp* and *dependent*, for recording its current reading and its related thermometer, respectively. The user application can determine the value of *temp* by using *aThermometer.get()*. Each thermometer has been initialized to the temperature of freezing water by its constructor function. If a thermometer has a dependent, that relationship can be established by calling *aThermometer1.addDependent (aThermometer2)*. The only other external operation on thermometers is *aThermometer.set(aNumber)*, which sets the thermometer to have *temp=aNumber*. Then it informs the dependent by the call

```
self.dependent.reset()if self.dependent <> nil
```

which means that if *aThermometer* has a dependent, that thermometer will be told to reset itself. This in turn uses *getAbs* and *setAbs* as explained above to determine the value to which it must be reset. Finally, inspection of the definitions of *getAbs* and *setAbs* in each of the classes *Centigrade* and *Fahrenheit* should convince you that the conversion takes place correctly. More importantly, inspection of the structure of these three classes and the protocol for communicating between them should convince you that adding a new type of thermometer is trivial. We link it into the class hierarchy, provide a constructor and provide conversion functions between its scale and our (quasi) absolute scale. It then inherits the cooperative behaviour of the existing thermometer types.

Since we have developed the Enact specification so completely we have the advantage that we can test it. This we would do progressively by calling the simpler operations first; for example, the sequence

```
F := fahrenheit().
F.get().
```

should result in the response *32*, the initial value for a *Fahrenheit* thermometer. Having similarly checked a *Centigrade* thermometer, we would link the two together using the calls

```
F.addDependent(C).
C.addDependent(F).
```

Now we can check their cooperative behaviour. Suppose we call

```
F.set(212).
C.get().
C.set(0).
F.get().
```

We would expect the two responses to be *100* and *32*, respectively, showing that communication in both directions is working.

The benefits of this Enact model are many. The first is that it detects errors earlier in the development process than might have been possible if we had to wait until we had a C++ version available (although this benefit really shows only on larger examples). The second is that in practice we are not usually totally satisfied with our first model, so we iteratively improve it by repeating some of the analysis and design. The models presented in this book are usually third- or fourth-generation, having been improved in the light of experience playing with earlier models. This iterative process is obviously worthwhile, as long as it is economical, if it builds in elements of future-proofing by making our models either simpler or more generic or, ideally, both. The third benefit is that we have tackled half of the implementation issues in a more abstract language than C++. When we move to C++ we still have problems to solve, but we have many solutions we can just lift whole from Enact into C++. In this example we have actually done considerably more than half of the implementation work already, because there are no serious memory management or performance issues to be resolved. What remains to be done is almost exclusively an act of translation.

```
class Thermometer {
protected:
  long temp;
  Thermometer* dependent;
  Thermometer(long);
public:
  void set(long);
  long get();
  void addDependent(Thermometer*);
  void reset();
  virtual void setAbs(long)=0;
  virtual long getAbs()=0;
};
```

Figure 5.12 The class **Thermometer** in C++.

The implementation in C++ is shown in Figs. 5.12, 5.13, 5.14 and 5.15. This implementation is arrived at largely by applying the rules of transliteration described at the beginning of this chapter and implicit in Fig. 5.1. For example, the class hierarchy is coded up exactly as in Enact, but using the C++ conventions. It has been necessary in the C++ to be more explicit about the types of variables, arguments to functions and return values. Temperatures are represented by **long** values. Thermometers are represented by pointers declared as **Thermometer***. The derived classes **Centigrade** and **Fahrenheit** shown in Figs. 5.14 and 5.15 are simpler than the base class **Thermometer**. They each inherit **Thermometer**'s public members **(void set(long), long get()** etc.) and provide implementations of their own constructors and of the two virtual functions **void setAbs(long)** and **long getAbs()**. They are also pleasingly symmetric. Adding a third type of thermometer would be a trivial procedure of copying the form and supplying new details.

```
Thermometer::Thermometer(long t):temp(t){}

long Thermometer::get(){
  return temp;
}

        void    Thermometer::addDependent(Thermometer*
aThermometer){
    dependent=aThermometer;
}

void Thermometer::reset(){
  setAbs(dependent->getAbs());
}

void Thermometer::set(long aNumber){
  temp=aNumber;
  if(dependent!=0)dependent->reset();
}
```

Figure 5.13 Member functions of class **Thermometer**.

```
class Centigrade: public Thermometer{
public:
  Centigrade();
  void setAbs(long);
  long getAbs();
};

Centigrade::Centigrade():Thermometer(0){}

long Centigrade::getAbs(){
  return(temp+273);
}

void Centigrade::setAbs(long aNumber){
  temp=aNumber-273;
}
```

Figure 5.14 The class **Centigrade** with its member functions.

```
class Fahrenheit: public Thermometer{
public:
  Fahrenheit();
  void setAbs(long);
  long getAbs();
};

Fahrenheit::Fahrenheit():Thermometer(32){}

long Fahrenheit::getAbs(){
  return((temp-32)*5/9+273);
}

void Fahrenheit::setAbs(long aNumber){
  temp=(aNumber-273)*9/5+32;
}
```

Figure 5.15 The class **Fahrenheit** with its member functions.

Now consider the base class **Thermometer**. Here we have made a few further implementation decisions. We have hidden the data members by making them **protected** (so that derived classes can see them) and we have also hidden the base class constructor in the same way. Note that we could have made **dependent** a private data member since the subclasses do not need it. Making the constructor hidden is one way of making sure no instances of the base class are created. However, in this case it was also unnecessary, because the fact that we have made **void setAbs(long)** and **long getAbs()** pure virtual ensures that the compiler will prevent the construction of objects of type **Thermometer**. Making these member functions pure virtual is the C++ way of indicating that their implementation is a subclass responsibility. We are not required (or allowed) to provide implementations of pure virtual functions for the base class, but they must be provided for all derived classes. Their appearance in the declaration part of the base class allows us to declare that they are virtual (and pure) and allows the compiler to check usages such as **aThermometer -> getAbs()** as being type correct even though **aThermometer** can only in practice be bound to a (pointer to a) **Centigrade** or **Fahrenheit**.

Although the C++ has been developed fairly automatically from the Enact, and although the Enact has been tested, and although the program we are aiming eventually to build is, so far, only half built, I would nevertheless test this C++ code at this stage. A suitable test would take the following form

```
Thermometer* C = new Centrigrade();
Thermometer* F = new Fahrenheit();
C -> addDependent();
F -> addDependent();
```

Here we have declared two **Thermometers** and allocated space for them on the heap. Then we have cross-linked them. Now we can run a simple test:

```
F -> set(212);
cout << C.get() << "\n";
C -> set (0);
cout << F.get() << "\n";
```

from which we would expect to see on the output screen the two answers 100 and 32. More testing would be appropriate to check such things as correct initialization, that it still works when the dependent is nil, that linking two **Fahrenheit**s together also works and so on. It is better that we detect those sorts of error in the scope of a small program like this than later, when its components are embedded in something larger (which is where we go to next). Now we will add a tolerable user interface.

5.3 USER INTERFACE OBJECTS

We continue our development in a different way. Now we cope with the fact that we are going to make use of an existing library of user interface objects. We have no control over what they are. They have been supplied from elsewhere and a (commercial) decision has been made to use them. Our job is to match our solution of the first half of the problem to this fixed target for the second half. Of course, we anticipated the nature of this library of components when designing the first half and therefore expect the marriage to be a straightforward, if not trivial, one. We expect to do some work, but not to encounter insurmountable problems.

The library of user interface classes we shall use is listed fully in Appendix 2. This is of course a pedagogical toy developed by the author. It is markedly simpler than any comparable commercial offering because it provides only the most trivial functionality, but it is sufficient to make the points we want to make about reusing existing code.

Had we bought this code commercially the first thing we would encounter is the user manual describing the protocol for using the objects. In all likelihood this would be described at the C++ level, giving examples of C++ calls invoking each of the facilities in turn. To make use of the library, apart from learning how, we have to have access to a file of declarations which describes (to the compiler) each of the classes which the library makes available for use. This is referred to as a header file. We **#include** it in our program in order that reference to classes can be understood by the compiler. The compiled code can then be linked to the compiled library, presumably also delivered by the supplier along with the header file. This means that the supplier of the library need not deliver the source code of its implementation, only of the declarations in the header file. Thus the supplier protects its investment.

In this section I want to simulate the process one goes through of familiarization with, and abstraction from, code which has been bought in in this way, so I shall start by looking at the C++ declarations for the library of user interface objects and describing them as they typically would be in a user manual for that library. Then I shall use the diagramming and pseudocode techniques to capture a more succinct model of the interface to this library. I shall effectively retrofit an abstract system to the library before proceeding to attach it to our application. In fact, I shall retrofit an Enact model which abstracts away from much of the (essential) cluttering detail of the C++. This will then enable us to fit the application code and the user interface code together very neatly. Of course we will ultimately have to add the detail (such as screen locations) which the C++ demands, but at a certain level of design ignoring it is an important designer's simplification.

```
class Display : public Window {
public:
  Display(int, int, int, int, char*);
  void put(long);
  void put(char*);
};

class Prompter : public Window {
public:
  Prompter(int, int, int, int, char*);
  long get();
  char* gets();
};
```

Figure 5.16 Classes **Display** and **Prompter** (from **userface.h**).

The essential features of the C++ header file (called **userface.h**, for future reference) are shown in Figs. 5.16, 5.17 and 5.18. There are four types of user interface object which we can create using this library, respectively **Display**, **Prompter**, **Menu** and **Selector**. Each of them creates and uses a window on the screen in a different way.

```
class Menu : public Scroller , public Event {
public:
    Menu(int, int, int, int);
    void _do();
};

class Selector : public Scroller {
public:
  Selector(int, int, int, int);
  void* get();
};
```

Figure 5.17 Classes **Menu** and **Selector** (from **userface.h**).

```
class Event {
  Set* dependents;
  char* _label;
public:
  Event();
  void addDependent(Event*);
  void doAllDependents();
  void setLabel(char*);
  char* label();
  virtual void _do();
};

class Scroller : public Window {
  ...
public:
  Scroller(int, int, int, int);
  void install(Set*, char*(void*));
};
```

Figure 5.18 Classes **Event** and **Scroller** (from **userface.h**).

A **Display** is used as an output device to display either a **long** or a **char*** in a permanently visible window. A **Prompter** is an input device which will appear when input is required and disappear when it has been entered. We can use this **Prompter** to read either a **long** or a **char***. A simple example of the use of these two devices is (we assume this is taken from the instruction manual):

```
Display d(2,2,1,20, "the value is");
Prompter p(10,20,1,50, "enter a value");
long x = p.get();
d.put(x);
```

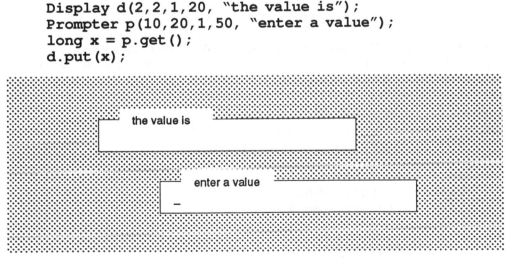

Figure 5.19 How a **Display** and a **Prompter** might appear on screen.

A **Display d** is opened on the screen with its top left corner at (character) position 2,2. It has space for 1 line of 20 characters. It has a frame with the title 'the value is' (see Fig. 5.19). A **Prompter p** also appears on the screen with its top left corner at 10,20 (tenth column, twentieth row) and with space for 1 line of 50 characters. Its frame exhibits the message 'enter a value' and the program waits for the user to type a response to **p.get()**. Once this is done (if it is a valid **long**) the value is assigned to **x** and then displayed on the screen in the **Display** by the statement **d.put(x);**. The prompter appears when **p.get()** is called and disappears when a valid response has been elicited. Thus **Display** and **Prompter** work together to provide a simple input–output means for **long** and **char*** values.

The **Menu** and **Selector** devices are more complex. They are both derived classes from the base class **Scroller**, shown in Fig. 5.18. A **Scroller** supports the notion of a scrollable list of strings which is an input device whose appearance on the screen is as shown in Fig. 5.20. A list of strings appears in a window. By moving the cursor up and down using the arrow keys on the keyboard one of these strings can be selected by the user. If the list of strings is longer than the window then the window scrolls up and down over the list, moving whenever the cursor (shown in reverse video) would disappear off the top or bottom of the window. A **Scroller** is not itself a usable device. We use two specializations of it, respectively a **Selector** and a **Menu**.

Figure 5.20 A **Scroller**, from which both **Menu** and **Selector** are derived.

The difference is in the nature of their use. A **Selector** allows us to choose an object from a collection of objects. It returns that object. A **Menu** allows us to select from a collection of special objects of class **Event**. Rather than return anything, the **Menu** sends the message **_do()** to the chosen **Event**, thus evoking further activity. Needless to say, setting up these devices is not trivial.

Let us look first at how we set up a **Selector**. Suppose we have a collection of objects, all of type **Book**, created perhaps as follows:

```
Set* list = new Set();
list -> insert(aBook1);
list -> insert(aBook2);
        .
        .
        .
```

In order to use a **Selector** we must also define a function which, when applied to any object in this collection, will return a string which can be displayed on the screen. Fortunately, **Book** objects have a string valued attribute accessed by **aBook** **->** **name()** so we can use this for what the **Selector** refers to as the label of the object. The selector expects to be provided with a function of type **char*(*) (void*)** which it can use to determine the label for each object, so we will supply

```
char* BookNameFunction(void* aBook){
     return ((Book*)aBook) -> name();
}
```

With this preparation, we can set up a **Selector** as follows

```
Selector aSelector(10,10,6,20);
aSelector.install(list,BookNameFunction);
```

Our **Selector** will not appear on the screen until we interrogate it with

```
aBook = aSelector.get();
```

whereupon it will appear with its top left corner at position 10,10. It will have space in the window for 6 lines of 20 characters, so it would indeed appear as Fig. 5.20 shows. As soon as the selection has been made (by hitting RETURN), the **Selector** disappears from the screen and the program proceeds with **aBook** set to point to whichever element of the collection has the selected name.

```
class testEvent : public Event{
public:
  testEvent();
  void _do();
};

void testEvent::_do(){
  aDisplay->puts(label());
}
```

Figure 5.21 A suitable event for testing **Menu**.

A **Menu** is a similar device, but uses one more new class, **Event**, which is shown in Fig. 5.18. The most important property of an **Event** is that it has a method **anEvent._do()**. A **Menu** is effectively a special type of **Selector** which selects an **Event** from a collection of events and invokes its **_do()** operation. To illustrate how this works consider the very simple derived class **testEvent** shown in Fig. 5.21. First we create a number of **testEvent** objects:

```
testEvent* event1 = new testEvent();
testEvent* event2 = new testEvent();
```

and then we use the inherited operation **setLabel** to give them unique labels:

```
event1 -> setLabel("event1");
event2 -> setLabel("event2");
      .
      .
      .
```

Now we create a collection to hold these events:

```
Set* events = new Set();
events -> insert(event1);
events -> insert(event2);
      .
      .
      .
```

and a function to derive their labels:

```
char* EventLabelFunction(void* anEvent){
    return ((Event*)anEvent) -> label();
}
```

Finally we can create a menu and install this collection of events, as follows:

```
Menu aMenu(10,10,6,20);
aMenu.install(events,EventLabelFunction);
```

With this preparation we can invoke the menu with the call

```
aMenu._do();
```

On reaching this point in the program, the menu pops up on the screen. The user can scroll through the (labels of the) **Events** listed using the arrow keys, and select an **Event** by hitting RETURN. Suppose the user selects **event2** from the list; then, because of the definition we have given to **testEvent::_do()** in Fig. 5.21, this selection will cause **aDisplay -> puts("event2")** to be invoked, presumably displaying an appropriate message elsewhere on the screen, confirming our use and understanding of the **Menu** device.

The final feature of this C++ library is the way in which it supports nested menus, that is, the ability of one menu selection to delegate the choice to a submenu. It does this because a **Menu** is a specialized type of **Event**, a subclass of **Event**. Since a **Menu** is also a subclass of **Scroller**, what we have here is an example of multiple inheritance.

Figure 5.17 shows that the derived class **Menu** has both **Scroller** and **Event** as base classes. This means that objects of type **Event** inherit the properties, and in particular the operations, of both base classes. In our case, a **Menu** is something which can present a scrollable list of strings on the screen (inherited from **Scroller**) and itself be a member of a set of **Events** responding to the message **_do()** (inherited from **Event**).

Setting up a submenu using this system is the same as setting up a top-level menu. Suppose we extend the example given earlier by declaring

```
Menu* subMenu = Menu(12,14,6,20);
subMenu -> install(subevents,EventLabelFunction);
```

where the **Set*** **subevents** has been set up to contain the **testEvents** **event6,event7,...** . We have chosen to refer to the **subMenu** via a pointer because that makes the remainder of this exposition simpler. In fact, when we come to use this C++ library in anger we will adopt a uniform policy of referring to all **Menus** (indeed all objects) by pointers.

What we have to do now is insert the **subMenu** as an **Event** in the top level **Menu**, but before we do that we have to ensure that it has a label:

```
subMenu -> setLabel("subMenu");
```

Having done this, we can add it to the top level **Menu** by the simple device of

```
events -> insert((Event*)subMenu);
```

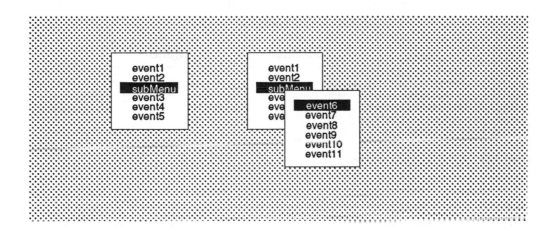

Figure 5.22 Submenu selection, before (left) and after (right).

The top-level menu is invoked by **aMenu._do();**, upon which it pops up on the screen as shown on the left of Fig. 5.22. By moving the cursor the user can select any of the **Events**. Suppose the user selects **subMenu**; then the screen will change to present the appearance shown on the right of Fig. 5.22, with both menus visible. Their relative positions on the screen were chosen by the programmer when creating the respective objects. The user can now move up and down the choices in the **subMenu**. On making a choice, that event is performed and the **subMenu** remains active. The user needs to know that pressing ESCAPE will cause the **subMenu** to disappear and return to the top-level menu. There is a fundamental difference here between a **Selector** and a **Menu**. A **Selector** disappears as soon as a selection is made. A **Menu** disappears only when explicitly told to go. This was the library designer's choice. It seems to be an effective one.

So, that is the C++ library **userface** described as it would be in the manual supplied with it. We have to understand it sufficiently that we can fit it on to the code we have already written for the thermometer exercise. The particular design chosen by the designer of the **userface** library is not ours to change: we don't have the source of the implementation, only the header file. Our way of proceeding will be to capture our knowledge about the way the library works in a more abstract model using the diagramming techniques and pseudocode which we have used, up until now, for design purposes. That is, we will build an abstract system for the **userface** library.

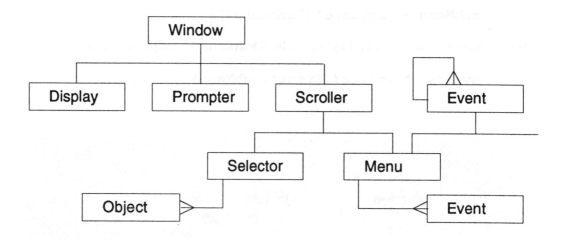

Figure 5.23 ER diagram for **userface**.

Drawing the ER diagram is a straightforward process of reading the base class information from the header file. Thus we get the ER diagram shown in Fig. 5.23. Each of the devices *Display*, *Prompter* and *Scroller* inherits from a class *Window*, which we will not be making direct use of. This class provides the commonality of operation which all three devices share, that they occupy a rectangular area of the screen and write to and/or read from that area. A *Scroller* is further specialized into a *Selector* and a *Menu*. A *Selector* has a collection of *Objects* (of any type) from which we can select. A *Menu* has a collection of *Events*. An *Event* is a base from which we are expected to derive specialized *Events*. The system already supplies one specialized *Event*, the *Menu*. We have just seen how to use this multiple inheritance. Its depiction in Fig. 5.23 is fairly obvious. We use the dangling leg of the subclasses of *Event* to indicate that we expect the user to supply specializations of that class. The fact that the *Selector* can have a collection of any type of *Object* does not excuse us from some responsibility to ensure that when we obtain a selected object we know what type it is, at least to the extent that we can do sensible things with it. Similarly, the fact that a *Menu* has a collection of *Events* means that when we select an entry from the *Menu* the only attribute we will be able to assume it has is the _*do ()* method.

```
aPrompter:=prompter()
aReply:=aPrompter.get()

aDisplay:=display()
aDisplay.put(aValue)
```

Figure 5.24 (Abstract) protocols for *Prompter* and *Display*.

Having reverse engineered the structure of the library to obtain the ER diagram, the next step is to capture the protocols which are the interface for the user of the libary. We would normally take the opportunity here to abstract from detail in order to make the modelling activity of the design step have the property that it allows us to test overall design validity without the clutter of (less relevant) detail. For example, here we shall ignore the requirement which the **userface** library places on the programmer to specify the screen positions of all the devices, and that some devices have messages coded into them. This is a detail which can safely be left until the implementation stage. The abstract protocols for the userface library are shown in Figs. 5.24 and 5.25. They are simple enough. A *Prompter* can be created and then we can *get* a value from it; in practice this will be a number or a string. A *Display* can be created and we can *put* a

```
aSelector:=selector()
aMenu:=menu()
aScroller.install(aCollection,aFunction)
anObject:=aSelector.get()
aMenu.do()

anEvent.doAllDependents()
anEvent.setLabel(aLabel)
anEvent.addDependent(anEvent)
anEvent.do()
```

Figure 5.25 (Abstract) protocol for *Selector*, *Menu* and *Event*.

value to it, again in practice a number or a string. We can create a *Selector* and a *Menu*, and since each inherits from *Scroller* we can install a *Collection* and a function in each one. The *Collection* will be the *Objects* and *Events* (respectively) presented to the user for him or her to choose. The function will be applied to each *Object* or *Event* to determine the label to be used to distinguish the selection on the screen. To a *Selector* we may apply the operation *get ()*, in which case we shall obtain, as a result, one of the objects from the collection installed in it. To a *Menu* we may apply the operation *do ()* in which case we will be allowed to select an *Event*, and then that *Event* will be sent the message *do ()* in turn. So we must ensure that every *Event* in the collection installed in a *Menu* has both a label and a *do* method if this protocol is to work.

*Event*s have one further important property. An *Event* has a collection of *Events* which are its dependents. We can add an *Event* to this collection using the *addDependent* method shown in Fig. 5.25 and we can also invoke the operation *doAllDependents* which sends the message *do ()* to all the *Event*s in the collection of dependents.

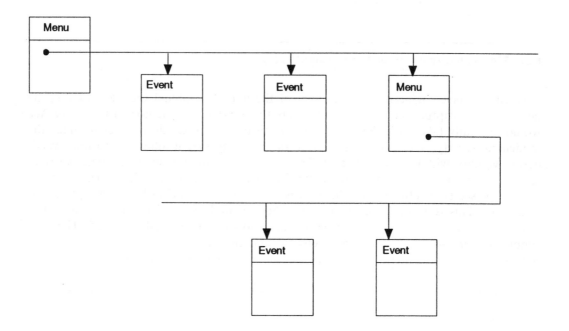

Figure 5.26 Object diagram for nested menus.

Finally, as part of the normal method of capturing our knowledge about an abstract system, we shall draw some object diagrams of typical arrangements of objects from the abstract system, showing how they can be used to solve simple problems. For example, Fig. 5.26 is an object diagram for the arrangement of *Menus* and *Events* which implements a nested menu system such as that shown in Fig. 5.22. We see that the top level *Menu* has a collection of *Events* one of which is a *Menu*. The user is asked to choose an *Event* from this collection. The chosen *Event* is sent the message *do ()* and then, when that completes, the choice is offered again. If the submenu is chosen then the user is offered (repeatedly) choices from that menu, each chosen *Event* being sent the message *do()*. This repeating subprocess can be terminated (by pressing ESCAPE), in which case we return to the top level *Menu*.

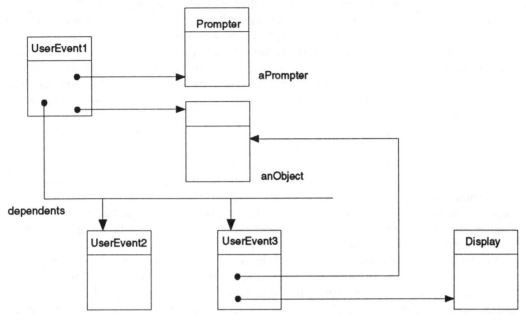

Figure 5.27 Object diagram for linked *Prompter* and *Display*.

Figure 5.27 is an arrangement of *Event*s which show how a *Prompter* can be used to elicit a value of an (attribute of an) application object and then a *Display* which is dependent upon that application object can be updated. We assume we have defined a number of application specific subclasses of *Event*, in this case *UserEvent1*, *UserEvent2* and *UserEvent3*. The object *aUserEvent1* knows *aPrompter* and *anObject*. When we say *do()* to *aUserEvent1*, *aPrompter* obtains a value which it uses to update *anObject*. Then we fire all of the *Event*s in *aUserEvent1*'s dependents. In this case, *aUserEvent3* is included, so it is fired. We assume *aUserEvent3* knows *anObject* and *aDisplay*, so it can update the display using the value of the updated *anObject*. We shall see examples of this sort in the next section, when we solve the remainder of the thermometers problem, and in the next chapter when we shall add a reasonably sophisticated user interface to my personal library.

The abstract system described here, retrieved from the concrete C++ implementation, is in fact implemented in Enact in such a way that models of the logic of the user interface can be tested. This implementation is listed, along with the C++ header file, in Appendix 2. It does not use anything more sophisticated than the normal line at a time input-output capabilities of a normal glass teletype, which makes it a lot less fun to use than the C++ itself. But for complex user interfaces such as the one that we shall build in the next chapter, it is a cost-effective way of getting the logic and reliability of that interface correct. We shall see how to use it in the coming sections.

5.4 A USER INTERFACE FOR THERMOMETERS

Now let us turn back to the problem which we set ourselves at the beginning of the chapter. The requirement is perhaps best recalled by looking again at Fig. 5.3, where we see that we have anticipated the use of the **userface** library showing a screen with a *Menu*, a *Prompter* and two *Display*s which we consider adequate to solve our problem. The anticipated behaviour of the underlying application was that it began with the user focused on the *Menu*. The user would select between thermometers whereupon a *Prompter* would appear allowing the user to enter a numeric value for the new temperature. On completing this entry satisfactorily, both *Display*s would change to indicate the new value of the temperature and the input focus would return to the *Menu*.

So far we have established the objects for implementing thermometers. We have designed them to have the external protocol shown in Fig. 5.6, with the property that, once they are cross-linked using the *addDependent* operation, setting the value of any thermometer automatically updates the value of its dependent with appropriate scale conversion. We have also developed an Enact working model and a tested C++ implementation of this part of the problem. This represents a substantial investment, not one we would wish to repeat, so we consider these components as building blocks with which we must build our solution.

We have also obtained and invested in a particular user interface library, our investment being the time we have now spent in developing the skill needed to be able to make use of it. We have determined that it is adequate to our purpose. We have already got access to it from C++ and even have an Enact model of it which we can use for testing our logic. So, our method of proceeding from here will be first to build on the

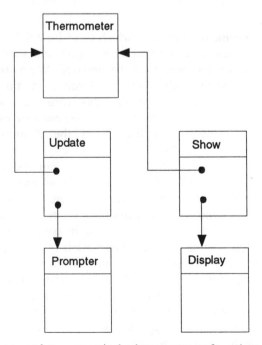

Figure 5.28 Linking the *Update* and *Show* events in the thermometer configuration.

abstract systems for thermometers (Figs. 5.4 – 5.6) and for user interface objects (Figs. 5.23 – 5.25), combining their objects to form a proposed solution to our problem. Then we shall complete the Enact pseudocode descriptions of the behaviour of our extension so that we can use the Enact implementation to debug the design at an early stage. Finally, we shall use the rules of transliteration from Enact to C++ to obtain a skeleton of the final implementation and add the detail which is required to make this a complete solution.

Hence we return to a creative stage, to an analysis activity which we believe will lead to a design which will work. In fact, the seeds of our solution are already laid in the abstract systems we have decided to build upon and in the way of using them that we have either developed or discovered. The seeds are that we have *Thermometer* objects which are used to hold current values of the temperature reading and we have *Event* objects which are used to establish the connection between the user interface objects and the application objects. In the previous section we showed how to link a *Prompter* and a *Display* which were connected with a particular application object. That is exactly our requirement here. We need to be able to update the value of a *Thermometer* and to display this updated value. We do this by introducing two new types of *Event*, shown in the object diagram of Fig. 5.28. *Update* is a subclass of *Event*. An *Update* object knows of a *Thermometer* and a *Prompter*. It can use the *Prompter* to obtain a new value, which it can then assign to its *Thermometer*. Similarly, *Show* is a subclass of *Event*. A *Show* object knows of a *Thermometer* and a *Display*. It can determine the current reading of the *Thermometer* and use the *Display* to display it on the screen. The corresponding *do()* methods for these two new classes should be trivial to write (we would conjecture at this stage).

As arranged in Fig. 5.28, we would need to fire the *Show* event after firing the *Update* event. We know that the *Event* structure of our user interface objects provides for this eventuality. We simply add the *Show* event to the dependents of the *Update* event and remember to *doAllDependents* in the *Update.do()* method, so that would seem to be an excellent component for our solution. We would need two such components, one for the *Centigrade* thermometer and one for the *Fahrenheit*. So now we try to extend our solution by combining two such components. This is what we have done in Fig. 5.29. Here we see two identical subsystems, one for each thermometer. The two *Thermometer*s are linked, as they should be, and we have added to each of the *Update* events a link showing its collection of dependents. This includes its own *Show* event and the *Show* event in the other subsystem. That we will discuss in a moment, for our analysis is almost complete. We simply have to be able to drive the entire system. So we add a *Menu*. It will have a collection of *Event*s which it can fire. We simply put the two *Update* events in that collection. Now we convince ourselves (and our colleagues) that this is a potential solution by running through a scenario of using the system.

We assume the system is driven from the *Menu* object (in Fig. 5.29). This allows the user (repeatedly) to choose and fire one or other of the *Update* events. When an *Update* fires, it opens its *Prompter* on the screen and elicits a numerical value. It uses this value to update its own *Thermometer*, which, because of the linking of *Thermometer*s, causes the *Thermometer* in the other subsystem to be reset appropriately. Next *Update* fires all of its dependents, which are its own *Show* event and the neighbour's *Show* event. Each *Show* event interrogates its *Thermometer* and displays its new value in its *Display*. Then the firing quiesces and the focus returns to the *Menu* for a repeat performance if required.

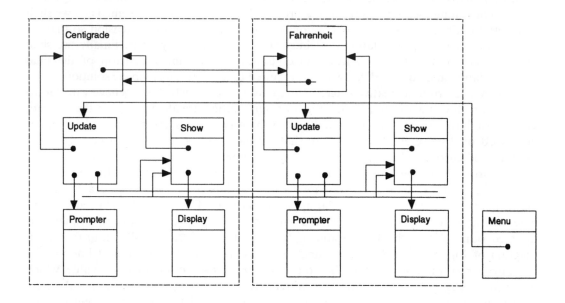

Figure 5.29 The configuration of objects on the thermometer example.

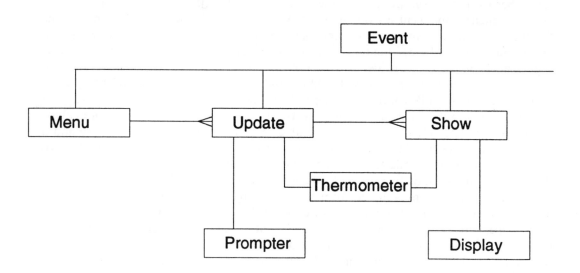

Figure 5.30 An ER summary of the configuration shown in Fig. 5.29.

This scenario seems convincing enough that we might now move on to design. Before we do that we complete the analysis stage by capturing the generic nature of our decisions so far in the form of an ER diagram. This we show in Fig. 5.30. It complements the object diagram of Fig. 5.29 by presenting the same information more concisely. It shows that *Update* and *Show* are new subclasses of *Event* and that (in this application) our *Menu* will contain a collection of *Update*s which in turn will contain a collection of *Show*s. Each *Update* will know of a unique *Thermometer* and a unique *Prompter*. Each *Show* will know of a unique *Thermometer* and a unique *Display*.

```
class Update < Event.

update(aThermometer,aPrompter):=
  new Update with thermometer=aThermometer
          with prompter=aPrompter
          with dependents=set().

Update.do():=
  (aNumber:=self.prompter.get();
   self.thermometer.set(aNumber);
   self.doAllDependents()).
```

Figure 5.31 Enact specification of *Update*.

Now let us show that we can design a detailed specification of the new classes in this system, which will produce the behaviour we have described in the foregoing scenario. We shall write sufficiently detailed Enact that we will be able to validate it by execution. Figure 5.31 shows the Enact specification for *Update*. It is a subclass of *Event* and has its own constructor and its own *do()* method. The constructor is *update (aThermometer,aPrompter)* which builds a new *Update* object with three attributes (respectively the *Thermometer* it knows about, the *Prompter* it knows about and its dependents), which is initialized to be the empty set. The method *Update.do()* first uses the *Prompter* to get a numerical value. Then it sets the value of its *Thermometer* using this number. Finally it invokes *doAlldependents()* on itself which sends the message *do()* to all of the *Event*s which have been added to this *Update* by *addDependent* (inherited from *Event*).

```
class Show < Event.

show(aThermometer,aDisplay):=
  new Show with thermometer=aThermometer
          with display=aDisplay
          with dependents=set().
```

```
Show.do():=
  (aNumber:=self.thermometer.get();
   self.display.put(aNumber);
   self.doAllDependents()).
```

Figure 5.32 Enact specification of *Show*.

```
C:=centigrade(). F:=fahrenheit().
C.addDependent(F). F.addDependent(C).

CP:=prompter(). CD:=display().
UC:=update(C,CP). SC:=show(C,CD).

FP:=prompter(). FD:=display().
UF:=update(F,FP). SF:=show(F,FD).

UC.addDependent(SC). UC.addDependent(SF).
UF.addDependent(SF). UF.addDependent(SC).

M:=menu(). events:=set().
UC.setLabel('upC). events.insert(UC).
UF.setLabel('upF). events.insert(UF).
M.install(events,anEvent::anEvent.label).
```

Figure 5.33 Setting up the thermometer configuration shown in Fig. 5.29.

The definition of *Show* is very similar. As Fig. 5.32 shows, it has a constructor *show(aThermometer,aDisplay)* which establishes a new *Event* of this type attached to a *Thermometer* and a *Display*. All that *Show.do()* does is to read the current temperature from the local thermometer and then poke this value into the local *Display* : quite simple really.

Now, if we combine the Enact specifications written in the first section of this chapter (Figs. 5.9 – 5.11) with the Enact specification for user interface objects listed in Appendix 2 and then with the Enact specifications of Figs. 5.31 and 5.32, we will have a complete working model of the system we have designed. We can experiment with this to determine whether or not it is complete, consistent and in conformance with our requirements. It is instructive to see how that would appear at this stage. You may find this to be a sufficiently interesting experiment that you wish to repeat it. The relevant files are included on the disk supplied with this book (see Appendix 1).

Having loaded all the necessary specifications we must build the arrangement of objects shown in Fig. 5.29. This is done by the sequence of Enact statements shown in Fig. 5.33. First the *Thermometers* *C* and *F* are defined, then they are linked together. Then for the *Centigrade* subsystem we define a *Prompter*, a *Display* and *Update* and *Show* events. We link these together appropriately. We repeat that for the *Fahrenheit* subsystem. Finally, we define a *Menu M* and add the *Update* events *UF* and *UC* to the collection of events which can be fired from that *Menu*.

The sequence shown in Fig. 5.33 builds the network of objects shown in Fig. 5.29 and then waits for us to test it. This we do by typing

        M.do()

whereupon the Enact interpreter asks the question

        Menu(upF,upC)?

and waits for a response. The only responses which will cause further activity are *upF* or *upC*. Anything else will terminate the experiment. So, say we respond *upF*; this will cause a *do()* message to be sent to the *UF* object. This in turn will cause a *Prompter* to open and ask another question

        Prompter(FP)?

which means that *Prompter FP* is expecting input. Now we must respond with a number. Suppose we respond 212; then this value will be assigned to *aNumber* in *Update.do()* and hence be used to set the value of the *Fahrenheit* thermometer. Then the *UF* event will fire all of its dependents, which in this case are the two *Show* events *SF* and *SC*. What will happen is that we will be asked two questions by the Enact interpreter. The first question is

        Display(SF = 212)?

which means 'the *SF* display has just changed to show 212, did you know that?'. This question must be answered before the system will proceed. The appropriate answer is *ok*. Next we are asked

        Display(SC = 100)?

which again requires the response *ok*. This pair of questions is of course the consequence of each *Show* event firing and using its local *Display* to display the value now held by its *Thermometer*. The success here has been that the *Centigrade* thermometer correctly shows a reading of 100. The test continues. The Enact interpreter has looped back to the top level *Menu* and asks

        Menu(upF,upC)?

again. So we continue testing until we are satisfied that everything is correct.

In practice, this process of building and testing a working model will lead to requirements for change, perhaps in the detail, perhaps in the overall structure. Sometimes the change will be required to correct errors, and sometimes to enhance the design, either by making it simpler or more generic. In any case, discovery of these change requirements at this early stage can lead to designs which are much more flexible against the possibility of future change. Also, the benefit of the working model means that we can step with confidence to the implementation stage, which is what we shall do now.

```cpp
class Update : public Event{
public:
  Thermometer* thermometer;
  Prompter* prompter;
  Update(Thermometer*,Prompter*);
  void _do();
};

Update::Update(Thermometer* aThermometer,
                      Prompter* aPrompter):Event(){
  thermometer=aThermometer;
  prompter=aPrompter;
}

void Update::_do(){
  long aNumber=prompter->get();
  thermometer->set(aNumber);
  doAllDependents();
}
```

Figure 5.34 C++ implementation of **Update** event.

```cpp
class Show : public Event{
public:
  Thermometer* thermometer;
  Display* display;
  Show(Thermometer*,Display*);
  void _do();
};

Show::Show(Thermometer*aThermometer,
  Display* aDisplay) :Event(){
  thermometer=aThermometer;
  display=aDisplay;
}

void Show::_do(){
  long aNumber=thermometer->get();
  display->put(aNumber);
  doAllDependents();
}
```

Figure 5.35 C++ implementation of the **Show** event.

```
char* labelFunction(void* anEvent){
  return(((Event*)anEvent)->label());
}

main(){

openScreen();

Thermometer* C = new Centigrade();
Thermometer* F = new Fahrenheit();
C->addDependent(F); F->addDependent(C);

Display* CD=new Display(2,2,1,20,"Centigrade");
Prompter* CP=new Prompter(10,20,1,50,"enter a Centigrade
value");
Display* FD=new Display(2,42,1,20,"Fahrenheit");
Prompter* FP=new Prompter(10,20,1,50,"enter a Fahrenheit
value");

Update* UC=new Update(C,CP);
Show* SC=new Show(C,CD);
```

Figure 5.36 C++ code for setting up the thermometer objects.

Once again we make use of the implicit rules of transliteration between Enact and C++ to obtain a skeleton for the implementation. By this means we get the code for the classes shown in Figs. 5.34 and 5.35. There is absolutely nothing unusual there, except that C++ expects us to be pedantic about types, so for example the type of _do is (we have no choice) a function with no arguments returning *void*, that is *void()*. Finally, Figs. 5.36 and 5.37 list the remainder of the program which implements our thermometers problem. Again, this is obtained by transliteration from Enact. We see that the details about positions of devices on the screen, titles on windows and labels in menus have been decided. Apart from that, there is a requirement to call a couple of global functions first to clear and restore the screen at the start and end of the program.

Testing this program is straightforward as long as it is correct (which it is), but in practice we should prepare comprehensive tests which allow us efficiently to detect bugs in case we have made any. We should normally build up the code progressively, adding a few lines at a time and testing them, so that bugs are localized and quickly eradicated. One way to do that here would be to build just the part of the program corresponding to a single thermometer with its *Update* and *Show* events. Then the test

```
    UC -> _do();
    UC -> _do();
```

would, if the code was valid, go through the sequence prompt, display, prompt, display. Successfully getting to the second prompt would be sufficient. Then we could add the second thermometer subsystem and repeat the above test or some slightly extended variant of it. If bugs are encountered they are local to a few lines of code and to some very simple logic. Detecting them and correcting them would then be simple.

```
Update* UF=new Update(F,FP);
Show* SF=new Show(F,FD);

UC->addDependent(SC);
UC->addDependent(SF);
UF->addDependent(SF);
UF->addDependent(SC);

Menu* topLevel=new Menu(14,32,3,12);
UC->setLabel("Centigrade");
UF->setLabel("Fahrenheit");
Set* events=new Set();
events->insert(UC);
events->insert(UF);

topLevel->install(events,labelFunction);
topLevel->_do();

closeScreen();

}
```

Figure 5.37 C++ code for setting up the thermometer objects (continued).

Finally we would add the top level *Menu* and run the program for some reasonably long series of interactions in order to ensure such properties as the fact that we are not progressively filling up memory.

5.5 CONCLUSIONS

We promised to return to a discussion of the extent to which our eventual software has achieved acceptable levels of quality and the contributions our methods have made to this achievement. Clearly the most important quality is correctness (or at least robustness against the consequences of error). This we have tried to achieve simply by having a clear, concise design and by making it have high visibility to ourselves and our colleagues. We have tested the design fairly comprehensively in three stages. We did a work-through of the proposed use of the abstract system using the object diagram of Fig. 5.29. We built and tested a working model in Enact. And we used simple rules to generate the C++ and tested that both progressively and exhaustively. Finally, we used components (**userface** and **collect**) which have been established for some time, used in other applications, and are generally to be trusted. In fact, we had little choice but to trust them. But this is what happens in all software development. To a very large extent, the quality of our product is dependent upon the quality of these trusted components.

On the negative side, with respect to correctness and robustness there are some programming conventions on which we should comment. In general the use of **void*** should be avoided. Because our implementation of **Collections** is done in terms of **void***, and because **Event** uses a **Collection** for its dependents and **Scroller** uses a collection for its list of objects, we are forced to use **void*** in the user interface. We have to be extremely careful to ensure that, once something has been cast (implicitly) to a **void*** by placing it in a **Collection**, when we take it out and cast it (explicitly) to the type we want it to be, we don't cast it to a type which is incorrect for it. In practice, we must cast it to (a pointer to) the type of the class whose constructor was used to make the object pointed to, or to one of that class's (direct or indirect) base classes. There are many potential pitfalls here. Fortunately, C++ provides the mechanisms for us to avoid using **void***. This is an advanced feature which we discuss in Chapter 10. We have taken care here in our use of **void***, but the correctness of the program is very dependent upon our correct understanding of casting from **void***. It would be better if we were not so dependent.

The other quality which we consider of great importance is flexibility, the openness to future change of the design and of the code we have developed. There are many reasons to believe that the quality of our product here is high in this respect. The object-oriented nature of the design, making a close relationship between entities in the real world (here thermometers, displays, prompters etc.) and corresponding objects in the implementation, means that changes to these entities have obviously parallel changes to the objects. One of the properties which this engenders in the code is a belief that there is a logical place for every piece of code to be and every piece of code is in that place. It is easy to find. We have a clear relationship between the design and the code, and, perhaps most importantly, we have clear descriptions of all the components. We have abstract systems for thermometers and for generic and specific user interface objects. We have diagrams of their deployment in our solution. We have written specifications of the protocols and we have a working model in Enact. A proposed change requires us to extend all these things, which may appear to increase the amount of work we have to do, but in fact the very existence of this additional information accelerates our ability to make change. It makes change more economical. It does that because it makes the structure and behaviour of our product clearly accessible. It makes apparent the design rules which have been followed in its development. It makes clear the architecture of the product. It reduces the cost of understanding it (for the designer charged with changing it) and increases the likelihood that this change will maintain the high quality of the product by retaining its architectural integrity. In the next chapter we shall build a more elaborate program with much the same architecture as the program we have developed here. This reuse of design will, we claim, allow us to build a high-quality product with low additional cost, because of the use of the investment we have in the architecture we have developed here.

5.6 EXERCISES

1. Revise the design of the interlinked thermometers (Figs. 5.9 – 5.11) so that each thermometer can be linked to many others. Changing one thermometer changes all its dependents.

2. Develop a model of a currency conversion program where the user can select, from a menu, an input currency. When prompted for an amount of cash in the input currency, the program then displays the value converted to each of the supported output currencies. Extend the model to allow the conversion rate to be easily changed.

3. Both the models in Exercises 1 and 2 can encounter the problem that cycles of linked events cause an infinite sequence of firing. Only careful design avoids that. How could the operation *Event.doAllDependents* be revised to ensure that such infinite sequences did not occur?

4. The design of menus in **userface.h** relies upon the fact that C++ supports multiple inheritance. Suppose it did not, or that you just wanted to avoid using it. How could the nested menus be supported if a menu was not also an event? It is possible. It may even be a neater solution.

5. We introduced an artificial standard value for communicating temperatures between thermometers: absolute scale. Could we have simply used the Fahrenheit temperature as the standard for communication? What difference would it make to the design?

6. Devise an abstract system for a subset of the user interface objects available on your machine. For example, you may have access to Windows 3 or some of the commercial libraries which are built on top of it. Or, you may have access to a library of widgets for X-Windows. Build an Enact model of the abstracted interface.

7. Devise an abstract system for a subset of the C++ stream classes as described, for example, in the manual for your compiler.

8. Devise an abstract system for a subset of the C++ collection classes described in the manual for your compiler, or otherwise available in your working environment.

6

A USER INTERFACE FOR THE PERSONAL LIBRARY

6.1 INTRODUCTION

Once again we are in the situation where we are required to elaborate an already established design. In Chapters 2, 3 and 4 we developed, as a running example, a simple system to record the coming and going of books from my personal library. To summarize the stage we have reached, the abstract system for my personal library is shown in Fig. 6.1. We have the ability to create persons, books and libraries. We have the ability to acquire books for a library and to join persons as members of the library. We have the ability to record that a person has borrowed a book and that eventually that book is returned. We can enquire which books a person has and we can enquire of a book, whether or not it is in the library, and if it is not, which person has it out.

```
aLibrary:=library()
aPerson:=person()
aBook:=book()
aLibrary.join(aPerson)
aLibrary.acquire(aBook)
aSet:=aLibrary.holding()
aSet:=aLibrary.members()
aLibrary.borrow(aPerson,aBook)
aLibrary.return(aPerson,aBook)
aBook.inlibrary()
aPerson.books()
aBook.borrower()
```

Figure 6.1 Abstract system for personal library.

```
aPrompter:=prompter()
aDisplay:=display()
aSelector:=selector()
aMenu:=menu()
avalue:=aPrompter.get()
aDisplay.put(aValue)
anObject:=aSelector.get()
aMenu.do()
```

Figure 6.2 Abstract system for user interface.

The other part of the development which we already have behind us is the user interface components. In Chapter 5 we saw how to use the **userface** library components. We saw how the various input–output devices, specifically prompters, displays, selectors and menus, could be used to update and interrogate a network of application objects. The abstract system for the user interface objects is summarized in Fig. 6.2. The task we have in this chapter is to develop a suitable user interface for the personal library, that is, we want to combine the two components defined by the abstract systems of Figs. 6.1 and 6.2 in some way to provide a satisfactory means of editing the network of application objects which represents the current state of the personal library.

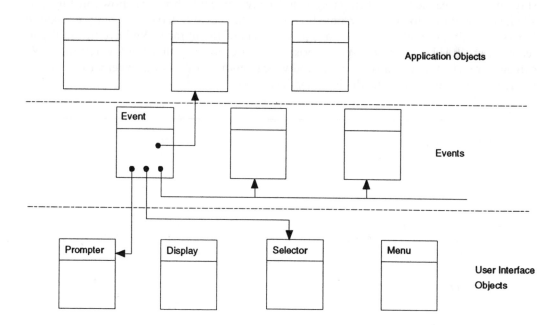

Figure 6.3 Idiom for event-driven user interface.

In Chapter 5 we discovered an architectural idiom for deploying the user interface objects which perhaps we did not bring out fully in that chapter. The idiom is depicted in Fig. 6.3. This shows three strata of objects linked in a particular way. The user interface objects are linked to the application objects via an intermediate strata of *Event* objects. The way that the application proceeds is by progressively firing *Events*, causing activity in both the user interface and in the application objects. A glance back now at Fig. 5.29 will show a concrete example of the abstract architecture shown in Fig. 6.3.

6.2 ANALYSIS

The starting point for our analysis step is to accept the existing components for a personal library and user interface and to see if we can exploit the idiomatic architecture of joining these two components using a layer of specialized *Events*. As always in analysis, we turn to what happens in the real world, and look for entities which we can model by objects in the computer-based solution. At this juncture the entities we are looking for are events. Let us look at the central transaction with the library, a person borrowing a book. The interface between the computer system and the real world arises when the person presents the book to the librarian to indicate that he or she wishes to borrow it. The librarian wishes to record this information in the computer system. Thus an obvious event is the librarian commencing a transaction with the computer system to record the allocation of this book to this person. There would be the need to check that the person was indeed a member of the library and the book had been acquired by the library and was available for loan. Then the allocation could be safely made.

There would be a symmetrical activity on returning a book. The event is the commencement of the transaction of recording the return. The checks required this time would be that the book is indeed one which has been acquired by the library and that it is indeed on loan. The record of borrowing would then be removed.

These two events are central to the operation of the library. Other obvious events in this category which we would require are ones which allow us to record a new book acquisition and which allow us to record a new person joining the library as a member. Of course, we would need many more events than just these for a practical system, but for the purposes of the exercise we are undertaking in this chapter these few are sufficient to illustrate the development methods we are trying to study.

Let us look more closely at the activity of borrowing. In the real world we have a person and a book. In the computer system we have an object representing the library, which has members (a collection of persons) and a holding (a collection of books). We must identify the object from each of these collections which represents, respectively, the real-world person and the real-world book. In terms of the user interface we have to obtain sufficient information about the real-world entity that we can identify the corresponding application object. One obvious way to do this would be to put up a prompter and allow the librarian to type in (or scan in) some identifying details. Another way, would be to display a list of possible candidate application objects and have the librarian choose. This latter solution seems attractive and we believe that we can use the *Selector* object to achieve it. In the case of borrowing we place the collection of all members of the library in a *Selector* and let the librarian choose one from among them. In the case of the personal library this is a practical solution since there will only be a few dozen members at most. Having identified the borrower we can use the same device to identify the book being borrowed. This time we install in the *Selector* those books which are known to be in the library. The librarian selects one from this collection. This may not be a practical solution, for I have a few hundred books in my personal collection, but for various reasons it seems worth a try.

This solution seems attractive primarily because it automatically implements the constraints that only members of the library may borrow books and only books currently in the library may be borrowed. It does this by only presenting objects which satisfy this criterion for selection. Another good reason for being attracted to this solution is that we deal with selection in the same way for people and for books. The fact that it may not be a practical solution for a holding of a few hundred books is a worry, but we believe that an experiment is worthwhile (and cheap) and that if we need eventually to change this decision that will not be too expensive for us to carry out.

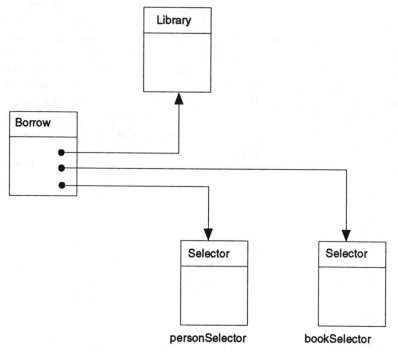

Figure 6.4 Arrangement of devices for *Borrow* event.

Figure 6.4 shows our attempt to capture this design decision. We have invented a new type of *Event* which we have called *Borrow*. A *Borrow* has access to a *Library* and to two *Selector*s. When fired, the *Borrow* event will open the *personSelector* to allow the user to select a person. It will then open the *bookSelector* to allow the user to select a book. Having thus obtained a person and a book identity it will inform the *Library* that this person borrows this book. The validity of this operation will be assured by virtue of the fact that the lists installed in the respective *Selector*s will have been obtained by the *Borrow* event from the *Library* object to which it is attached.

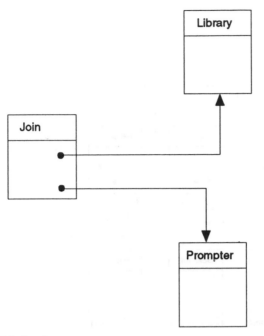

Figure 6.5 Arrangement of devices for *Join* event.

A similar arrangement of objects would suffice for a *Return* event, which we would use when returning a book. When a new person is to be joined to the library as a member we need a slightly different arrangement, as shown in Fig. 6.5. Here we have created a new type of event, *Join,* which opens a *Prompter* to obtain details of the new member and then creates an object to represent that person and informs the *Library* of the enrolment. Finally, acquisition of books is achieved in a similar way using a new event *Acquire.*

The layout of these objects in our architectural idiom is shown in Fig. 6.6. Here we have added a *Menu* device to drive the selection of *Events* in the usual way and have arranged the objects in a uniform way which shows their relationship to each other and to their roles within the system. The ghost *Event* indicates our expectation that extension will take place and our evidence that the architecture is open to it.

Let us run through a scenario of driving the system devised in Fig. 6.6. The *Menu* offers a choice of events. We can repeatedly fire the *Acquire* event to record new books. Each time it fires we see a *Prompter* open which asks for details of the book. These details are recorded in the *Library* object which all events share. In a similar way we can use the *Join* event to record the details of members. Selecting the *Borrow* event from the *Menu* causes the use of both the *Selectors* to determine first who is doing the borrowing and second which book is being borrowed. This allocation is then recorded in the *Library.* Similarly, the *Return* event uses the same devices to determine first who is returning the book and second which book it is. We can quibble (at this analysis stage) about whether or not the look-and-feel details of each of these transactions is exactly what is required, but in practice we won't really know until we have a prototype to try. More important then is our ability to persuade ourselves that the changes of detail which will undoubtedly

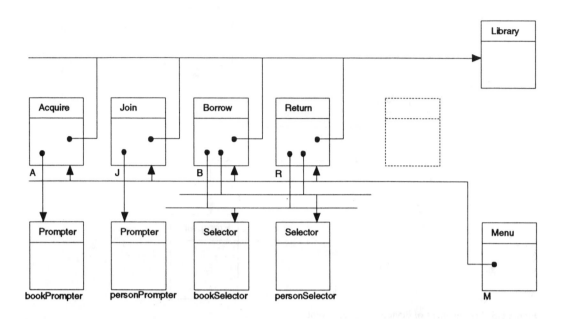

Figure 6.6 Arrangement of devices for interface to library.

be required will not cause expensive upheaval to our design. We should consider some possible changes and work out how they would affect our design before we proceed, for example, if books were returned anonymously. The *Return* event would not require the *personSelector*. We would either need to make its use of the *personSelector* optional, or (possibly better) have a specialized event for anonymous returns. Neither of

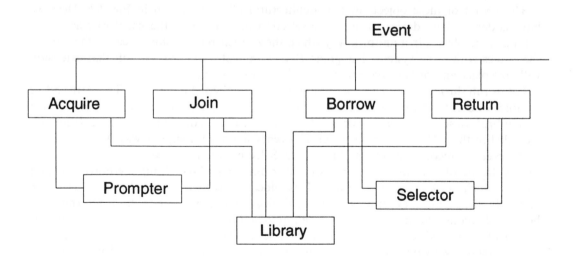

Figure 6.7 ER diagram.

these changes would be an upheaval. They would affect exactly one event and possibly one small change to the menu. This observation should make us confident to proceed with the architecture as we have it, expecting the detail to become more focused as we proceed through design and into implementation.

The result of our analysis has been a proposed exploitation of the idiomatic architecture of the last chapter. The only protocol which we need to design is a *do ()* method for each new subclass of *Event*. The generic structure of our proposal is shown in the ER diagram of Fig. 6.7. Now we need to turn our attention to the detail, that is, we need to commence the design step.

6.3 DESIGN

If we can design the *Borrow* event, the rest should follow very simply. The first thing the *Borrow* event will do when fired is to determine the borrower by a call such as

```
aPerson := personSelector.get()
```

For this to work, the *personSelector* will need to have been properly initialized. We said that the selection would be made from among the members of the library, so we might initialize *personSelector* as follows:

```
personSelector.install(aLibrary.members(),...)
```

The collection thus installed in the *Selector* is a set of persons. We must also supply, as a second argument to *install*, a function which, given a *Person,* will return a suitable string to display in the *Selector* on the screen. Unfortunately, the only attribute that a *Person* currently has is the collection of books which that person has borrowed (see Fig. 3.34) so we must extend this design to include an additional attribute.

```
class Person < Object.

person(aName) := new Person with books=set()
                            with name=aName.

Person.allocate(aBook) :=
    self.books.insert(aBook).

Person.deallocate(aBook) :=
    self.books.remove(aBook).
```

Figure 6.8 Named *Person* (cf. Fig. 3.34).

This we have done in Fig. 6.8, where a *Person* now has the attribute *aPerson.name* which is set by the constructor *aPerson := person(aName)* and never subsequently altered. It means that we can complete the installation process for *personSelector* as follows:

personSelector.install(aLibrary.members(),aPerson::aPerson.name)

which means that when we say

> *aPerson := personSelector.get()*

we shall be offered a list of names of members of *aLibrary* from which to choose. On choosing one, the corresponding *Person* object will be assigned to *aPerson*.

The next thing the *Borrow* event will do is to select the *Book* to be borrowed using *bookSelector*. The books to be offered for selection are just those in the library which are not out on loan. Thus we need to construct the set

availableBooks := aLibrary.holding.select(aBook::aBook.
>> *inlibrary())*

which constructs the subset of *aLibrary.holding* which are available to be borrowed. Before we can install this collection in *bookSelector* we have to extend the *Book* object to have a printable name, as we did for *Person*. This we have done in Fig. 6.9. So we can install as follows:

> *bookSelector.install(availableBooks, aBook::aBook.name)*

and then use this selector as follows:

> *aBook := bookSelector.get()*

```
class Book < Object.

book(aName):= new Book with borrower=nil
                   with name=aName.

Book.borrow(aPerson):=
    (self.borrower:=aPerson; aPerson.allocate(self)).

Book.return():=
    (self.borrower.deallocate(self); self.borrower:=nil).

Book.inlibrary():=
    self.borrower=nil.
```

Figure 6.9 Enact specification of a named *Book*.

Now that we have both *aPerson* and *aBook*, all that remains to be done is to allocate this book to this person, which is achieved by

```
aLibrary.borrow(aPerson, aBook)
```

```
class Borrow < Event.

borrow(aSelector1,aSelector2,aLibrary):=
  new Borrow with personSelector=aSelector1
          with bookSelector=aSelector2
          with library=aLibrary.

Borrow.do():=
  (self.personSelector.install(self.library.members,
                            aPerson::aPerson.name);
   aPerson:=self.personSelector.get();
   availableBooks:=
     self.library.holding.select(aBook::aBook.inlibrary());
   self.bookSelector.install(availableBooks,aBook::aBook.name);
   aBook:=self.bookSelector.get();
   self.library.borrow(aPerson,aBook)
  ).
```

Figure 6.10 (Detailed) Enact specification of *Borrow* event (without tests).

At this stage in the design process we have every reason to be confident. The main path through the most detailed of the operations (*Borrow.do()*) has been designed and it has turned out to be very simple. Our confidence in it should be high. But we should not be complacent or too optimistic. We need to test the design, which we can do by completing the detail in Enact. This we have done for the *Borrow* event in Fig. 6.10. The constructor we have designed expects two *Selectors* and a *Library* as arguments, so we can initialize it as follows:

```
personSelector := selector().
bookSelector := selector().
aLibrary := library().
B := borrow(personSelector, bookSelector, aLibrary).
```

Before we can test it we need to acquire some books for the library and join some members. Once this is done we can execute the test

```
B.do()
```

and answer the questions which each *Selector* poses. When completed we can inspect the objects which we expect to have changed to see if this has indeed happened.

```
class Borrow < Event.

borrow(aSelector1,aSelector2,aLibrary):=
  new Borrow with personSelector=aSelector1
              with bookSelector=aSelector2
              with library=aLibrary.

Borrow.do():=
  (self.personSelector.install(self.library.members,
                              aPerson::aPerson.name);
   aPerson:=self.personSelector.get();
   availableBooks:=
      self.library.holding.select(aBook::aBook.inlibrary());
   (availableBooks.size()>0)then
   (self.bookSelector.install(availableBooks,aBook::aBook.name);
     aBook:=self.bookSelector.get();
     self.library.borrow(aPerson,aBook))
  ) if self.library.members.size()>0.
```

Figure 6.11 Enact specification of *Borrow* event with tests.

Exhaustive testing of *Borrow* should lead us to detect two potential bugs, both to do with empty collections. If there are no members of the library then *aPerson* will not be assigned a sensible value. If either there are no books in the library or all books are out on loan, then *aBook* will not be assigned a sensible value. To guard against both of these eventualities we insert tests, as shown in Fig. 6.11. Placing the tests where we have ensures that the user is not asked to select from an empty collection, which we assume would be found a little tedious.

```
class Return < Event.

return(aSelector1,aSelector2,aLibrary):=
  new Return with personSelector=aSelector1
             with bookSelector=aSelector2
             with library=aLibrary.

Return.do():=
  (self.personSelector.install(self.library.members,
                              aPerson::aPerson.name);
   aPerson:=self.personSelector.get();
   (aPerson.books.size()>0)then
    (self.bookSelector.install(aPerson.books,aBook::aBook.name);
     aBook:=self.bookSelector.get();
     self.library.return(aPerson,aBook))
  )if self.library.members.size()>0.
```

Figure 6.12 Enact specification of *Return* event.

A very similar process of design leads to the specification of the *Return* event shown in Fig. 6.12. This time we see that the *personSelector* is used to select the *Person* returning the book and then only the books on loan to that person are shown for selection. Only if the book is actually on loan to this person can it be returned. Alternative strategies for implementing return logic are left as an exercise for the reader (see the exercises). Again the design has been tested exhaustively. This time the bugs which would arise if collections were empty have been avoided and tested for.

```
class Acquire < Event.

acquire(aPrompter,aLibrary):=
   new Acquire with prompter=aPrompter
               with library=aLibrary.

Acquire.do():=
   (aName:=self.prompter.get();
    self.library.acquire(book(aName))).
```

Figure 6.13 Enact specification of the *Acquire* event.

```
class Join < Event.

join(aPrompter,aLibrary):=
   new Join with prompter=aPrompter
            with library=aLibrary.

Join.do():=
   (aName:=self.prompter.get();
    self.library.join(person(aName))).
```

Figure 6.14 Enact specification of the *Join* event.

The remaining events *Acquire* and *Join* are shown in Figs. 6.13 and 6.14 respectively. They are virtually identical. Consider only *Acquire*. It has a *Prompter* and a *Library* as attributes. When the event is fired, the prompter opens and elicits a string from the user which it uses as a name for a new *Book*. The new *Book*, *book(aName)*, is then acquired by the library.

A good way of testing this event is as follows:

```
A := acquire(bookPrompter, aLibrary).
A.do().
B.do().   % which is the Borrow event from earlier
```

whereupon, having entered the details of the new book, we should immediately be able to see that it is available to be borrowed.

```
lib:=library().
AP:=prompter(). A:=acquire(AP,lib).
JP:=prompter(). J:=join(JP,lib).
personSelector:=selector(). bookSelector:=selector().
B:=borrow(personSelector,bookSelector,lib).
R:=return(personSelector,bookSelector,lib).


M:=menu(). events:=set().
A.setLabel('acquire). events.insert(A).
J.setLabel('join).     events.insert(J).
B.setLabel('borrow).  events.insert(B).
R.setLabel('return).  events.insert(R).

M.install(events,anEvent::anEvent.label).
```

Figure 6.15 Setting up the library interface devices (see Fig. 6.6).

To complete the design step all that remains is to establish the *Menu* object, but this is trivial. It is exactly as we have done it for the thermometers example of the previous chapter. For completeness it is listed in Fig. 6.15, which should be compared with the object diagram of Fig. 6.6. Together these two descriptions form a top-level specification of the artefact which we have designed.

6.4 IMPLEMENTATION

And so finally we turn to implementation. We begin the implementation step when we begin to concern ourselves with the additional requirements which C++ imposes upon us if we are to achieve a working product. There are the usual comparatively trivial requirements of transliterating the pseudocode of our design into C++ and adding the details, such as screen location of devices. However, in addition in this particular implementation we do have a major issue to deal with, the use and reuse of heap memory. Because we are frequently using the *select* operation we are creating new collections which occupy heap space. We drop the pointer to these temporary collections when we leave the function in which it is used locally (in this case, for example, *Borrow.do()*). We need to recover the space once we have done with it. Another major problem which we might anticipate is one of performance, in that the collection classes which we are using are far from fast. When we have developed the C++ we will discuss both these major potential problems.

Transliterating the Enact specification of Fig. 6.8 we obtain very directly the C++ of Fig. 6.16. This is identical to the code which we developed in Chapter 4 (Figs. 4.48 and 4.49) where we had anticipated the need for a name attribute. There we adopted a convention that the data member should be hidden and accessed only by a member function. Thus **Person::name()** is a function in C++ where it was simply an attribute in Enact. The C++ code for **Book** is similar. It appears in Figs. 4.50 and 4.51, so is not repeated here.

```
class Person{
  char* _name;
  Set* _books;
public:
  char* name();
  Set* books();
  Person(char*);
  void allocate(Book*);
  void deallocate(Book*);
};

Person::Person(char* n):_name(n),_books(new Set()){
}

char* Person::name(){return _name;}

Set* Person::books(){return _books;}

void Person::allocate(Book* aBook){
  _books->insert(aBook);
}

void Person::deallocate(Book* aBook){
  _books->remove(aBook);
}
```

Figure 6.16 C++ for class **Person** (cf. Figs. 4.48 and 4.49).

Again, the **Borrow** class shown in Figs. 6.17 and 6.18 is a direct transliteration of the corresponding Enact from Figs. 6.10 and 6.11. The usual rules of transliteration apply. Every object is accessed via a pointer, hence we see **->** replacing dot. Name clashes must be avoided, therefore *do()* is replaced by **_do()** since **do** is a keyword in C++. The constructor initializes its base and its attributes in a conventional way. The need for a function as a parameter means a global function **inlib** must be defined, since C++ does not have the equivalent of lambda expressions.

```
class Borrow : public Event{
  Selector* personSelector;
  Selector* bookSelector;
  Library* library;
public:
  Borrow(Selector*, Selector*, Library*);
  void _do();
};

Borrow::Borrow(Selector* aSelector1,
        Selector* aSelector2, Library* aLibrary)
  :Event(),personSelector(aSelector1),
   bookSelector(aSelector2), library(aLibrary){
}
```

Figure 6.17 C++ code for **Borrow** event (part).

```
int inlib(void* aBook){
return(((Book*)aBook)->inlibrary());
}

void Borrow::_do(){
if(library->members()->size()>0){
 personSelector->install(library->members(),
                         PersonNameFunction);
 Person* aPerson=(Person*)(personSelector->get());
 Set* availableBooks=
            (Set*)(library->holding()->select(inlib));
 if(availableBooks->size()>0){
   bookSelector->install(availableBooks,
                         BookNameFunction);
   Book* aBook=(Book*)(bookSelector->get());
   library->borrow(aPerson,aBook);
   }
  delete availableBooks;
  }
}
```

Figure 6.18 C++ implementation of **Borrow::_do**.

It is deep in the definition of **Borrow::_do()** that our potential storage problem arises. We assign a temporary collection to the local variable **availableBooks**. We install this collection in the selector **bookSelector**, but once we have assigned to **aBook** using **bookSelector->get()**, this collection is no longer required. To return the storage which it occupies we must delete it with

```
delete availableBooks;
```

which we have done. We explained in Chapter 4 how this works, but it is worth recalling. Since **availableBooks** points at a collection, the destructor for collections is called. This takes the responsibility for returning to the heap all of the storage allocated to the collection. None of the objects in the collection will be destroyed, only the record that they were part of this temporary collection.

The question should arise in our minds as to whether this is the only responsibility we have with respect to storage in **Borrow::_do()**. We want to be sure that on exit from **Borrow::_do()** the only additional space occupied is that required to record the borrowing. We need to inspect each call to subroutines which return objects which get assigned to local variables, including to the temporaries required to hold arguments to functions. For example, the first argument to install is **library->members()**, which is a **Collection*** value. But no new storage is allocated to implement it, so no obligation to recover is imposed. Similarly, the assignment to **aBook** is only a pointer, so no heap space is used. I believe that the only requirement upon us to recover storage is the one we have dealt with. But the only way to determine this in practice (given the nature of our collection classes) is by careful analysis and a full understanding of the way that heap storage is utilized. This is an onerous and important responsibility. We discuss memory management more fully in Chapter 9, where we explain how C++ provides the tools for the programmer to organize memory management more automatically.

The pitfall which we avoided here, more by luck than planning, is the following. Suppose we had not needed a local variable such as **availableBooks** and had instead been able to call directly

```
bookSelector->
  install(library->holding()->select(...), ...)
```

The temporary collection **library->holding->select(...)** would have been created, used to initialize the argument to **install**, and then our pointer to it lost when we exited **install**. We would have no way of recovering the storage which it allocated. We are not the suppliers of **install** so we cannot change that. Nor could the suppliers, because we do not always hand **install** something which it can delete. This example is one of the commonest ways in which garbage can be accidentally created by C++ on its heap. The implementor should always be on the lookout for it.

The collection classes provide a crude means of testing that storage is not being lost. There is a global variable **long cellcount** which counts the number of cells currently allocated to collections. This value can be printed before and after a call to a function such as **Borrow::_do()**. If a book is successfully borrowed this value should go up by a small amount (probably 1). The following tests were used to create some reassurance that the solitary **delete** in the implementation of Fig. 6.18 was satisfactory. The value of **cellcount** was displayed in a specially created **Display**. **Borrow::_do()** was called with no available books. The value of **cellcount** did not change. **Borrow::_do()** was called with **delete** commented out and 10 books available for borrowing. The value of **cellcount** increased by 11. The **delete** was made operational and the test repeated. The value of **cellcount** went up by 1. The display of **cellcount** was left enabled for a period of subsequent testing and the behaviour of its value observed. It appeared to behave as it should, going up and down by appropriate amounts. Figure 6.19 shows some obvious global functions required by **Borrow::_do()** and elsewhere. We omit the C++ for **Return** which is trivially comparable to **Borrow**.

```
char* labelFunction(void* anEvent){
  return(((Event*)anEvent)->label());
}

char* BookNameFunction(void* aBook){
  return(((Book*)aBook)->name());
}

char* PersonNameFunction(void* aPerson){
  return(((Person*)aPerson)->name());
}
```

Figure 6.19 Global functions required by **Borrow** event.

```
class Acquire : public Event{
  Prompter* prompter;
  Library* library;
public:
  Acquire(Prompter*, Library*);
  void _do();
};

Acquire::Acquire(Prompter* aPrompter,
            Library* aLibrary)
  :Event(),prompter(aPrompter),library(aLibrary){
}
  char* aName=prompter->gets();
  library->acquire(new Book(aName));
}
```

Figure 6.20 C++ code for the **Acquire** event.

Instead, we show the C++ for **Acquire** in Fig. 6.20. Here we have to deal with one further local storage requirement. **Acquire** uses a **Prompter** to obtain a string which is used to create a new **Book**. We recall that **Book** does not allocate space for that string. We have to be sure that the space allocated by **Prompter** does not get deleted. The call

```
aName = prompter -> gets();
```

assigns a **char*** to **aName**. Is the space allocated for the string protected? If not, we had better create memory here and copy the string to it. It is the case that **Prompter** allocates space on our behalf, which we may trust to stay around or explicitly **delete** if we do not need it. In this case we need it, so we do not **delete** it.

```
openScreen();

Prompter* AP=new Prompter(10,20,1,50,"enter a Book
name");
Prompter* JP=new Prompter(10,20,1,50,"enter a Person
name");

Menu* topLevel=new Menu(14,32,6,12);
Selector* bookSelector=new Selector(4,12,12,12);
Selector* personSelector=new Selector(4,52,12,12);
Set* events=new Set();
Acquire* A=new Acquire(AP,lib);
Join* J=new Join(JP,lib);
Borrow* B=new Borrow(personSelector,bookSelector,lib);
Return* R=new Return(personSelector,bookSelector,lib);

A->setLabel("acquire");  events->insert(A);
BB->setLabel("books");   events->insert(BB);
J->setLabel("join");     events->insert(J);
B->setLabel("borrow");   events->insert(B);
R->setLabel("return");   events->insert(R);

topLevel->install(events,labelFunction);

topLevel->_do();

closeScreen();
```

Figure 6.21 C++ to establish the user interface for library (cf. Fig. 6.6).

Finally, Fig. 6.21 shows the **main()** which creates our network of **Events** and other objects to implement our architecture. As explained in the previous chapter, this would be progressively built up and exhaustively tested before being considered to be of adequate quality for further development or for delivery to the customer.

6.5 CONCLUSIONS

The qualities we are most concerned with are correctness and flexibility, for which the comments of the previous chapter hold true. We have considerable confidence in the correctness because of the cleanness of the design, the clearness of its exposition, the close relationship between design and delivered code and the careful testing which has been applied. The flexibility comes from the openness of the architecture which we have amply illustrated here. A third quality which may not be so high, however, is performance. This can only be ascertained by testing. Well, not quite: we can do a bit of predictive sizing before committing ourselves to a particular architecture. We did that when I suggested that my library would only have a few hundred books (say 500). The performance would be dominated by the speed of **select** on a collection this size. I thought that C++ had a fighting chance of being tolerably fast on that size of collection, so I thought that an investment in implementation was probably worthwhile. But now I need to test my conjecture. This is not very convenient with the implementation as far as we have got in this chapter, for the only way to create a holding of 500 books is to type them all in (or write a program to do it). In the next chapter we shall develop the means to store our data in a file, thus enabling it to persist over time. This will make performance testing much easier, and so we will delay that essential quality assessment until the end of the next chapter.

6.6 EXERCISES

1. Extend the user interface to the library to include a new event for anonymous returns: that is, a book is returned but we do not know who has borrowed it. Give a complete design, including detailed Enact comparable to that shown in Fig. 6.10.

2. One of the advantages of personal returns, where we know who has borrowed a book, is that the selector, when it appears on the screen, only contains a short list of choices. These are the names of the books borrowed by that reader. One way of obtaining a similar advantage for borrowing (where currently the selector lists all available books) would be to organize the books into groups, where the selection is perhaps group, then subgroup, then book. With just 10 groups, each with about 10 subgroups, each with about 10 books we could have 1000 books more easily selected. Suppose I mark all my books with two symbols, being group and subgroup respectively. Design a new structure for my personal library, and for its interface, to present this revised method of accessing its data.

3. An alternative way to locate books in collections is to do string matching on their names. Postulate a function which gives a numerical measure of the distance between two names. Now, when the librarian wishes to identify a book, he or she can enter an approximate name in a prompter. The system will retrieve (say) the 10 nearest matches. Design such a system, in particular its user interface. Develop that as far as C++ and experiment with various distance functions. For example, the distance between two strings could be the number of characters in the union of their constituent characters which are not in the intersection.

4. Devise a user interface for the currency converter described in Exercise 2 of Chapter 5 based on the generic model of Fig. 6.3.

7

PERSISTENCE

7.1 INTRODUCTION

The implementation we have made of my personal library has a major drawback. When the program terminates, all record of who has which book has been lost. This is because the data is stored in the memory (RAM) allocated to C++ data structures, which disappears (is returned to the operating system) upon exit from the program. So, in order to make use of the program as we have implemented it so far, we must ensure that once we have begun to make serious use of it, we never allow it to terminate.

This is a plausible, but not very practical measure. The version of the program completed in the last chapter will run happily in a window on my machine while I get on with other work in other windows. The operating system is quite capable of sharing the resources between the separate programs in each window. As long as I never switch my machine off and never use any of the methods for terminating the program (such as escaping from the top-level menu or closing the host window) then my information about who has which book is intact, up to date and accessible. But if my machine breaks, or power is lost, or an upgrade to the operating system is required, or any of many disruptive events happens, then all this information will be lost.

So our implementation is not complete. We need to ensure that data collected by our program will be available for reuse after normal or abnormal termination. The standard way of doing this is to record it not in RAM but on disk. When this is achieved we are able to claim that our data will persist. We say that our objects have persistence. In this chapter we shall address the problem of persistence for applications of the kind we have been developing. We shall develop a method which is reasonably generic (a fact we shall demonstrate in the next chapter) and which has adequate performance characteristics. It is also reasonably simple to implement.

Persistence of objects is the abstract notion that we want to achieve. It is achieved logically by the never-terminating program, so our requirement can be stated simply by equating the behaviour of a terminating program to that of a non-terminating one. Quite simply, what we want to achieve is the ability to terminate our program and then to restart it so that on resumption all data is intact in exactly the arrangement it was just before termination. With a conventional machine, since we must assume that during execution anything can happen, including the removal of power, if our data is to persist it must have been recorded on a non-volatile medium, such as a magnetic disk. That is, we must ensure that prior to termination, sufficient data is copied to a file on disk that all internal data structures can be constructed once the program is resumed.

There are a number of strategies we can adopt. In a realistic commercial environment our first consideration should be to investigate available libraries for adding persistence to objects and for interfacing C++ programs to databases. For large applications this is the mechanism we would expect to give us maximum flexibility for least cost. We could still apply our methods by building an abstract system for the commercial product and then interfacing that with the abstract system for our library. Rather than do that, we shall adopt an approach which is sometimes an economically viable alternative. We will try to reuse a 'design idea'. By this I mean that, at the analysis stage, we are aware of a general method (the 'idea') which has been used successfully elsewhere and which we wish to reuse even though it means some additional implementation on our part. If we can make this additional implementation sufficiently generic that we can reuse it in future projects, then the extra investment at this stage will be justified.

So what is the reusable idea? It is simply that a collection of objects can be streamed out into a sequential file as a sequence of characters. Let us look at the informal justification of this idea and then rehearse some of the arguments we would make to justify taking it into design and implementation. Every simple object, such as an integer or a string, can be represented by a sequence of characters. So can a simple user-defined object, such as a *Point*, or a *Thermometer* or a *Book*, simply by having its attributes listed in some prescribed order in the sequence. What about when one object refers to another, just as when a *Book* refers to a *Person*? Then we need to put into the sequence of characters some identifying information about the object referred to. In an extreme case we could give each object in the sequence a unique name (or a number) and ensure that all objects appear in the sequence before they are referred to by other objects. Collections of objects can be represented in the sequence by delimiting the beginning and end of the collection in some way and by placing the representative of each object sequentially between these delimiters.

That should suffice as an initial argument to justify the generality of this solution, of this idea. However, we can reinforce it by the observation that all the data is collected sequentially in the first place and each collection activity is represented at the interface between the user and the program as a sequence of characters (from the keyboard). So, in an extreme case, we could represent the database of collected data by the sequence of original keystrokes used to create it. In practice we would expect to be a great deal more economical than that (but see the exercises for further discussion). However, before proceeding further with this idea it is sensible to consider whether or not it is economical in its use of machine resource. Let us do that now for the personal library.

The two aspects of performance which interest us are the amount of disk space used up by our file and the time to read and write that file. Previously, when discussing sizes, we have assumed a library of a few hundred books and a few tens of people. For the sake of argument, let us say 1000 books and 100 people, which is larger than any realistic figure for my personal collections of books and colleagues. Each book and each person can be represented by a character string, for which 50 characters should suffice. The number of books on loan at any time is unlikely to exceed 100 and I could (at worst) represent this loan arrangement by repeating the strings representing book and borrower, respectively. This means that the total file size could be at most

$$50\,000 \; + \; 5\,000 \; + \; 10\,000$$

for the books, the people and the borrowings respectively. 65,000 characters is a small file compared with most on my disk. The only remaining problem would be whether the time to read and write it would be acceptable.

A small experiment would serve to reassure us in that respect. By constructing a program to write a file of known size and then to read it back, while timing both operations, we can perhaps predict whether or not saving our objects sequentially will be reasonable. On the target machine for this application this experiment yielded interesting results. A file of 65K characters was created and read, each operation taking approximately 0.5s. To confirm this rate of operation, a file of 300K was created and read, each operation taking about 3s. The target machine was not a particularly fast one, so the experiment was repeated on a faster machine. On this occasion, even the 300K file was created and read in less than 0.5s. So the conclusion from this is that, for the size of file we anticipate, the actual disk input and output will not be significant. At this level of consideration, at this stage of the development, we might consider that a time of 2 or 3s to read or write a 65K file, including building the internal data structures (representing the objects in RAM) is realistic. It would also be acceptable from the user's point of view. If we can make it faster, so much the better. But no part of this consideration would discourage us from abandoning this approach (at least, not yet).

7.2 ANALYSIS

With this background, let us turn to the analysis of persistence for our personal library, bearing in mind that we are trying to build a program which is open to future change, a program which is flexible. The basic nature of simple, sequential files is shown in the protocol of Fig. 7.1. A *TextObject* is either a string of characters or a number (for our

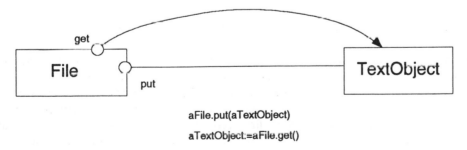

Figure 7.1 Protocol for sequential files.

purposes). We can put such an item into a file, in which case it will be appended to the end of the file. We can get an item from a file, in which case it will be taken from the front of the sequence. In practice, we know that we shall need further operations to open and close files, to determine whether we are allowed to read or write or both, and to determine, before reading, whether there is anything there to be read. But for the purposes of analysis we can ignore those details and deal only with the essential nature of a sequential file, as a queue or first-in, first-out collection of what are basically strings.

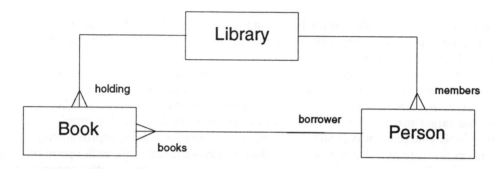

Figure 7.2 ER diagram for library (cf. Fig 3.7).

The structures we have given to the essential data in the library are recalled in Fig. 7.2. In the solution presented in earlier chapters we only have one *Library* object. The relationship between a *Library* and the *Book*s which it contains is represented by the collection-valued attribute *holding*. We say a *library* has a collection of *Book*s, its *holding*. Similarly, a *Library* has a collection of *Person*s, its *members*. So, for our single *Library* object we can record its relationship with the *Book* and *Person* objects by copying each of these collections, somehow, to the sequential file. This begs two questions. How are we to record objects of type *Book* and *Person*? And how are we to record collections?

For objects from the classes *Book* and *Person*, the application only requires that we record a string, the name used to display the object on the screen. For a collection we have to deal with the fact that there can be an arbitrary number of members of the collection. We need to delimit the beginning and end of the collection. One simple way to do this would be to reserve the strings **collection** and **end** for these respective purposes. So a holding might be recorded in the file as the sequence of strings

collection Stroustrup Proust Hardy end

where the three books have been represented by the strings which are their authors' surnames. What we are doing here is choosing a syntactic representation for our data structures. The syntax we are using is shown in Fig. 7.3. In this description, the syntactic categories *<Library>*, *<Holding>* etc. all define sequences of strings. Thus a *<Library>* is the sequence obtained by first recording the sequence for *<Holding>* and then the sequence for *<Members>*. A *<Holding>* is recorded as the string **collection** followed by zero or more (that is what the asterisk means) sequences representing *<Book>*, finally followed by the string **end**. Similarly *<Members>* records a sequence of *<Person>* representations. Finally, each of *<Book>* and *<Person>* is simply a *<string>*.

```
<Library>  ::= <Holding> <Members>
<Holding>  ::= collection <Book>* end
<Members>  ::= collection <Person>* end
   <Book>  ::= <string>
 <Person>  ::= <string>
```

Figure 7.3 Syntax for *Library* when streamed out to disk (part).

This seems satisfactory, as far as it goes. We still have to deal with the borrowings which have not yet been recorded in our sequential file. Figure 7.2 reminds us that these were recorded by a collection-valued attribute of *Person*, namely the individual's *books*, and redundantly by the *borrower* attribute of *Book*. It is not necessary to record both links in the sequential file, although we could do that. It should be sufficient to record one or the other, as long as we remember to reconstruct the one which we do not record explicitly. If we choose to record the collection-valued attribute *aPerson.books* then we need to replace the syntactic rule for *<Person>* with the revised rule shown in Fig. 7.4. Immediately after the string identifying the *Person* we will place the collection of *Books* currently on loan to that *Person*.

```
<Person>  ::= <string> collection <Book>* end
```

Figure 7.4 Further synax for *Library*.

```
collection Stroustrup Proust Hardy end
collection David collection Stroustrup Proust end
          Hugh collection Hardy end
          Stephen collection end
end
```

Figure 7.5 A library with three books, three persons and some borrowings (cf Figs 2.4 and 3.21).

An example of a sequence of strings representing a *Library* with three books, three persons and some borrowings is shown in Fig. 7.5. We see that *David* has two books, *Hugh* has one and *Stephen* has none. Some careful consideration at this time, comparing the abstract structure of our library shown in Fig. 7.2 with the proposed syntactic representation of Figs. 7.3 and 7.4 and the example of Fig. 7.5 should convince us that the proposed syntax is adequate for its purpose. We would no doubt recognize that other alternatives are possible, such as recording the *Person* with the *Book* rather than the *Book* with the *Person*. And there are others which may or may not be better (see the exercises). At this stage of analysis I am reasonably confident that the solution proposed here will be satisfactory and I am prepared to proceed to design.

Before doing so, we should be convinced that the sequential representation we have chosen will be reasonably straightforward both to write to and read from disk. In fact, the technique we are using here is based on the 'idea' that data structures can be represented sequentially by syntactic structures. The associated technique for reading such structures is called parsing, and we are aware of many parsing techniques for recognizing sequences such as that of Fig. 7.5 according to the syntax of Figs. 7.3 and 7.4. One obvious technique which will be valid here is recursive-descent parsing. In the case of our syntax of Fig. 7.3 this means that we would parse as follows. To get a *<Library>*, first get *<Holding>*, then get *<Members>*. To get a *<Holding>*, get a collection of *<Book>*. To get a collection, get each item in turn until **end** is encountered. To get a *<Book>*, just get a string, and so on. The corresponding operations for creating the sequential file are just the reverse of those for reading it. This kind of analysis of our proposal should serve to convince us that we have taken everything that we can into account and that we are in a good position to proceed to add the detail which we normally do at the design stage.

7.3 DESIGN

Our analysis of the problem has resulted in a proposed sequential representation of the data structures for a *Library* and a proposal that we use recursive-descent parsing to read and write such a sequential representation. Now we must design the detail of those algorithms. As ever, we will detail that design in Enact and in fact build a working model of our proposal, on the basis that we can do this very quickly, try alternative designs and remedy any design faults very cheaply.

```
class File < Object.

file():=new File with members=nil.

File.put(anObject):=
  (self.members:=append(self.members,anObject:())).

File.get():=
  (result:=hd(self.members);
   self.members:=tl(self.members);
   result).
```

Figure 7.6 Enact specification for sequential file.

First we must build a model of a sequential file. This we have done in Fig. 7.6, according to the protocol which we gave in Fig. 7.1. It is not necessary (nor even very desirable) to understand the detail of how the Enact in Fig. 7.6 actually works. It uses the list processing operations defined in Appendix 1. Using this definition of *File*, we can construct a sequential file by the calls

```
aFile := file().
aFile.put(aTextObject1).
aFile.put(aTextObject2).
```

and once we have constructed such a file we can read it using

```
aTextObject := aFile.get().
```

repeatedly.

Let us define the operations for building a sequential representation of *Library* first and deal with parsing second. It is quite straightforward to organize the operations for putting a representative of each object on to a file according to the type of the object being put, so we can have operations *aBook.put()*, *aPerson.put()* and *aLibrary.put()*. For example, *aBook.put()* will simply put the string representing its name on to the file. Similarly, *aPerson.put()* will put the name of the person and then put the collection of books. A solution organized in this way is shown in Fig. 7.7. We carry the object *aFile* along as a parameter. We have added an operation to *Collection* which puts a whole collection out to a file and here we have taken the liberty of revising the proposed file format. Rather then delimit a collection by the words **collection** and **end** we have chosen instead to prefix the sequence by a number, being a count of the number of objects to be collected. This change is minor. It is clearly equivalent to the proposed structure. The revised format is shown in Fig. 7.8. Logically, I prefer to think of it as having the structure of Fig. 7.5, while knowing that physically it is as in Fig. 7.8.

```
Book.put(aFile):=
  aFile.put(self.name).

Collection.put(aFile):=
  (aFile.put(self.size());
   self.forEachDo(anObject::anObject.put(aFile))).

Person.put(aFile):=
  (aFile.put(self.name);
   self.books.put(aFile)).

Library.put(aFile):=
  (self.holding.put(aFile);
   self.members.put(aFile)).
```

Figure 7.7 Enact model for creating file from library.

```
3 Stroustrup Proust Hardy
3 David   2 Stroustrup Proust
Hugh    1 Hardy
Stephen 0
```

Figure 7.8 What the file will look like.

Note that the operation *aCollection.put(aFile)* makes use of the object-oriented device of sending the message *anObject.put(aFile)* to each of its members. Thus each member will respond to this message according to its type. So when we call *aPerson.books.put(aFile)*, since *aPerson.books* is a collection of *Book*s, each will be put on the file simply as a string. But when we call *aLibrary.members. put(aFile)*, since each element of *aLibrary.members* is a *Person*, then what will be sent to the file this time is all the information representing a *Person*, which includes a collection of books.

To check that the specification of Fig. 7.7 will do what we want we should examine each operation in turn. First, *aBook.put(aFile)* indeed puts just the name of *aBook* to the file. However, *aPerson.put(aFile)* first puts the name of the person and then puts the collection of books currently on loan to that person. Finally, *aLibrary. put(aFile)* puts out two collections, the first being the holding and the second being the members. Note that each member has an embedded collection of books which is put automatically by the embedded call within *aLibrary.members.put(aFile)*. Another reassuring property of this specification is that its textual relationship with the syntax of Figs. 7.3 and 7.4 is very obvious. Given an extension to the syntax we feel confident we could extend the specification cheaply and correctly using the rules implied by this simple correspondence.

Notwithstanding this confidence it is still worthwhile executing the specification as a means of testing it. This we can do already with Enact if we load up our earlier prototype of the library and extend it with the definitions in Figs. 7.6 and 7.7. If we have created and used for some time a *Library* called *aLibrary*, so that it contains some books, some persons and some borrowings, then the test

```
aFile := file().
aLibrary.put(aFile).
aFile.members.
```

should yield a list which has the expected members. For example if we had created a library with three persons, three books and some borrowings we might expect to see a list of the form

```
(3 Stroustrup Proust Hardy 3 David 2 Stroustrup...)
```

which is the Enact representation for the structure shown in Fig. 7.8. Once we have achieved this we can be fairly confident that our design is correct. As always, we would run a series of tests, especially testing extreme cases of empty collections. Any bugs encountered here would be easily eradicated. The solution in Fig. 7.7 has no such bugs.

```
   <Library> ::= <Holding> <Members>
   <Holding> ::= <Book>*
   <Members> ::= <Person>* <Borrowings>
<Borrowings> ::= <Book2>*
      <Book> ::= <string>            acquire
    <Person> ::= <string>            join
     <Book2> ::= <string>            borrow
```

Figure 7.9 Simplified syntax with appropriate semantic actions for input.

The elegance of this solution for putting data to a file is difficult to repeat for getting data from a file. There are two reasons. The first is that the information about what type of object is encountered is not available to be read from the file. We have to determine that implicitly from the syntax. The second reason is that, quite what we do with an object when we get it depends upon context. In particular, when we first encounter a book, we have to create it and add it to the library's holding. When we subsequently encounter it, we have to locate it in this holding in order to ensure that we have only a single object representing each book. To make this requirement more specific, look at the revised syntactic description in Fig. 7.9. Here we show collections again by decorating the syntactic category with an asterisk (and remember that is now recorded by prefixing the collection with a count). Alongside each syntactic category, where it is appropriate, we have added a semantic action **acquire**, **join** or **borrow**. This means that, for example, when we encounter each *<Book>* in *<Holding>* we will invoke the method *aLibrary.acquire(aBook)* to record the acquisition of that book in the library. Similarly, for each *<Person>* we invoke *aLibrary.join(aPerson)* and for each *<Book>* in that *<Person>*'s borrowings we will invoke *aLibrary.borrow (aPerson, aBook)*. What we are proposing is that we begin with an empty *Library* and, as we encounter each item on the file, we update the library to record the relevant facts about that item.

The usual way to encode a recursive-descent parser is to provide one subroutine for each syntactic category. That subroutine is charged with recognizing the corresponding sequence and building its internal representation. The benefit of this form of encoding is that there is a simple correspondence between the syntax and the code of the program. Since this is a very desirable property for us, we shall seek to achieve it here. In that sense, we shall ignore the object-oriented nature of our design and allow our program to be structured by the syntactic structure of our sequential representation. The corresponding Enact specification is derived as shown in Figs. 7.10, 7.11 and 7.12, respectively. Note that there are exactly seven subroutines corresponding to the seven syntactic categories of Fig. 7.9. The definitions are an obvious transliteration of the corresponding syntactic rules, except where we have carefully had to carry along appropriate parameters. By and large, it is necessary to carry along the two objects which we are regularly updating, *aLibrary* and *aFile*, respectively. Note how, when we call *getBook(aLibrary, aFile)*, a single name is taken from *aFile*, a *Book* with this name is created and then that is acquired by *aLibrary*. This means that the effect of *getHolding(aLibrary, aFile)* is to acquire a whole sequence of books and install them as *aLibrary. holding*.

```
getBook(aLibrary,aFile):=
  (bookName:=aFile.get();
   aBook:=book(bookName);
   aLibrary.acquire(aBook)).

getHolding(aLibrary,aFile):=
  (size:=aFile.get();
   (size>0)loop(getBook(aLibrary,aFile);
               size:=size-1)).

getLibrary(aLibrary,aFile):=
  (getHolding(aLibrary,aFile);
   getMembers(aLibrary,aFile)).
```

Figure 7.10 Enact specification of parser.

```
getPerson(aLibrary,aFile):=
  (personName:=aFile.get();
   aPerson:=person(personName);
   aLibrary.join(aPerson);
   getBorrowings(aLibrary,aPerson,aFile)).

getMembers(aLibrary,aFile):=
  (size:=aFile.get();
   (size>0)loop(getPerson(aLibrary,aFile);
               size:=size-1)).
```

Figure 7.11 Enact specification of parser (continued).

In the definition of *getHolding*, (Fig. 7.10) we see the use of an idiom

```
size := aFile.get();
(size > 0) loop (... ; size := size -1)
```

which is repeated elsewhere in the Enact specification. Having obtained the *size* of a collection from *aFile*, this idiom then carries out that many actions by counting down. Each action (represented above by ellipsis) must obtain exactly one collection member from the file if the integrity of the file is to be preserved. Enact does not really provide suitable means for avoiding this explicit use of loop. We could define a function

```
DO_N_TIMES(n, ACTION) :=
    (size := n;
        (size > 0) loop (ACTION();size := size -1)).
```

and then replace the definition of *getHolding* by

```
getHolding(aLibrary, aFile) :=
    DO_N_TIMES(aFile.get(), ()::getBook(aLibrary, aFile))
```

but, for a specification as short as ours I feel the idiom is rather easier to handle than the higher order function *DO_N_TIMES*. For bigger problems we might prefer the hiding of the loop which the higher order function achieves.

```
getBook2(aLibrary,aPerson,aFile):=
  (bookName:=aFile.get();
   aBook:=aLibrary.holding.locate(aBook::aBook.name=bookName);
   aLibrary.borrow(aPerson,aBook)).

getBorrowings(aLibrary,aPerson,aFile):=
  (size:=aFile.get();
   (size>0)loop(getBook2(aLibrary,aPerson,aFile);
            size:=size-1)).
```

Figure 7.12 Enact specification of parser (continued).

Most of the specification given in Figs. 7.10, 7.11 and 7.12 is unremarkable. Note how *getPerson* calls *aLibrary.join(aPerson)* and then calls *getBorrowings*. This latter call has an extra parameter, *aPerson*, required eventually when we allocate each borrowed book. The call of *getBorrowings* calls in turn the subroutine *getBook2*, which, as its name implies, expects a *<Book>* on the input file but is going to treat it differently from *getBook*. This is the only really exciting part of this design. Having obtained the name of the book from the file we do not create a new *Book* object; rather we *locate* the existing object which represents this book. This is accomplished by the call

```
aBook := aLibrary.holding.locate(aBook::aBook.name = bookName)
```

which assumes such a book exists in *aLibrary.holding* and, finding it, returns it by assigning it to *aBook*. Now we have the names of both the borrower and the book, so we can record the allocation by

```
aLibrary.borrow(aPerson, aBook)
```

which we do for every book on loan to this particular person. And in turn, we do this for each person. The net effect is that, beginning with an empty *Library*, we succeed in acquiring a collection of books, a collection of members and then reinstating the record of the allocation of books to persons.

Despite the fact that the simple relationship between the syntax and the design means we should be reasonably confident about its correctness, the fact that we have an executable Enact specification means that we will be able to raise our confidence even more by testing it. A suitable test is to construct in *aFile* a sequence which truly represents a sensible *Library*. A sensible way to do this is by calling

```
aLibrary.put(aFile).
```

At this stage *aLibrary* will be unchanged, but a sequential representation of it will be recorded in *aFile*. So if we now call

```
aLibrary2 := library().
getLibrary(aLibrary2,aFile).
```

we should obtain an exact copy of *aLibrary* in *aLibrary2*. This we can check by browsing it.

Have we achieved persistence? If we can represent *aFile* on disk we surely have, for the above sequence of operations demonstrates that we can break the execution after *aLibrary.put(aFile)* and resume at a later time as long as *aFile* is held on persistent storage. We have made certain that the operations on *aFile* are sufficiently simple that the usual file operations provided by C++ will indeed make copying it to disk very simple. That is what remains to be done, and is what we shall do next.

7.4 IMPLEMENTATION

As always, when we move into implementation, we have much to bring forward from our explicit design and we have a few remaining problems to solve. Mostly, the remaining problems are to do with the detail of how C++ handles the specific operations which we propose to use. On this occasion however, we have one reasonably substantial detailed design problem still to solve. This relates to the nature of what, in the previous section, we have taken to calling strings. We will need to take care of the fact that, in practice, the strings which will be used to identify *Book*s and *Person*s may ultimately contain any character, including spaces and digits and most delimiters. We will need to design input and output routines which cater for this eventuality.

To begin with however, we will elaborate our design using just the facilities which C++ provides for input and output to files. Sequential files are implemented in C++ as streams. We have already seen the use of the standard output stream **cout** in expressions of the form

```
cout << n << "\n"
```

where the stream operator **<<** expects an output stream as left argument and a printable expression as right argument. The side-effect of the **<<** operator is to append the printable value to the output stream and the result returned by the **cout << e** expression is a value representing the output stream **cout**. This means that **<<** operators can be cascaded as above. More important is the fact that the **<<** operator's behaviour is determined by the type of the expression to be printed. Thus **cout << n** will print **n** according to its type. If **n** is an **int** it will be printed as a string of decimal digits. If **n** is a **char*** it will be printed as a sequence of characters.

Much the same facilities are available for input from streams. Suppose we have declared **int i;** and **char s[100];** the following expression

cin >> i >> s

reads an integer and then a string from the input stream **cin**. Some conventions are obeyed. The most important one is that white space is skipped. White space includes space, newline, and tab characters. In the case of the string, leading white space is skipped, the first non-white space character being the first to be taken as part of the string. The characters are read until the string is terminated by a white space character, hopefully before we have filled our array. We shall see that this interaction between white space and the input of **char*** will cause us some difficulties, which we will ultimately rectify.

The predefined streams **cin** and **cout** are normally connected to the keyboard and the screen, respectively. We want to connect streams to a file. This is accomplished by declaring an appropriate type of object. The necessary type definitions are usually found in the file **fstream.h**. For input file streams we define, for example,

ifstream aFile("library.db");

The variable introduced here is **aFile** and its type is **ifstream**. The constructor **ifstream::ifstream(char*)** is called to build and return an object representing an input stream attached to the file whose name is given by the **char***, so the above declaration attaches **aFile** to the file **library.db** in the current directory. The **ifstream** object which is built in this way can be tested to see whether or not attaching it to the file has been successful. In the statement

if (aFile) { .... };

the guarded portion is only executed if the opening of the file has been successful. So within that section we can use **aFile** in much the way we would use **cin**.

A file is opened for output by a similar device, this time declaring its type to be **ofstream.** C++ provides many facilities for both types of file and indeed allows files to be opened simultaneously for both reading and writing. We shall not require that. Files are automatically closed by the implicit invocation of the destructor, which happens on exit from the block in which the declaration is made. If, however, we require to close a file explicitly, we can do this, for example, by the call **aFile.close();** .

The way in which the **<<** and **>>** operators work, by determining their specific action on the basis of the types of their arguments is called operator overloading. C++ allows us to overload the operators further to output our own application types. Figure 7.13 shows the definition of two functions, overloading the **<<** operator, respectively to print the representations of **Book*** and **Person***. The convention for defining a function which overloads **<<** is to give the function the name **operator<<**. The type of this function must be that its first argument is an **ostream&** (a reference to an **ostream**) and its result must be an **ostream&**. It must have a second argument, whose type is distinct from any other definition of **operator<<**, including the built-in definitions. This convention, we can see, has been followed in Fig. 7.13. The relationship between the various types in use here is shown in Fig. 7.14.

```
ostream& operator<<(ostream& aFile, Book* aBook){
aFile<<aBook->name();
return aFile;
}

ostream& operator<<(ostream& aFile, Person* aPerson){
aFile<<aPerson->name();
return aFile;
}
```

Figure 7.13 Overloaded stream operators.

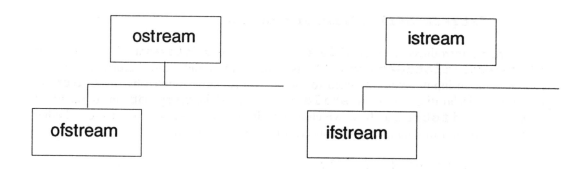

Figure 7.14 Relationship between some stream types in C++.

With this preparation we can begin the transliteration of our Enact design of Fig. 7.7 into a C++ implementation. This we have done in Figs. 7.15 and 7.16. It would have been nice to have overloaded **<<** to output a **Collection** but this is not possible because we do not know the type of members of a **Collection**. We can, however, still define a generic function **putCollection**, as in Fig. 7.15, where we have parameterized this with a function **void putObject(ostream&, void*)**, which has the responsibility for putting the representative of each member onto the **ostream**. Within the body of **putCollection** we have made use of the method **Collection::index** to retrieve each member in turn (see Appendix 2). The definition of **putBook** in figure 7.15 is a suitable candidate for **putObject**, so a call of the form

```
putCollection(aFile, aCollection, putBook);
```

will work, assuming **aCollection** is indeed a collection of **Book***s.

```
void putCollection(ostream& aFile, Collection*
    aCollection, void putObject(ostream&,void*)){
  aFile<<aCollection->size()<<" ";
  for(int i=aCollection->size();i>0;i--)
    putObject(aFile,aCollection->index(i));
}

void putBook(ostream& aFile, void* aBook){
aFile<<(Book*)aBook;
}
```

Figure 7.15 C++ for streaming out **Collection** and **Book**.

```
void putPerson(ostream& aFile, void* aPerson){
 aFile<<(Person*)aPerson;

putCollection(aFile,((Person*)aPerson)->books(),putBook);
}

ostream& operator<<(ostream& aFile, Library* aLibrary){
  putCollection(aFile,aLibrary->holding(),putBook);
  putCollection(aFile,aLibrary->members(),putPerson);
  return aFile;
}
```

Figure 7.16 Operations for outputting **Person** and **Library**.

We can see such a call in the body of **putPerson** in Fig. 7.16. Here the books currently on loan to **aPerson**, that is **aPerson->books()** are put on to **aFile** in this way. Note that **putPerson** is our implementation of *Person.put(aFile)* revised to be in the shape required by **putCollection**. So now we are in a position to copy the whole library to **aFile**, which we accomplish by the overloaded **operator<<** in Fig. 7.16. Using this operator, and opening **aFile** for output, is accomplished as follows:

```
ofstream aFile("library.db");
if(aFile)aFile<<aLibrary;
```

By building a sample library in **aLibrary**, we can test this much of the implementation at this stage, and should do that.

Our tests will reveal a problem, which we predicted at the beginning of this section. The problem arises because of the possibility of white space occurring in the middle of one of the names we have used for a **Person** or a **Book**. It is not unreasonable for us to allow space characters; it is even desirable. For example, two of my colleagues may be called **David** and I may wish to distinguish them as, say, **David1** and **David2**. The appearance on screen with a space between **David** and the digit is more elegant. Unfortunately, if the characters placed in the file include the space I will have difficulty reading that back. A simple, universal solution for storing strings will be adopted. This prefixes the string with a count of the number of characters in it, thus:

```
7:David 1
15:Stephen Dedalus
```

The colon is ignored, but is necessary in case the first character of the name is a digit. Functions for printing such strings to an **ostream** and reading back from an **istream** are shown in Fig. 7.17. The new output function is easily incorporated in our implementation by revising the overloaded operators for **Book*** and **Person***, as shown in Fig. 7.18.

```
void getName(istream& aFile, char*& name){
int length; aFile>>length;
name=new char[length+1];
aFile.get(name[0]);
for(int i=0;i<length;i++)aFile.get(name[i]);
name[length]='\0';
}

void putName(ostream& aFile, char* name){
int length;
length=strlen(name);
aFile<<length;
aFile.put(':');
for(int i=0;i<length;i++)aFile.put(name[i]);
aFile.put(' ');
}
```

Figure 7.17 Functions for reading and printing universal strings.

In these definitions we have used the more basic operations on streams for outputting and inputting single characters. The advantage of using **istream::get(char&)** is that it reads the very next character, even when it is white space. The reason for using **ostream::put(char)** is simply for symmetry in the definitions. Note that these two definitions collaborate quite well. The fact that **getName** skips white space until it encounters the integer part of the string makes this quite a robust function. The fact that **putName** uses ':' in the middle of the string and ' ' at the end is arbitrary, although some character is necessary. These characters make the output reasonably readable for debugging purposes.

```
ostream& operator<<(ostream& aFile, Book* aBook){
putName(aFile,aBook->name());
return aFile;
}

ostream& operator<<(ostream& aFile, Person* aPerson){
putName(aFile,aPerson->name());
return aFile;
}
```

Figure 7.18 Revised operators for **Book** and **Person**.

```
istream& operator>>(istream& aFile, Library*& aLibrary){
  getLibrary(aLibrary,aFile);
  return aFile;
}
```

Figure 7.19 Overloaded operator for reading **Library**.

```
void getBook(Library* aLibrary, istream& aFile){
  char* bookName;
  getName(aFile,bookName);
  Book* aBook=new Book(bookName);
  aLibrary->acquire(aBook);
}

void getHolding(Library* aLibrary,istream& aFile){
  int size; aFile>>size;
  while(size>0){
    getBook(aLibrary,aFile);
    size--;
  }
}

void getLibrary(Library* aLibrary, istream& aFile){
  getHolding(aLibrary,aFile);
  getMembers(aLibrary,aFile);
}
```

Figure 7.20 C++ parser for reading **Library** objects (cf. Fig. 7.10).

All that remains to be done to complete our persistent personal library is to implement the input procedures which will read the file created by **aFile<<aLibrary**. We need to define the overloaded operator which will allow us to evaluate **aFile>>aLibrary**. Such an operator is shown in Fig. 7.19. This is achieved largely by a straightforward transliteration of our Enact design, as shown in Figs. 7.20, 7.21 and 7.22. Exactly the same names have been used, so the correspondence between the Enact model and the C++ implementation should be obvious. The only non-trivial bit is where we have had to lift the lambda expression used as an argument of **Collection::locate**, up to the top level and give it a name **bookwithName**. This function is defined as shown in Fig. 7.23, where the free variable **char* bookName** is made global and carefully assigned before the call to **locate**, according to the simple idiom we have previously used in this situation.

```
void getPerson(Library* aLibrary, istream& aFile){
  char* personName;
  getName(aFile,personName);
  Person* aPerson=new Person(personName);
  aLibrary->join(aPerson);
  getBorrowings(aLibrary,aPerson,aFile);
}

void getMembers(Library* aLibrary,istream& aFile){
  int size; aFile>>size;
  while(size>0){
    getPerson(aLibrary,aFile);
    size—;
  }
}
```

Figure 7.21 C++ parser for **Person** and **Members** (cf. Fig. 7.11).

```
void getBook2(Library* aLibrary, Person* aPerson,
              istream& aFile){
 char* bookName;
 getName(aFile,bookName);
 ::bookName=bookName;
 Book* aBook=(Book*)aLibrary->holding()
                          ->locate(bookwithname);
 aLibrary->borrow(aPerson,aBook);
}

void getBorrowings(Library* aLibrary,
                   Person* aPerson,istream& aFile){
  int size; aFile>>size;
```

```
  while(size>0){
    getBook2(aLibrary,aPerson,aFile);
    size--;
  }
}
```

Figure 7.22 C++ parser for **Borrowings** (cf. Fig. 7.12).

```
char* bookName;

int bookwithname(void* aBook){
  return strcmp(((Book*)aBook)->name(),::bookName)==0;
}
```

Figure 7.23 Lifted lambda for use in locate in **getBook2**.

We put the whole of our implementation together now by adding the necessary file opening and closing operations to **main** as shown in Fig. 7.24. After the **Library* lib** has been declared we attempt to initialize it from **aFile**. If there is no file **library.db** then statement **inFile>>lib** will not be executed. If however it is executed we take the precaution of also closing **inFile** so that at the end of the program we can open it (i.e. **library.db**) again for writing. The program executes as normal by invoking **toplevel->_do()** which eventually returns when the user escapes from the menu. At that time we open **outFile** for writing and stream the contents of **lib** back into the file **library.db**, thus ensuring that exactly the same data is available the next time the program is run.

```
main()
{
Library* lib=new Library();

ifstream infile("library.db");
if(infile){infile>>lib;
infile.close();
}

... set up user interface

topLevel->_do();

ofstream outfile("library.db");
if(outfile)outfile<<lib;

}
```

Figure 7.24 Persistence added to top level of library program.

Comprehensive testing can now be performed, including setting up test **library.db** files by hand and checking that the system is robust against such eventualities as a non-existent **library.db** and against the use of spaces and other unusual characters in the names of books and persons. Also at this point we are now well placed to carry out some sensible performance testing to see if our actual behaviour is anything like that which we predicted. Recall that we had estimated that a worst case would be 1000 books and 100 people in the library with about 100 books on loan at any time. We estimated a file size for this data not exceeding 65K and tested that we could read that file in less than a second. We predicted that the time to build the internal data structure would be acceptable. So now we must test that.

This was done by writing a program which used the **putName** function to define a database with a given number of **Book**s and a given number of **Person**s. Each book was given a unique name, for example **Book 232** and each person called, for example, **Person 478**. Each **Person** borrowed exactly five **Book**s. The data for various sizes of library are shown in Fig. 7.25. The figures for 1000 books and 100 persons are adequate if not brilliantly fast. The implementation was also extended to display (in a **Display** at the bottom left of the screen) a count of the number of cells currently allocated to collections. We watched this go up and down by exactly the right amount on each transaction.

number of books	250	500	1000	2000
number of persons	25	50	100	200
books per person	5	5	5	5
file size	4.5 K	9K	18K	37K
cell count	406	808	1606	3209
secs to open	1	3	10	50
secs to borrow	0	< 0.5	1	3
secs to close	1	2	6	20

Figure 7.25 Comparative performance on data sets of different sizes.

Since the performance of 1000 **Book**s was poor, we inspected the code a little more closely. The call to **locate**, used each time a borrowing is encountered, is the cause of most of the loss of performance. This was checked by performing a test with this line commented out. The 10s load time reduced to 3s. There are many ways in which performance could be improved here, which are left as exercises for the reader. The other possible source of poor performance is when the borrow option is exercised, for then the entire stock of **Books** needs to be scanned using **select** to ensure we only offer for borrowing books which actually are in the library. As Fig. 7.25 shows, this performance was satisfactory. With these tests giving confidence in correctness and showing reasonable performance at the limits of its expected operating range, the program was passed as satisfactory for daily use. It now forms part of my usual desktop and the primary objective with which we began this book has been achieved: a program to look after my personal library. But this is not the end of the story. We had other objectives to do with flexibility and it is those that we address next.

7.5 EXERCISES

1. Suppose the library holds both books and videos, organized as in Fig. 3.10 (see also Exercise 3 in Chapter 3). Revise the syntactic description of Fig. 7.3 to include this additional data. Extend the Enact model of Figs. 7.7 and 7.10–7.12 to include this further requirement.

2. How might the design of the entire library system be modified to include an element of safeguard against machine failure. Use the fact that the database may be written to periodically and recommend ways in which this may be used to record checkpoint information. Suppose it was absolutely essential that no information would be lost in the case of machine failure, but that writing the entire database after each update was considered too expensive. What intermediate measures could be taken?

3. Rather than streaming out and in the data structures, we could record on the database a series of acquire, join and borrow commands, which, upon reading, execute the corresponding events just as if the commands had been typed in or selected from menus. Design such a persistent system.

4. What modification is required to the design given in this chapter if the database is to record the borrowings from more than one library? Give syntax, Enact and C++ modifications.

5. Suppose that, rather than reconstruct the inverse relationship, we were to record both *aPerson.books* and *aBook.borrower* in the database. Would this have any advantages? Repeat the calculations with respect to database size and expected performance to help you decide if this is a better design.

8

GENERIC APPLICATIONS

8.1 INTRODUCTION

We took as our original objectives that our programs should be correct, robust and have adequate performance. We also took as a major objective that they should be flexible in their openness to future change. The properties of correctness, robustness and adequate performance we have obtained by means of careful design and testing of our product. The property of flexibility is rather more difficult to quantify and hence more difficult to test for. We are aware that during analysis and design we iterated rather a lot, experimenting with alternatives, finding a balance between the eventual development cost of the software and the perceived quality of the eventual product. We attempted to reduce the cost of the eventual development by various kinds of reuse. We attempted to improve the quality of the product by the care we took and the eventual simplicity of the design. And it is on these qualities that flexibility also resides. The components we have reused are obviously generic (meaning they can be used for more than one purpose) but so are the new components we have built. It is this property of reusability and the more general concept of being generic which we shall discuss in this chapter.

In what sense is our library application generic, that is, reusable in future developments? It is generic in the very simple sense that we can imagine for it a lifetime of future change. In what sense is our library application flexible, that is, open to future change? A measure of openness would be the amount of effort required to make a change. Since the architecture of our library application is comparatively simple we anticipate that there is a wide range of changes which, because they would fit into the architecture in an obvious way, would be comparatively cheap to make. For example, moving the application to a different windowing environment would simply involve replacement of the **userface** component. Changes in user requirements, such as organizing books into groups according to subject, to simplify browsing (for the user), would be equally straightforward. Such extensions are worthy of contemplation, but are left as an exercise

86

for the reader (see exercises). We shall go on to consider other ways in which the library application is generic. When we break the library application down into its component parts we see that it is generic in quite a more generous sense. Many of its parts are reusable, as we shall show. Clearly those parts which we reused from previous applications, specifically the collections component and the user interface component, are reusable in further applications. Also the 'reusable idea' which we exploited, that data structures can be represented by a string which contains (effectively) the instructions to rebuild the structures, can clearly be reused. We feel confident that any object structure which we can represent as an ER diagram we can stream out to and in from a sequential file, based on the obviously simple relationship between the syntax which we adopt and the code we must then write. There are other generic components. For example, there is the way in which we tie together the events which comprise the user interface, exemplified by the designs shown in the object diagrams in Fig. 5.29 (for the thermometer example) and Fig. 6.6 (for the library example). This gives us a means of designing user interfaces of a particular kind. Clearly this design method is reusable for a wide range of applications. Integrated with that reusable design method is the close relationship, which we have exploited, between the ability to represent relationships using collections and the mechanism of selectors which allow the user to pick objects from collections.

The sense in which the library application is built from a generic architecture is the following. We have four reusable components:

1. The collection component **`collect.h`**
2. The user interface component **`userface.h`**
3. Design method for events
4. Persistence by syntax

and one specific component for the library application itself:

5. The personal library component

We have abstract systems for 1, 2 and 5 and we can think of 3 and 4 as being the glue which we use to bind these together. Changes to the application will require us to modify 3, 4 and 5 while keeping them clearly separate, so that the architecture remains simple for future changes. In this way we can see how flexible the design is. However, we can see better how generic it is if we remove the application-specific component altogether and re-use the others in a completely new application. This is what we will do in the next section. After that, we shall show how a whole family of applications can be implemented as a single generic application (subsuming both the library and our new application) and eventually we shall return to the nature of what it means to be a generic application.

8.2 A HIERARCHY EDITOR

Of course, our choice of alternative application cannot be entirely free. It must fit into the family of applications which reuse the basic components supporting our personal library. However, the application we shall tackle is quite different from the personal library.

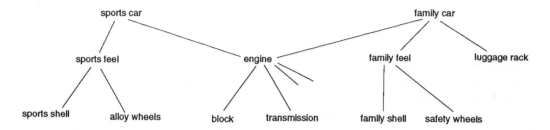

Figure 8.1 Simplified design parts structure for two motor cars.

Other examples, quite different again, are listed among the exercises at the end of this chapter.

A hierarchy editor is a tool which is used to manipulate, and keep in good order, a description of a hierarchical organization. We have in mind a particular type of hierarchical organization, that which is used to describe how products are built from components. For example, a *motor car* consists of a *chassis* and an *engine*, some *wheels* and a *body shell*. The *engine*, in turn consists of *engine block*, *transmission* and so on. If we are referring here to design parts as opposed to actual physical parts then we can imagine two separate designs sharing the same design parts.

For example, a (grossly simplified) description of two motor cars is shown in Fig. 8.1. Here we see that the *sports car* is an assembly of two components which (in the company marketing this model) are referred to as the *sports feel* and the *engine*. The *sports feel* is also an assembly (remember, it is a design part) of the *sports shell* and the *alloy wheels*. Similarly, we have an assembly referred to as a family car. Both cars share the same engine, which is also an assembly of many parts. Our analysis of this problem yields the entity relationship diagram of Fig. 8.2. We have distinguished two types of *Component*, respectively *Basic* and *Assembly*. A *Basic* is a component which is not further decomposed. In our example, *sports shell* and *alloy wheels* are examples of *Basic* components. An *Assembly* is a component which is further decomposed into parts. In our examples *sports car* and *sports feel* are examples of *Assembly* components

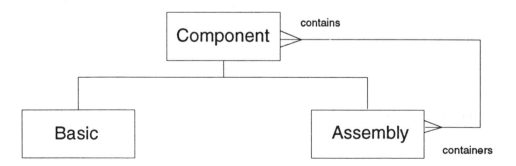

Figure 8.2 ER model of hierarchical structure.

We note that an *Assembly* has many *Components* which we call its *contains*. We also note that each *Component* may be in more than one *Assembly*. We call the *Assembly*s which a *Component* is in its *containers*. So the components of *engine* are *block*, *transmission* etc., while the *containers* of *engine* are *sports car* and *family car*. The way in which objects, organized according to the ER diagram, are used to record the data of our example is shown in the object diagram of Fig. 8.3. Here we see that only an *Assembly* has a *contains* but every *Component* has *containers*.

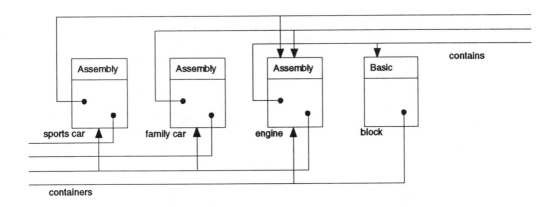

Figure 8.3 Object diagram for part of motor car data.

Our editor is required to build a database of descriptions of which assemblies contain which components and allow us to change this structure and to browse it. First we must complete our abstract system for manipulating *Components*. What remains to be done is to define the protocol which we will use to create, update and interrogate *Components*. In fact, we shall present here a design which was the final outcome of an iterative process. We will comment in passing on the alternatives that were rejected. Most of the iteration took place within an Enact prototype. The only iteration which took place in C++ was the aesthetics of where to place various devices on the screen.

```
anAssembly:=assembly(aName)
aBasic:=basic(aName)
anAssembly.addComponent(aComponent)
anAssembly.delComponent(aComponent)
aName:=aComponent.name
aCollection:=aComponent.containers
aTruthValue:=aComponent.isAssembly
aCollection:=anAssembly.contains
```

Figure 8.4 Protocol for manipulating assemblies and components.

Figure 8.4 shows the protocol for manipulating *Component*. We can create the two types of *Component* using the constructors *assembly()* and *basic()*. Each component is given a name to identify it when it is on the screen. Once we have an *Assembly* we can *addComponent*s to it. We can use *anAssembly.contains* to access it subsequently. For example, after *anAssembly.addComponent(aComponent)* we should find that

> *anAssembly.contains.member(aComponent)*
> *aComponent.containers.member(anAssembly)*

are both true. We can remove a *Component* from an *Assembly* using *anAssembly.delComponent* and we can determine whether or not a *Component* is an *Assembly* using *aComponent.isAssembly*, which we will need to test as a precondition before using *anAssembly.contains*.

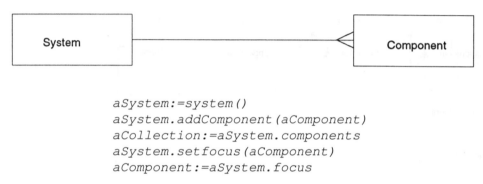

> *aSystem:=system()*
> *aSystem.addComponent(aComponent)*
> *aCollection:=aSystem.components*
> *aSystem.setfocus(aComponent)*
> *aComponent:=aSystem.focus*

Figure 8.5 The top-level object gives access to the collection of all components.

Just as we did in the personal library, we will need an object which will act as the root of our entire data structure. Accordingly we define *System* as in Fig. 8.5. The intention is that every component that is created is stored in the collection of *Component*s referred to by the root *System* object. The *System* object contains one more device, which was arrived at after iteration within the Enact prototype. This is called the *focus*. We shall see that, as a result of browsing within the editor, we shall keep a record of where we are currently located in the entire system in the *aSystem.focus* attribute. The normal editing process will be to browse until the *focus* is the *Assembly* to which we must add or delete a *Component*. Having arrived at that place in the structure, we will ask the user to select the *Component* to be added or deleted, the selection being made from an appropriate collection of *Component*s.

The kind of user interface which we are contemplating is shown in Fig. 8.6. In the top left corner of the screen there is a display which shows the current *focus* of browsing. The menus appear on the screen below that and on the right there is a selector which is used to choose components either when navigating or when adding and deleting. The top-level menu entries allow us to choose *newBasic* or *newAssembly,* whereupon a prompter will pop up allowing us to type in a name for this new component. If we select *Browse* from the top-level menu we are first offered a selector with all *Component*s in it, to set the initial *focus*. Then we are offered a submenu with entries *up* and *down*. If we choose *up*, we will be offered a selector with all the `containers` of the focus to choose from. If we choose *down* we will be offered a selector with all the `contains` of the focus to choose from. When we make our choice that becomes the new focus and we are still positioned at the submenu, with the ability to move further up and down. By this means we can position ourselves anywhere in the structure. Having done so, we escape from the submenu back to the top-level menu, where we are able now to choose either *add* `Component` or *delComponent*. Doing so will cause the selector to open with a collection of `Components`. In the case of *delComponent*, it will be the components in the `Assembly` which are the focus. In the case of *addComponent* it will be a collection of all `Component`s known to the system.

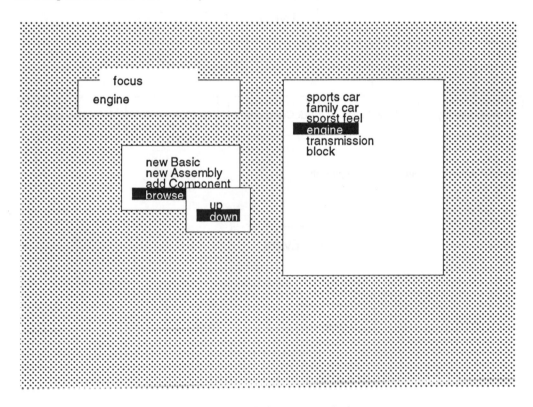

Figure 8.6 The proposed user interface, with focus display, menus and selector.

This was not the first user interface proposal. We considered and built an Enact prototype of a simpler model which didn't use a focus but rather used two selectors, one for the assembly to be edited and one for the component to be added or subtracted. Use of the Enact prototype, while convincing us that the basic design was correct, also led us to contemplate the use of what we have called the *focus*. A redesign and revision of the Enact prototype was sufficient to convince us that this would give a more usable interface for the eventual use. This second version is still not ideal, in ways which we shall discuss in the exercises, where the reader is invited to consider how these further shortcomings might be addressed.

Clearly our user interface is designed to reuse the **userface** objects. We also propose to reuse the design method of configuring *Event* objects to glue the application abstract system to the user interface abstract system. Thus we define seven new subclasses of *Event*, as shown in Figs. 8.7 and 8.8. The *NewAssembly* and *NewBasic* events each have a *Prompter*. *AddComponent* and *DelComponent* each have a *Selector* and *Browse* has a *Menu*. *Up* and *Down* do not have associations with any other devices. All seven new events have access to the *System* object, which is where the actual data is available.

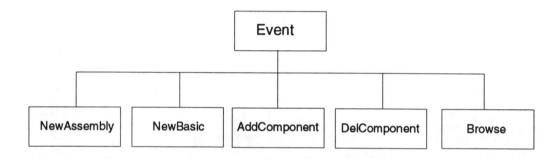

Figure 8.7 Events for manipulating components.

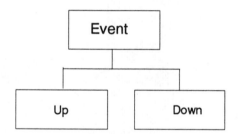

Figure 8.8 Events for moving up and down the hierarchy.

Figure 8.9 shows how the top-level events are organized to be evoked from the top-level *Menu*. Each of the five events has access to *aSystem*. So, for example, if we fire the *NewBasic* object, it opens up *basicPrompter* to get a name for the component from the user. Then it creates a new *Basic* component and adds it to the collection of all components held in *aSystem*. When we fire the *AddComponent* event, it will check that the focus of *aSystem* is an *Assembly* and then place the collection of all *Components* in *componentSelector* for the user to choose a *Component*. This choice is then added to the *contains* of the *Assembly* which is the current focus. The *Del Component* event is very similar, except that the collection of components installed in *componentSelector* is just those that are actually part of the contains of the *Assembly* which is the focus of *aSystem*. As an illustration, the Enact specification of *DelContains* is shown in Figure 8.10.

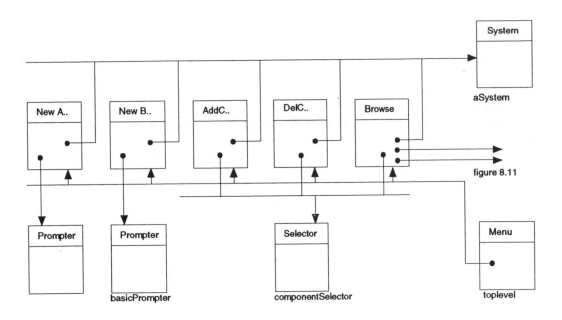

Figure 8.9 Object diagram for events and interface objects.

The situation that arises when we fire *Browse* at the top level is a little more complex. The layout of objects is shown in the object diagram in Fig. 8.11. The *Browse* event has access to *aSystem* and to *componentSelector*, so it can initially offer the user a choice from all components which it then sets as the new focus. Next, the *Browse* event fires the submenu *upDownMenu*, which gives the user access to the *Up* and *Down* events. Each of these events has access to *aSystem*. If the user chooses *Up* and it is possible to go up (that is, there are some containers of the component which is the current focus) then the user is offered a choice by installing *aSystem.focus.containers* in *componentSelector*. This choice is then taken as the next focus. For definiteness the Enact specification of *Up* is shown in Fig. 8.12.

There is one more feature of this design which needs to be explained. This is the mechanism used to refresh the *Display*, which displays the current focus. For this we borrow an idiom which we introduced in the thermometers exercise. We have an event *Show*, which, when fired, interrogates *aSystem* and presents the current value of the focus to the *Display*. We ensure that *Show* is fired at appropriate times by adding it as dependent to each of the events which change focus, in this case *Browse*, *Up* and *Down*. Each of these events must fire *Show* by the call *doAllDependents()*. This we can see happening in Fig. 8.12 for the *Up* event.

```
class DelContains < Event.

delContains(aSelector,aSystem):=
  new DelContains with componentSelector=aSelector
                  with system=aSystem.

DelContains.do():=
    (self.system.focus<>0 and
    self.system.focus.isAssembly())then
      (anAssembly:=self.system.focus;
      availableComponents:=self.system.focus.contains;
      (availableComponents.size()>0)then
          (self.componentSelector.install(availableComponents,
                                    aComponent::aComponent.name);
            aComponent:=self.componentSelector.get();
            anAssembly.delComponent(aComponent)
            )
      ).
```

Figure 8.10 Enact specification of `DelContains` event.

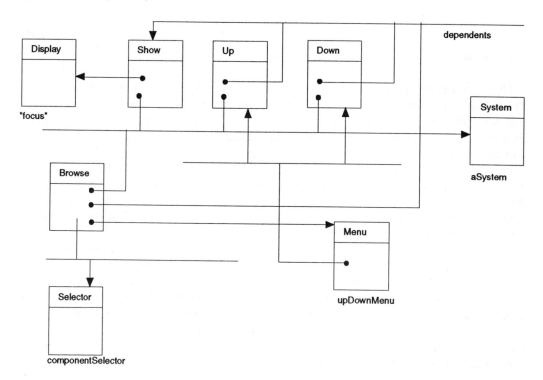

Figure 8.11 Object diagram for moving up and down hierarchy and refreshing focus.

```
class Up < Event.

up(aSelector,aSystem):=
  new Up with componentSelector=aSelector
        with system=aSystem
        with dependents=set().

Up.do():=
  (self.system.focus.containers.size()>0)then(
   self.componentSelector.install(self.system.focus.containers,
                          aComponent::aComponent.name);
   aComponent:=self.componentSelector.get();
   self.system.focus:=aComponent;
   self.doAllDependents()
).
```

Figure 8.12 Enact specification of *Up* event.

So much for the event handling in the user interface. The remaining events are very similar in design to those we have detailed here. Persistence required that we devise a syntax for the data held in the *System* object. The syntax we have chosen is shown in Fig. 8.13, which should be compared to the ER model given in Figs. 8.2 and 8.5. We have separated the components out into *<Basics>* and *<Assemblies>* as a way of distinguishing them on input. Each is put on the file as a collection of what are ultimately the strings used to represent them on the screen. All the components have to be dumped before any of the *<Contains>* for the simple reason that an *Assembly* may contain anything (cyclic structures were not forbidden, but see exercises). The *<Contains>* is a collection of *<Contain>*s each of which lists an *<Assembly>* and the collection of *<Basic>*s which it contains. The semantic action on input of each of the *<string>*s is shown on the right of the syntax. On first encountering a *<Basic>* or an *<Assembly>* we simply add it as a component to the top level *System*. However, when we encounter a *<Component>* as part of a *<Contain>* we shall need to locate the corresponding component in the collection of all components and then add it as a component of the *Assembly* we are currently concerned with.

```
<System>    ::= <Basics> <Assemblies> <Contains>
<Basics>    ::= <Basic>*
<Assemblies> ::= <Assembly>*
<Contains>  ::= <Contain>*
<Contain>   ::= <Assembly> <Component>*
<Basic>     ::= <string>          aSystem.addComponent
<Assembly>  ::= <string>          aSystem.addComponent
<Component> ::= <string>          anAssembly.addComponent
```

Figure 8.13 Syntax for persistence of assemblies and other components.

Although we have shown only a small part of the detailed design, the rest is very straightforward and can be considered an exercise for the reader. The implementation in C++ is also very straightforward and is not included here. For completeness we show in Figs. 8.14 and 8.15 the detailed C++ corresponding to the Enact specification of Figs. 8.10 and 8.12. There is nothing at all remarkable about this C++; it has been obtained by a very simple and obvious transliteration of the Enact.

As usual, there is the need, when going to C++, to consider the problems of memory management. We need to inspect each of the occasions when we create new collections to see if we accidentally lose space by failing to **delete** it. In the C++ of Figs. 8.14 and 8.15 no new collections are created, so the problem does not arise. In Fig. 8.14, where we construct **Set* containedComponents** we do not allocate new space for it, but simply copy the pointer into the local variable.

```
class DelContains : public Event{
Selector* componentSelector;
System* system;
public:
DelContains(Selector*,System*);
void _do();
};


DelContains::DelContains
    (Selector* aSelector,System* aSystem):
   Event(),
componentSelector(aSelector),system(aSystem){
}


void DelContains::_do(){
if(system->focus()!=0 &&
   system->focus()->isAssembly()){
    Assembly* anAssembly=(Assembly*)system->focus();
    Set* containedComponents=anAssembly->contains();
    if(containedComponents->size()>0){
        componentSelector ->
           install(containedComponents,componentName);
        Component* aComponent =
           (Component*)componentSelector->get();
        anAssembly->delComponent(aComponent);
          }
     }
}
```

Figure 8.14 C++ code for **DelContains** event.

```
class Up : public Event{
Selector* componentSelector;
System* system;
public:
Up(Selector*,System*);
void _do();
};

Up::Up(Selector* aSelector, System* aSystem):
   Event(),componentSelector(aSelector),
     system(aSystem){
}

void Up::_do(){
 if(system->focus()->containers()->size()>0){
   componentSelector->
       install(system->focus()->containers(),
         componentName);
   Component* aComponent=
     (Component*)componentSelector->get();
   system->setFocus(aComponent);
   doAllDependents();
   }
}
```

Figure 8.15 C++ code for the **Up** event.

8.3 A MORE GENERIC APPLICATION

There is considerable similarity between the two applications, a personal library and a hierarchy editor. The obvious question arises, is there a more generic application of which these two are special cases? We shall discuss in the next section the nature of what it means to be generic and the various ways in which this can be achieved. Before doing that, we shall briefly describe an application which could indeed replace both the specific applications we have developed, providing at least the same functionality, but at some cost in terms of convenience to the user. We shall discuss the relative merits of the more generic and the more specific applications in the next section.

The feeling of comparability between our two specific programs arises because of the correspondences shown in Fig. 8.16. In both applications we are able to search lists of named objects and to add and remove these objects from collections.

If we put into the hands of the user the power to determine which object types the application manipulates and which collections are associated with each object, then we will be able to devise an application which users can tailor to their own uses. Not least of all, they will be able to specialize it to serve as a personal library or as a hierarchy editor. The scheme we have in mind is shown in Fig. 8.17. Here we have conjectured some events which may appear at the user interface of our more generic application. They give the user the ability to name new *Entity Types*, new *Entities* and collection-valued attributes of *Entities*. Associated with each conjectured event we have shown the action we would expect to be performed by the event in terms of *PROMPT* and *SELECT* activities. So, for example, if the user fires the new *Entity Type* event he or she will be prompted for a name for the *Entity Type*. Similarly, if the user fires new *Collection* he or she will first be asked to select an *Entity Type* from those previously defined and will then be prompted for the name of the collection.

Personal library	Hierarchy editor
list of Books, Persons	list of Components
assign Book to Person	assign Component to Assembly
browse Books, Persons	browse Components

Figure 8.16 Correspondence between two specific applications.

```
new Entity Type          PROMPT for name of Type
new Collection           SELECT Type,
                         PROMPT for name of Collection
new Entity               SELECT Type,
                         PROMPT for name of Entity
add Entity to            SELECT Type,
     Collection          SELECT Entity
                         SELECT Type, SELECT Entity
                              SELECT Collection
```

Figure 8.17 Generic events available to user.

Figure 8.18 shows the actions of the user in creating the *Entity Type* **Person**, giving it the collection valued attribute **books** and then creating an *Entity* of this type with the name **David**. Assuming a similar sequence of events has created the book **Stroustrup**, then this **Book** can be added to **David**'s collection by the sequence of events shown in Fig. 8.19.

```
      FIRE addEntityType
      PROMPT "Person"
      FIRE addCollection
      SELECT Person
      PROMPT "books"
      FIRE addEntity
      SELECT Person
      PROMPT "David"
```

Figure 8.18 Using generic application events to create some library objects.

```
FIRE addEntityToCollection
SELECT Book
SELECT Stroustrup
SELECT Person
SELECT David
SELECT books
```

Figure 8.19 Using generic events to add a book to David's collection.

This is only a beginning, but clearly we can elaborate this design to enable us to use it either as a personal library or as a hierarchy editor. Many problems remain to be solved (or avoided), such as the need for relations to be modelled by pairs of collection-valued attributes (e.g. *contains* and *containers* in the hierarchy editor). We could revise the design to make all relationships two-way or we could make this an option. We need to be able to specify constraints on what assignments of entities to collections are allowed. For example, a book can be borrowed only if it is not already on loan to someone else. Finally, we would need to provide means for accelerating the sequence of events which must be performed for frequent operations. For example, the sequence in Fig. 8.19 would be very tedious to carry out every time someone borrowed a book. Nevertheless, the more generic application described here could be built and could serve as both a personal library and as a hierarchy editor. Consequently, it could no doubt serve as many other things. That is the sense in which it is generic. What we have designed is the structure of a rather trivial object-oriented database package which users are required to tailor to their own needs.

8.4 ON BEING GENERIC

We have shown how the personal library and the hierarchy editor are members of a family of applications. We have also shown how a more generic application (also a member of this family) can subsume their behaviour and hence serve to replace them. However, this more generic application has been achieved only at some cost. Clearly it is more expensive to build. The bits of it which are not yet designed, to take care of the inadequacies mentioned at the end of the previous section, are rather more difficult than anything we have actually had to design for either of the more specific applications (see exercises). This is therefore a cost to the company developing the more generic application. Either way, there is a cost to end users in that either they cannot tailor the application exactly as they would wish, or they can, but the work required is less trivial than simply learning to use the more specific application.

Of course there are benefits to both producer and consumer of a more general purpose product. The former implicitly gets access to a wider market, while the latter gets a tool which may be evolved over time to more sophisticated uses.

We have used the term generic applied to two quite different concepts in our discussions in the chapter. We began by referring to the generic nature of the components we were building from and the evidence that they were generic was our ability to reuse them for various purposes. We have ended by demonstrating an application which we claim is generic by virtue of the fact that its users can tailor it to various purposes. If we think of ourselves as owners of the generic capability embedded in the four reusable parts of the personal library listed earlier in the chapter, then we can seek to export this genericity in two distinct ways. Either we can provide a *platform* upon which applications can be more easily built, or we can make a general purpose *programmable* application which end users can tailor to their own purposes.

The platform use is exemplified by our development of the hierarchy editor based on the platform which we had previously used for the personal library. Clearly this platform can be reused for many similar applications. The programmable application use is what we have begun with the more generic application. When completed, the facilities provided to users to constrain what events may happen and what they actually do will amount to asking them to program the application themselves, in the sense that (for example) spreadsheets are programmed by formulae and macros. Presumably, this programmable application will be a great deal easier to use than C++ (for average users) and will therefore be preferred by them to the platform use. The value of the platform to the owner of the technology is that it gives the owner, via C++, access to a much wider range of systems facilities than are ever going to be provided in a generic application. Therefore, it retains the ability to move its products into new markets at a cost which is acceptable in the sense that the owner builds upon its existing investment while adding to it as it develops further capability. Being generic in either or both of the senses we have discussed is clearly very desirable. We shall return briefly to discussing it in the wider context of systems development as a whole in Chapter 10.

8.5 EXERCISES

1. Extend the design of the hierarchy editor so that the `AddComponent` event makes use of a second focus. Each focus is set by browsing. `AddComponent` then adds the value of the second focus as a new contained component of the assembly which is the value of the first focus. Try to achieve a design which is a small evolution of the design in Fig. 8.10.

2. Extend the design of the hierarchy editor so as to prevent the construction of cyclic nesting of containment. One way to do this (which may not be the best) is to define an operation which determines whether one component is directly or indirectly contained in another and to use this to detect cycles *before* they are established.

3. Design, using our methodology, a class hierarchy browser which would enable the classes of an object-oriented design to be built up and browsed. Include multiple inheritance and the ability to select attributes of classes and browse their class in turn. Would this be a suitable problem for our more generic application?

4. Complete the design of a new interface for the more generic application, including the choice of events. Give a complete Enact working model of your design. If you have access to a suitable user interface library, develop the model into a working C++

application. This will necessarily involve you in some quite complex C++ coding. Take care.

5. The design of the hierarchy editor is slightly flawed. We choose at the outset to determine that a component is either basic or an assembly. Suppose we change our mind after a description has been entered. This involves first removing the unwanted component and then adding the new component, remembering to add it into all the relationships which the removed component had. Redesign or extend the design to make this operation more straightforward.

SOME FOUNDATIONAL ISSUES

9.1 INTRODUCTION

Throughout the earlier chapters we have used terms such as *specification* and *abstract data type* in a relatively informal way. Our use, however, has not been inconsistent with the more formal meanings attached to these concepts in the theoretical literature. My objective in this book was to cover the whole of the software development process, from analysis, through design, to implementation. I chose not to use very formal mathematical methods because my experience is that, as yet, these methods are too immature for me to be able, convincingly, to develop the applications which I have developed here. This is not to say that others, more expert than I in mathematical methods, could not have done so. Nor is it to say that the methods I have described are to be preferred over more formal mathematical ones. I firmly believe that, in the fullness of time, those methods which will have survived and which will form the foundation of professional software engineering are the ones whose theoretical basis has been fully understood. Rather, what I have done is to use methods which are state-of-the-art and which move some way towards the fuller deployment of more theoretically sound methods. In this chapter I shall illustrate the proximity which I see between these methods. In the next I shall set the methods we have deployed in the larger context of systems development methods as a whole. First we shall illustrate two popular methods of formal specification, the algebraic method and the model-oriented method. Then we shall discuss their relationship to functional programming. We shall define the notion central to all these methods, the abstract data type. From that base we shall illustrate the relationship between these methods and object-oriented methods and address the issue of our having referred to Enact as an object-oriented specification language. Finally, in this chapter we shall consider the use of C++ as a target for our design method and as a potential host for other paradigms than the object-oriented paradigm.

9.2 METHODS OF SPECIFICATION

Formal specification in software engineering is the use of mathematical concepts to give a precise definition to the components from which the software is to be built. Usually, it is only the interface to these components which concerns the specifier and the normal way in which a specification is organized is to view each of these components as an abstract data type. The operations applied to this abstract data type are given a precise meaning by the mathematics deployed by the specifier without concern for how the abstract data type is ultimately to be built. The specifier is concerned with *what* the component is supposed to do, rather than *how* it is supposed to do it. The specifier is guided by a desire to achieve a description which clearly defines the meaning of each operation. A simple specification will be more amenable to the argument that it does specify exactly what is required. Once agreement has been reached on this point, the specification can be used to guide implementation and even to check that the implementation is correct by setting up formal proofs of consistency between specification and implementation.

```
library  :   → Library
borrow   : Library × Person × Book → Library
onloan   : Library × Book → TruthValue
borrower: Library × Book → Person
return   : Library × Book → Library
```

Figure 9.1 Signature for operations on ADT *Library*.

```
onloan(library(),b) = false

onloan(borrow(l,p,b),b') = true              if b=b'
                         = onloan(l,b')       otherwise

borrower(borrow(l,p,b),b') = p               if b=b'
                           = borrower(l,b')   otherwise

 return(borrow(l,p,b),b') = l                 if b=b'
                          = borrow(return(l,b'),p,b) otherwise
```

Figure 9.2 Algebraic definition of operations on ADT *Library*.

Algebraic specification is based on a very direct attempt to state exactly the relationship between operations available at the interface of an abstract data type. Figures 9.1 and 9.2 specify an abstract data type *Library*. The signature in Fig. 9.1 shows the functionality of five operations upon this abstract data type. This is a rather simpler library than we have used in the earlier chapters, in that it does not record which books the library has acquired nor which persons have joined the library. These simplifications have been made in order to shorten this presentation. The type of each operation is shown by listing the types of its arguments and the type of its results. Thus, for example, *borrow* has three arguments of types *Library*, *Person* and *Book*, respectively. Its result is of type *Library*. It is important to note that all these operations are pure functions. They do not have a side-effect. So, for example if *l* is a *Library* and *p* is a *Person* and *b* is a *Book* then *borrow(l,p,b)* is a *Library*. Similarly if *b'* is also a *Book*, then *borrower(l,b')*, if defined, is a *Person*. We intend *borrower(l,b')* to be defined whenever *onloan(l,b')* returns *true*. The only unusual operation given a functionality in Fig. 9.1 is *library*, which takes no arguments and constructs (what we shall see is) an empty library.

The pair of operations *library* and *borrow* have privileged status. They are generators (or constructors). Every representable *Library* object can be generated using just these two operations. Thus, for example,

```
borrow(library(), David, Stroustrup)
borrow(borrow(library(), David, Stroustrup), Hugh, Proust)
```

are two expressions, each of which denotes a *Library*. We shall see that they are different in that they are distinguishable using the *onloan* operator. However, not all distinct expressions denote distinguishable libraries. For example,

```
borrow(borrow(library(), Hugh, Proust), David, Stroustrup)
```

is not distinguishable from the second expression above using the operations of Fig. 9.1.

The important point about algebraic specification is that it is sufficient to define the meaning of operations by giving their values when applied to the results of generators. In the case of our example, we have given the meaning of the operations *onloan*, *borrower* and *return* by defining their values when applied to the generators *library()* and *borrow(l,p,b)*. Figure 9.2 shows four equations (usually called axioms) which are always true for the operations of this abstract data type. Each of these equations can be taken to be a rewrite rule. If the pattern on the left of the = is encountered in an expression it can be replaced by the pattern on the right. The equations of Fig. 9.2 are sufficient to reduce any expression involving *onloan*, *borrower* or *return* to an expression not involving those operations. This is the sense in which these operations are given a meaning. For example,

```
borrower(borrow(borrow(l, p1, b1), p2, b2), b1) =

    borrower(borrow(l, p1, b1), b1) = p1
```

and

```
return(borrow(borrow(l, p1, b1), p2, b2), b1 ) =

    borrow(return(borrow(l, p1, b1), b1), p2, b2) =

        borrow(l, p2, b2)
```

show the reductions which illustrate the meaning of *borrower* and *return* for a simple transaction. We stated at the beginning of this section that it is the abstract data type *Library* which is being defined in Figs. 9.1 and 9.2. We assume the abstract data types *Book* and *Person* are defined elsewhere. The signatures of Fig. 9.1 are captured on what is usually referred to as an ADJ diagram in Fig. 9.3. Each operation is a single-headed, multi-tailed arrow. The diagram shows at a glance how a *Library* is created, modified and interrogated. The reader will recognize that it is the ADJ diagram which we have extended in the earlier part of this book to depict also operations with side-effects. The signature, however, contains the notion of what we mean by an abstract data type. The only operations which are allowed upon *Library* are the five shown in Fig. 9.1. We can create *Libraries* by compounding sequences of operations *library*, *borrow* and *return*. Any expression composed of these operations can be reduced to one not containing any occurrences of *return*. Any expression which denotes a library can only be interrogated using *onloan* and *borrower*.

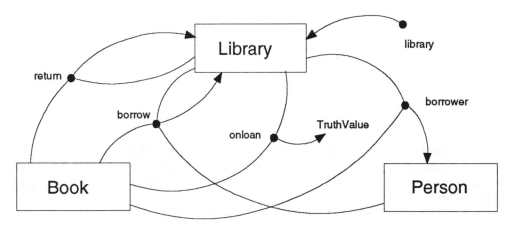

Figure 9.3 ADJ diagram for signature of *Library*.

A model-oriented specification takes a slightly different approach. We are still trying to define the interface to an abstract data type, but our method now is to build a model of that component in some mathematical system, usually set theory. Figures 9.4 and 9.5 show a simple model-oriented specification of the same library which we specified algebraically. The *Library* is modelled as a set of pairs (called *Association*s here) each pair containing a *Book* and a *Person*. The intention is that the pairs record the borrowings. In practice, more sophisticated mathematical machinery would be used here (relations or maps) but there is no need for us to delve that far into this issue. The constructors in Fig. 9.2 show that the initial library is just modelled by the empty set and that the act of borrowing is modelled by constructing a new set of pairs containing all the old borrowings and one new one. In terms of this model, the three remaining operations can be defined as shown in Fig. 9.5. The definition of *onloan(l,b')* reads: 'there exists a pair *(b,p)* contained in *l*, such that *b=b'*'. The definition of *borrower(l,b')* reads: 'the *p* corresponding to *b'* in *l*'. The definition of *return(l,b')* reads: 'the set of all *(p,b)*, where *(p,b)* is in *l* and *b* is not equal to *b'*'. With little more set theory than we have used here it has been found possible to define, quite succinctly, interfaces to components many times more complex than this one. Hopefully, the example in Figs. 9.4 and 9.5 will convince the reader that this is at least possible.

```
Library = set of Association
Association = Book  →  Person

library() = {}
borrow(l,p,b) = l  U  {(p,b)}
```

Figure 9.4 A model oriented specification of the `Library` ADT.

```
onloan(l,b') = exists (b,p) in l . b=b'

borrower(l,b') = l[b']

return(l,b') = {(p,b) | for each (p,b) in l where b<>b'}
```

Figure 9.5 Model oriented specification of `Library` ADT (continued).

The definitions of Fig. 9.5 are constructive in the sense that they are tantamount to a program for computing their results, as we shall show in the next section. Model-oriented specifications need not be constructive. Usually the use of what are sometimes called implicit specifications leads to a simpler definition. An implicit specification for `return` is shown in Fig. 9.6. This defines a property of the result `l'` of `return(l, b')`. Effectively it says that `l'` and `l` agree everywhere except `b'` and that `b'` does not occur in any of the pairs of `l'`. Although this particular implicit specification is not simpler than our constructive one, in general for more complex problems it is possible to find implicit specifications which are much simpler than the simplest constructive one. Not surprisingly, perhaps, the implicit specifications are not noticeably easy to discover, which perhaps explains why most published model-oriented specifications are constructive.

```
return(l,b') = l' where
       l[b]=l'[b] if b<>b'
       and dom l' = dom l - {b'}
```

Figure 9.6 An implicit specification of the `return` operation.

These two methods of specification are not so different as their names imply. Both are in fact algebraic and both use models. But the names I have used have become associated with the two styles illustrated here. For more details of real specification languages and methods see the books in the bibliography by Hayes, Jones, Nelson and Turner.

9.3 FUNCTIONAL PROGRAMMING

Specifications are used to give a precise meaning to the interfaces of components we propose to build or propose to build from. We have said that specifications can be constructive, by which we mean that they define the meaning of the result they are specifying by giving a means of constructing it. In that sense a constructive specification is a program. In algebraic and model-oriented specifications, because each operation is defined as a pure function, the program which each specification forms is a functional program. This means that we could check the specification for inconsistencies by transcribing it into a functional programming language. Languages such as ML and OBJ (see the bibliography) are ideally suited to this task. If you have access to these or similar languages you are strongly encouraged to investigate the relationship between formal specifications and functional programming by executing the specifications given here and set as exercises at the end of the chapter.

```
class Book < Object.

class Person < Object.

class Library < Object.

class Empty < Library.

class Borrow < Library.

book():=new Book.

person():=new Person.

empty():=new Empty.

borrow(aLibrary, aPerson, aBook):=
        new Borrow with library=aLibrary
                    with person=aPerson
                    with book=aBook.
```

Figure 9.7 Enact implementation of algebraic specification.

By way of illustration we have prepared functional programs in Enact which are executable versions of the algebraic and model-oriented specifications, respectively. The algebraic specification is shown in Figs. 9.7 and 9.8. The pattern matching is simulated by creating two subclasses of *Library*, specifically *Empty* and *Borrow* (see Fig. 9.9). The constructors for these two subclasses *library()* and *borrow(aLibrary, aPerson, aBook)* act as the generators of structures to represent each of the possible configurations of a *Library* that results from borrowing activities. The subclass relationships and the constructors are shown in Fig. 9.7. The four function definitions in Fig. 9.8 correspond to the axioms of the algebraic specification.

```
Empty.onloan(aBook):=false.

Borrow.onloan(aBook):=
  true if self.book=aBook else
  self.library.onloan(aBook).

Borrow.return(aBook):=
  self.library if self.book=aBook else
  borrow(self.library.return(aBook),self.person,self.book).

Borrow.borrower(aBook):=
  self.person if self.book=aBook else
  self.library.borrower(aBook).
```

Figure 9.8 Enact implementation of algebraic specification (continued).

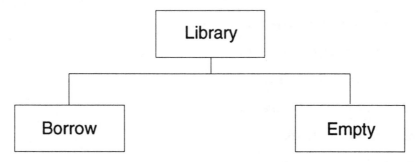

Figure 9.9 Pattern matching is simulated by creating two subclasses.

There is a very direct and obvious relationship between these definitions and those in Fig. 9.2. This functional program can be executed as follows. Assume *Stroustrup*, *Proust* and *Hardy* have been created as *Book*s and *David* has been created as a *Person*. Then

```
lib := library().
lib := borrow(lib, David, Stroustrup).
lib := borrow(lib, David, Hardy).
```

establishes *lib* as a *Library* with two borrowings. Note that there are no side-effects here, apart from the trivial (and strictly unnecessary) one at the top-level of overwriting the global variable *lib*. Once set up in this way we can test the definitions of the other operators by evaluating such expressions as

```
lib.onloan(Stroustrup)
lib.borrower(Stroustrup)
```

The model-oriented specification can also be established and tested in this way, although with a little more preparation. In Fig. 9.10 we define a class *Association* which will be used to represent our pairing of *Book* with *Person*. We also add an operation to *Set* so that *aSet.including(anObject)* is a function which returns a set containing all the members of *aSet* and also the member *anObject*. Figure 9.11 shows that *Library* is represented this time as a set of *Association*. In Fig. 9.12 we give the definition of each of the operations for interrogating a *Library*. These definitions should be compared with the corresponding model-oriented specification shown in Fig. 9.5. It turns out that the operations available on *Collections* in Enact are sufficient to model most constructive mathematical definitions. In particular the operations *select* and *collect* (which you will recall were taken from Smalltalk) combine to enable us to compute set-valued expressions according to the correspondence illustrated in Fig. 9.13.

```
class Assoc < Object.

assoc(d,r):=
  new Assoc with dom=d
            with rng=r.

Set.including(anObject):=
  new Set with members=(anObject:self.members).
```

Figure 9.10 Associations are needed for model-oriented specification.

```
class Book < Object.

class Person < Object.

class Library < Object.

book():=new Book.

person():=new Person.

library():=
  new Library with borrowings=set().

Library.borrow(aPerson,aBook):=
  new Library with borrowings=
      self.borrowings.including(assoc(aBook,aPerson)).
```

Figure 9.11 Enact implementation of model-oriented specification.

```
Library.onloan(aBook):=
  self.borrowings.exists(anAssoc::anAssoc.dom=aBook).

Library.borrower(aBook):=
  (self.borrowings.locate(anAssoc::anAssoc.dom=aBook)).rng.

Library.return(aBook):=
  new Library with borrowings=
    self.borrowings.select(anAssoc::(not (anAssoc.dom=aBook)).
```

Figure 9.12 Enact implementation of model-oriented specification (continued).

$\{ e \mid x \in S \}$	$S.collect(x::e)$
$\{ x \mid x \in S ; p \}$	$S.select(x::p)$
$\{ e \mid x \in S ; p \}$	$S.select(x::p).collect(x::e)$
$\{ e \mid G ; H \}$	$\{ \{ e \mid H \} \mid G \}.UNION()$

Figure 9.13 Correspondence between set expressions and Enact collection operations.

The important feature of both of these Enact programs is that they are purely functional. Although at the top level, where the user is interacting with the Enact system, we allow assignment to global variables, we do not allow any side-effect within the definition of operations. This means that expressions in a purely functional program enjoy the nice mathematical property that every expression denotes a value, and that is all. This makes functional programming easier to reason about and, theoretically at least, easier to get right. So why haven't we adopted functional programming more directly in the earlier part of this book? The answer is that it is not yet known how to deal effectively with the representation of state change, which is essential because it models corresponding state change in the real world. There are two aspects of this which we shall deal with here, one more trivial than the other.

The more trivial aspect comes from the potential implementation problems that arise because a functional program constantly builds and rebuilds complex objects. For example, if we construct

```
lib2:= return(lib, Hardy).
```

then our functional program now has two objects `lib` and `lib2` which represent the state of the library respectively before and after the return of the book `Hardy`. This can be expensive in both time and space. If, however, we call

```
lib:= return(lib, Hardy)
```

then we have a second potential problem, that the new value of `lib` is built but the storage used for the old value is not recovered. The reason I referred to this as a more trivial problem is that there are well-known solutions. To begin with, performance is not as significant an issue as it once was. There are now very fast implementations of functional languages. Secondly, the storage recovery problem has been solved for functional languages by the provision of automatic garbage collection. It has also been solved for C++ by the provision of hooks which allow programmers to supply their own garbage collection in a way we shall describe in the last section of this chapter.

The more fundamental reason why functional programming was not adopted as the leading paradigm in this book is that, when it comes to representing state change, in the essential way in which it is embodied in a real-world exercise such as our personal library, no one has yet discovered how to do that in a purely functional way. There are research solutions, as Turner's book shows. But, as yet, these solutions are far from trivial, involving higher order functions mapping streams to streams. At this time it seems that the object-oriented model of system design captures the notion of state change more succinctly than does functional programming. But this is just the state of the art. I have written this book as much to understand this phenomenon as for any other reason. By expanding the methods chosen in the earlier chapters I have taken a position with respect to what I think is good practice today. But I have also set a prospectus for further research, especially for functional programmers, for I would clearly like to see a purely functional implementation of the personal library, user interface, persistence and all, which is markedly simpler than the object-oriented one I have given here. I conjecture that the current functional solutions to input and output by streams will produce a solution which most readers would find much more complex. But eventually some reader will, I am sure, prove me wrong.

9.4 OBJECT-ORIENTED SPECIFICATION

Whenever in this book I have written some Enact I have variously referred to it as a specification, as a model, as a working model and as a prototype. Its role in our methods is to serve as a pseudocode to capture details of our object-oriented design and, when sufficiently complete that it can be executed, to provide a working model which gives us early feedback on the consequences of our design decisions. In what sense is an Enact description a specification and in what sense is it different from traditional, mathematical methods of specification?

One of the major roles of a specification in software development is as a means of communicating design ideas and design decisions among designers. This may be between members of a design team charged with a collaborative development or between two designers in the roles of supplier and consumer of a component. The use of a specification by an individual, as a means of communicating with him- or herself over a period of time, is just a special case of use by a group. To be efficient as a means of communication, a specification language should provide for easy comprehension by allowing use at a high level of abstraction and by having a precise and agreed meaning. The mathematical based methods clearly have both those properties. We have illustrated, we trust, the comparative ease of comprehension of Enact and ask the reader to accept that it has a precise meaning (which we attempt to define in Appendix 1) which is supported by a tool, the interpreter, which can be used to check its meaning.

Enact, however, is different from mathematical specification languages in that it allows the direct description of side-effects. It allows assignment. It directly supports the description of state-change. It uses the notion of object as holder of state. Objects have identity and state. Operations upon an object change the state of the object without changing its identity. The object-oriented method which we have described models the real world by associating objects with real-world entities in such a way that changes in the real world are modelled by corresponding changes in the related objects. This means that, in order to understand better the real-world system which we are charged with supporting, we can build a working model with a very direct relationship to reality. This model serves as a means of communication among those working on the system. It serves therefore as a specification. It is used to reach agreement between individual designers and themselves (as a means to convince themselves), between designers and their collaborators and between the designers and the Enact interpreter. Each of these agreements serves to improve the quality of the design. If used properly, Enact specifications are sufficiently economical to build that agreement is reached by iterative improvement of the initial proposal until all parties to the agreement are satisfied. This is exactly the same as the process of agreement which is used with more mathematical methods.

Given that we are taking object-oriented design as our central paradigm, this means that there are other obvious alternatives for object-oriented specification or model building. Indeed, all the mainstream object-oriented languages could serve this purpose as well. In particular, Smalltalk is an obvious substitute providing all of the functionality of Enact and more. Enact's sole virtue as far as the author is concerned is that it is an implementation which he can freely give to others, as we have done with this book.

An obvious question which must arise in the mind of the reader, however, is why not use C++ directly as the specification and modelling language? This is especially true now that very high quality interactive development environments such as Borland's Turbo C++ for Windows is available. In fact, if one uses the library **collect.h** and a great deal of discipline to 'think Enact, write C++', all the benefits of working at the higher level of abstraction afforded by sets and higher order operations upon them is indeed obtained. Moreover, the working model then becomes part of the eventual product. But C++ reduced to Enact is a very small part of C++ and the temptation to stray from the more constrained language can quickly lead to trouble. Trouble takes the form of lots of time spent on hacking details which are not in fact relevant to the early design decisions. This investment in detailed design becomes something which it is difficult to abandon when a high-level design decision requires change. It may be so difficult to abandon (insufficient time or money left in the project to allow it) that it is not done and a second-best design is allowed to prevail. Now, clearly, if C++ with restraint is every bit as good as Enact and all that is required for restraint is a professional attitude, then for some among us this will form a viable route. Enact then serves the role simply of providing a framework of concepts for the rapid development of applications directly in C++. Such a user would probably begin to extend Enact as pseudocode to encompass some of the more advanced features of C++ which we have not covered in this book. For the reader who will venture further into C++ we conclude this chapter with some of the highlights of the advanced C++ which we have avoided. In the next chapter we shall return to the role of specification and modelling in the software development process.

9.5 ADVANCED C++ CONCEPTS

Perhaps the most important C++ concept which we have avoided in earlier parts of this book is the template. This is a feature which became available in version 3 of the language and which is clearly destined for a central role. It allows classes (and functions) to be parametrized, in particular with other classes. One good use we could have made of this feature would be to revise our definitions of **Collection** classes to ensure that, when we extract an element from a **Collection** we know what type it is. For example, if we defined the classes **Collection** and **Set** as in Fig. 9.14, this would mean we could declare new sets, respectively for **Books** and **Persons**, as follows:

```
Set<Book>* books = new Set<Book>();
Set<Person>* persons = new Set<Person>();
```

Now, when we come to call, for example,

```
books -> insert(aBook)
```

then the exact type of **aBook** must be **Book*** or the compiler will signal a type error. The definition of **insert** is shown on Fig. 9.15. Similarly, when we call

```
Book* aBook = books -> locate(...);
```

then the result we get back from **locate** is a **Book***, so there is no requirement for us to cast it. This means that we both get cleaner code and greater type security.

```
template <class T>
class Collection{
...
public:
    virtual void insert(T*);
    ...
};

template <class T>
class Set : public Collection<T>{
...
public:
    Set();
    void insert(T*);
    ...
};
```

Figure 9.14 Definition of templated classes for sets.

```
template <class T>
void Set<T>::insert(T* e){
    ...
}
```

Figure 9.15 Definition of templated **Set** member function **insert**.

In order for this to work all our **Collections** must be homogeneous, that is, they must contain objects of the same type. But in all the applications we have written here this has been the case, so the benefits to be gained from reimplementing **Collections** this way would repay the investment in so doing. Doing so here, however, is beyond the scope I have taken for this book, and so is left as an exercise for the reader.

I mentioned earlier that C++ provides the means for programmers to implement their own garbage collector. What I meant by this is that it is possible to implement a scheme whereby objects allocated on the heap are automatically returned for reallocation once there are no valid references to them. So, for example, assignment to a pointer-valued variable may result in the object it was pointing to now being inaccessible to the programmer because there are no outstanding pointers to it. When this happens we can arrange that the object is implicitly deleted, making it available for reallocation. It is the implicit, as opposed to explicit, return of the memory which is important. It not only saves programmers from a detailed analysis of the memory behaviour of their programs, but ensures that all memory is traced, even that allocated to temporaries, which is done on the programmers' behalf by the compiler.

The scheme which C++ provides is described by Stroustrup and by Coplien. It is not trivial. It hinges on the fact that C++ gives the programmer the ability to define a number of special functions. These are:

1. constructors
2. destructors
3. the assignment operator
4. the copy constructor

The C++ compiler undertakes to compile code which implicitly uses these special functions in all circumstances where objects are created, copied or destroyed.

The garbage collection strategy to be used is called reference counting. We undertake to organize that each object that we wish to be able to collect will have a reference count (an **int**), probably as part of the record which represents it. Then we define a new class of objects which are to be used as handles on the traced objects. We always refer to the traced object via its handle (see Fig. 9.16). It is the handle which gets copied around and assigned to variables. It is the four special operations on the handle which we use to update the reference count. The constructor sets the reference count to **1**, its initial value. Whenever the handle is copied, such as for example when it is handed to a function as a parameter, the copy constructor is called and this increments the reference count by **1**. Assignment can overwrite a handle, so the reference count of the traced object will be decremented. Similarly, when a handle is deleted (for example by leaving the block in

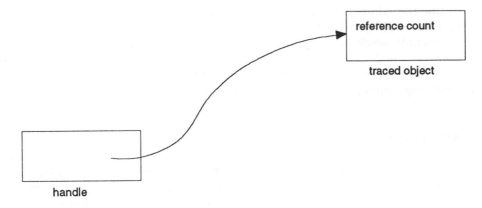

reference count

traced object

handle

Figure 9.16 C++ idiom for memory management using reference counts.

which it was declared) the reference count of the traced object is also decremented. Whenever the count is decremented we check to see if it has been reduced to **0**. If so, then we call the destructor of the traced object

Because the traced object can have fields which are themselves handles and because C++ will automatically call destructors on fields of an object whenever an object is **deleted**, we see that it is possible that dropping the last reference to a list of objects may cause a cascade of **deletes**, with the result that the entire list is returned to free storage. Although the details of this method of memory management are complex (or intricate), its implementation adds only a couple of operations to each of the above special functions. It is not massively expensive in terms of run-time overhead, and the freedom it gives the programmer is enormous. It was this single property of C++ which made me a convert to it, for as Coplien shows, it means that many of the idioms familiar to a functional programmer can be reproduced quite elegantly in C++. I have no doubt that automatic garbage collection, as provided in LISP is a fundamentally important programming concept which will ultimately find its way into all languages, even the most basic. Until that day, C++'s provision of the tools whereby one can have the benefit (if required) without penalizing those who don't need it, will do me fine. I note that Modula 3 is a systems programming language with automatic garbage collection, which may mean that one day C++ will also provide that feature.

Other advanced C++ topics which we shall only note here are well covered by Stroustrup and Coplien respectively. They include the notion of **friend** functions and classes which have privileged access to the private parts of the class to which they are a friend. Also, we have seen the overloading of the C++ operators **<<** and **>>**, but C++ allows overloading of almost all its operators. Although they retain their precedence, their meaning for user-defined classes can be defined, and so C++ can host application-oriented languages of a very exotic variety. Another advanced feature of C++ which lends itself to astute idiomatic use is the automatic invocation of user-defined type conversion functions. Combined with operator overloading, this can lead to the definition of very succinct, expressive forms in C++. We have seen the use of references in C++, but their uniform treatment is a more advanced topic. In particular, the ability to have reference-valued C++ functions means that we can devise selector functions which delve deep into a structure and then allow us to assign to the field which they find.

In the next, and final, chapter, we shall look at the relationship between the object-oriented methods which we adopted in the early part of the book and the specification techniques we have discussed in this chapter. All along we shall be concerned for the fact that our target language is C++ and that we want to make good use of its many features while producing a product of high quality at reasonable cost.

9.6 EXERCISES

1. In the specifications of the library, for example the algebraic specification given in Figs. 9.1 and 9.2, the *borrow* operation must not be applied if the book is already on loan. Consider the consequences of the fact that this precondition is not enforced. What does the specification say about a misapplied *borrow* operation? How can the specification be corrected so that this problem does not arise?

2. Extend the specifications given in Figs. 9.1–9.5 to include the specification of the operation

   $$books \; : \; Library \times Person \; \rightarrow \; set\,(Book)$$

   which determines the set of books currently on loan to a given person.

3. If you have access to the implementation of a purely functional language, such as ML (see Paulson's book), translate each of the specifications into a functional program in that language, so that they can be executed. Alternatively, if you have access to a Smalltalk implementation, restrict yourself to a purely functional subset of that language and translate each of the specifications as literally as possible. These experiments should increase your awareness of the perceived proximity between the various topics introduced in this chapter.

4. Take the executable Enact specification (Figs. 9.10–9.12) and translate it as literally as possible into C++. Now consider the storage management issues which this involves. Inspect every expression which creates storage and every one where reference to storage is lost (e.g. in *remove*). How can this storage be recovered? Revise the C++ to include the necessary **delete** operations.

5. Revise the entire collections library given in Appendix 2 to use templates. Take any of the C++ programs given earlier in this book and modify them to make use of the new classes (thus avoiding **void***). Even with great care, this is not just a trivial cosmetic exercise.

10

OUR METHODS IN CONTEXT

10. 1 INTRODUCTION

In this chapter we shall review what we set out to achieve. We shall discuss again the various elements of the methods which we have advocated, in the context of having seen them demonstrated. We shall consider alternatives to the methods used here in the spirit of encouraging the reader to investigate them further. You will want to determine how best to fit the methods which we advocate into your normal way of working and to the class of problems which you have to tackle. This will be best done by considering the alternatives and then adopting a judicious mix of your conventional methods, those advocated here and the alternatives which I suggest should be investigated. Although we have targeted this book on C++, the methods are applicable to other languages. We shall briefly discuss their use in this respect among the other alternatives which we consider. Finally, the chapter concludes with the author's view of where software engineering is headed and some of the issues it must tackle in the coming years.

10.2 WHAT WE SET OUT TO ACHIEVE

What I wanted to study by writing this book was the entire software development process from analysis to implementation. I wanted to explore the relationship between the very informal methods which we must use early in the process and the severely formal ones which we are forced to use at the end of it. I wanted to understand the role that a formal specification technique might play in establishing the link between the iterative process of problem exploration and the eventual delivery of a chosen alternative in the formal medium of a real programming language. I wanted also to concern myself with the achievement of quality in the delivered product, not least of all the quality of flexibility, openness to change, which I believe is absolutely essential to cost-effective software engineering now and in the future.

I was aware, from experience, that early in a new software engineering task, whether it be a completely new product or, as is normal these days, the re-engineering of an existing product, that the methods we use are necessarily informal. It is some time before we are in a position to be able to write down any of the requirements. When we are in a position to do that we traditionally use diagrammatic techniques to do it. Understanding the problem in hand is sometimes referred to as domain analysis. Evidence that we have understood the domain usually surfaces as our ability to name the entities (or entity types) with which we are concerned and to outline the process (or events) in which they are involved. Object-oriented methods seem, at this date, to be a convincingly practical way of proceeding from this informal understanding to a more formal model which captures this understanding.

I was also aware, again from experience, that formal mathematical methods of specification can capture knowledge about a domain in an extremely precise form, a form which can lead to very high levels of agreement between the cooperating users of such a specification. But at this date, use of these methods can be extremely expensive. It may well be that the costs which they eventually save more than compensate for the investment which they require. What I hoped to achieve with the object-oriented specification technique adopted here was some of the benefit of the more mathematical techniques but at rather lower cost. So a subsidiary objective was to demonstrate the effectiveness of this object-oriented specification technique, especially at the interface between a high-level domain model and the need to represent this in the code of a real programming language.

10.3 WHAT WE ACTUALLY DID, AND SOME ALTERNATIVES

The central concept in our approach has been the identification of what we have called an abstract system. This is the building block from which we propose all systems should be built. It is the component of a modular design structure. An abstract system is a collection of related abstract data types, (or related classes, to use the object-oriented terminology), which together describe a separable part of the problem domain. Thus, we might expect to have abstract systems for the reusable components imported from suppliers of other products and we might expect to develop an abstract system for the application specific part of a new product. It is this separation into parts and the setting of the interface to these parts at a high level of abstraction which gives our product its flexibility to change. The abstract system finds a balance between being sufficiently generic that future change is cost-effective and sufficiently specific to the problem in hand that the cost of developing our immediate solution is also acceptable.

The life-cycle within which we set the development of the abstract system is shown in Fig. 10.1. We separate the steps of analysis, design and implementation. Although it is perhaps oversimplifying, I like to think of these three stages as the stages at which we decide respectively 'what' it is we have to do, 'how' we are going to do it in overall terms and 'how, precisely' we are going to do it, given that our target is a specific programming language. Clearly the interfaces between these stages are going to be a little blurred, especially when our problem involves, as it usually does, reusing some existing components which have already been coded. But we see the general flow of development through this process as being one of adding more and more precision.

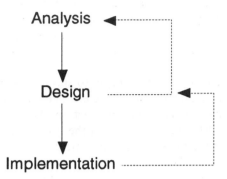

Figure 10.1 The system development life-cycle.

The application-specific abstract system is really the product of the design stage. As part of that design, we show how it interfaces with the abstract system which we inherit (or devise) for the components which we are reusing. We have recommended, and illustrated, various methods for capturing the abstract system, some more applicable at the analysis/design interface, some more applicable later. We shall briefly review these and mention the alternatives which the reader is encouraged to investigate. All of the alternatives are covered by the various books listed in the bibliography.

We described a diagramming technique, adapted from Coad and Yourdon, which we referred to as augmented entity relationship (ER) diagrams. It is a means of capturing the outline of the abstract system when all we can enumerate are the classes and the relationships between entities from these classes. Similar diagramming techniques are recommended by Booch and by Rumhaugh *et al*. These authors provide means for capturing, on the diagram, much more detail than I have used on the diagrams in this book. My way of working is to use the diagrams to iterate my understanding at a very high level of abstraction and when moving to a lower level of detail to invest in a working model in a suitable executable specification language. As well as looking at the object-oriented techniques recommended by the authors which I have mentioned, it is also worthwhile studying the more traditional structured analysis techniques, in particular data flow diagrams which give an orthogonal view of the structure of a system being analysed or of a proposed solution.

A diagramming technique which we have advocated and find particularly useful is the object diagram, where we illustrate a typical arrangement of objects representing a typical state of our system. By using diagramming techniques which organize related arrows (i.e. pointers) into buses we gain many of the readability benefits enjoyed by hardware designers through circuit diagrams. I find the object diagram useful at two distinct stages of the development process. Early in the analysis, when 'feeling' for an understanding of the problem, aware that there is a constraint on the model we propose, that it should be economically buildable, I will often casually draw alternative possible solutions as object diagrams. This serves to convince me that my investigations are heading in the right direction. The second, more obvious, role for object diagrams is when we move from design to implementation and we must consider the implications, in particular for storage management, of the design decision which we have taken. Although the object diagram provides only the same information as the ER diagram, I find that it is much easier to use when making arguments supporting the efficiency of a design proposal. When presenting a walk-through of a design proposal, the case for support is more convincingly made if accompanied by an object diagram. We trust that we have amply illustrated this in the earlier chapters of the book.

As we move from analysis to design we begin to specify the interfaces to the objects in our abstract system, that is, we define the protocol which we intend its user to deploy. It is the protocol which embodies the notion of abstraction. Access to the functionality of the abstract system is restricted to the operations in the protocol, and so details of how this functionality is provided are hidden. We give two means of denoting a protocol, a textual one and a diagrammatic one. Our advice is that the textual method is better for the iterative stages of refinement and improvement and that the diagrammatic method is useful for giving a potential user of an abstract system an overall 'feel' for the way the operations in its interface cooperate.

The big departure for us from other authors is our use of an object-oriented specification language. We suggest that it can be used in two ways, either as a pseudocode where outlines of the proposed design are sufficient, or as an executable specification language where a working model is considered an appropriate tool to assist the iterative refinement of the proposed design. Our provision of Enact as a language for this purpose makes a choice for its users of the level of abstraction at which they will specify their design. This level of abstraction includes decisions about the way that one object refers to another (semantically it is a pointer) and about the way that collections of objects will be operated upon. It also makes a suggestion about the way that relationships between objects will be represented by collection-valued attributes, an idea which in databases is referred to as the functional data model.

Clearly there are alternatives to Enact. We could choose the more mathematical specification languages such as Z, VDM, LARCH and OBJ (see bibliography). Each of these is supported by tools, and OBJ in particular is supported by an interpreter which allows execution of the specification in a way very similar to Enact. But perhaps the most obvious alternative to Enact is Smalltalk. Although this is a programming language and not a specification language, it provides all the functionality of Enact (and more), at the same level of abstraction. Smalltalk would be an ideal target language for our implementation. But if our implementation language has been chosen for us by other, usually commercial considerations, then that need not preclude the development of a prototype in Smalltalk which eventually gets transcribed into the target implementation language. A third alternative to Enact, and one which falls a little closer to the mathematical methods, is to use a functional programming language. Perhaps the best known and most widely available of these is ML, but there are alternatives to this (see for example Turner's book). I have used ML quite effectively in the role for which Enact has been deployed in this book. It is very good at the role of iterative refinement of our understanding of the domain. It is a strongly typed language which leads to a disciplined organization of types which is consistent with the object-oriented approach. However, functional programs are not always the most obvious models of state change in the real world, and so the gap between the executable specifications in ML and the imple-mentation in C++ is quite wide.

Along with the specific diagramming and specification techniques which we have deployed we have illustrated means of improving the quality of the product by careful testing, at as early a stage as possible, and by benchmaking as a way of maintaining control over the delivered performance. Our particular choice of implementation language, C++, was motivated by its undoubted commercial importance and by the facilities which it provides for object-oriented programming. If, however, the commercial considerations of a project require us to use other languages it does not mean that methods advocated here are of no use. For example if the implementation language must be C or FORTRAN or a 4GL, which has been the case in recent circumstances I have encountered, then the methods advocated here need to be augmented with ways of encoding the object-oriented concepts in those languages. These ways of encoding are presented as house rules for the idiomatic use of the implementation language. Coplien gives an example of hosting the object-oriented paradigm in C, simply by obeying the convention of handing the (pointer to an) object as the first parameter of a method.

Increasingly, implementation languages will provide direct support for object-oriented concepts. We already hear of object-oriented COBOL and object-oriented Ada. More modern languages such as Modula 3 go beyond what C++ has attempted and provide garbage collection for objects. I would expect that particular feature of implementation languages to become increasingly important and personally hope to see a garbage-collected C++. In the race to be at the front of the (never-ending) race to be best programming language, at various times different languages break through. The leaders are almost always chosen by commercial considerations. C++ is clearly a leader at the time of writing. Its designers have made an important and judicious extension of an earlier leader, C, and this link with the past has made it commercially sensible for the compiler suppliers to provide high-quality compilers for C++, presumably because they could be confident of the ability of their C customers to evolve gradually and economically to the new product. I expect C++ will be with the leaders for a long time.

10.4 ON WHAT WE CAN CONCLUDE, AND WHERE NEXT

We have presented a set of methods which work particularly well for us and demonstrated that they do work on at least one reasonably large example. We have dealt with every stage of the development process and candidly described the decisions we made, those we rejected and those which were mistakes. We have, we trust, shown you how to use these methods, in particular the object-oriented method and how to adapt it to your own way of working.

We have majored on the use of an executable specification language while nevertheless dealing realistically with the requirement that we must produce real code in C++. Perhaps the closeness of our particular specification language and our way of coding in C++ has left the reader unconvinced. In particular, the collection classes are clearly contrived to provide one for one the same facilities in C++ as we provided in Enact. I could argue that that is not a weakness because, if you want to target on a better library of collection classes (and there are certainly nicer and faster libraries available) then all you have to do is build an abstract system in Enact for that library (see Exercise 8 in Chapter 5) and proceed as before in Enact but using these collections rather than mine. But this may lose one of the major benefits of Enact. The speed of production of an Enact working model is critical to the economic use of executable specifications. As a rough guide one ought to be able to produce a number of iterations of a working model while using up only about 10% of the time (budget) allocated to the project. I think there may well be a relationship between my ability to do that in Enact and the very high-level operations provided on collections. As I showed in Chapter 9, this is not an arbitrary choice, but is based on a well-known and, from experience, entirely adequate modelling technique using sets, as in model-oriented specification. So in some sense this is a warning, with a benchmark you can use to test for danger. If you must avoid using the set theoretic collections of Enact and your model-building activity begins to take a long time, begin to worry if you have already used up 10% of your budgeted time and haven't yet got at least one prototype.

So where to next? Within the object-oriented paradigm there is still some considerable way to go to integrate fully some mathematical methods with the inherent notion of state changes. There are other paradigms of course, and C++ is a language well suited to hosting idiomatic use. It is not only an object-oriented language. Coplien for example explores a variety of paradigms, including functional programming. I would dearly like to see functional programming integrated with object-oriented or functional programming capable of the simple expression of solutions to problems of state change in the way that object-oriented programming appears to be. Both paradigms have great strengths and are applicable in different areas. If you doubt that functional programming has any real applications, then just read the later chapters in Paulson's book, where he develops a far from trivial theorem-proving application. Rather, the message I am trying to convey is that many applications are like the ones I have treated in this book and for each application, at the time of writing, the object-oriented solution appears to have the greater simplicity.

But the history of programming has seen us pile layer upon layer of abstraction upon the basic machine. To expression evaluation we added subroutines and then parameters, creating a class of languages isomorphic to FORTRAN. Then we added data structures to get the Pascal family which includes C and most languages of the 1970s. Classes, attributable to SIMULA and to frames from AI, added a dimension of user-defined types, called abstract data types. The functional languages made functions first-class citizens and demonstrated the power of high-order functions. Logic programming has given us the means to abstract from search. We are only just beginning to understand the abstractions which will allow us to hide concurrency. The state of the art in software engineering seems to have reached consensus on these topics as far as object-oriented programming, but not yet beyond that. So some of the future layers of abstraction are perhaps clear, but many, I am sure, are not. C++ seems to me to have been a barometer for programming language evolution in the 1980s. It will be interesting to watch it in the 1990s and beyond.

Appendix 1

ENACT REFERENCE MANUAL

A1.1 GETTING STARTED

The implementation of Enact is invoked as a traditional read–eval–print loop. The user may define functions and evaluate expressions. The following shows the screen during a sample interaction with Enact.

```
C:\>enact
Enact 1.00, Copyright Peter Henderson, 1993
f(x,y):=x+y.
  aFunction
f(1,2).
  3
f(f(1,2),3).
  6
1+2*3+4*5+6.
  33
a:=new Object.
  a
a.x:=99.
  99
a.x+1.
  100
```

You will see that functions can be defined and expressions containing them can be evaluated. Note how each expression to be evaluated is terminated by a *hard full stop*, a period followed immediately by white space, usually an end-of-line. The expression will not be evaluated until the hard full stop has been read. The value of each expression above is indented slightly from the left margin. Enact is based on expression evaluation. Expressions are built from operators and operands. Operators have a precedence which dictates the order of evaluation. For example,

```
a+b*c
```

is an expression with three operands *a*, *b* and *c*, and two binary operators plus (+) with precedence 5 and multiply (*) with precedence 4. The precedence dictates that multiplication with the higher precedence binds more tightly than addition. Thus the above expression is equivalent to

```
a+(b*c)
```

There are thirteen levels of precedence, with 1 being the highest, most binding, level. The Enact operators, each with their precedence, are listed later in the appendix. In Enact, identifiers are made from letters, digits and the underscore character. The first character of an identifier cannot be a digit. Numbers are made from digits. Negative numbers are prefixed with tilde (~99). Comments can be included in files following a % symbol; everything between this symbol and the next newline is ignored.

A1.2 FUNCTIONAL PROGRAMMING

As the previous section has shown, Enact is based on the idea of defining functions and calling them to effect computation. By defining functions which call others, which in turn call yet others, substantial programs can be written which use only this method of computation. This style, which avoids assignment and side-effect, is called functional programming. Enact supports a full range of functional programming concepts (with the exception of lazy evaluation) which we describe in this section. Enact also supports object-oriented programming and assignment as an extension to functional programming. These additional techniques are introduced in the following sections.

The usual definition of *factorial*, a well known example from functional programming, is written in Enact as follows:

```
factorial(n) := n=0 then 1 else n*factorial(n-1).
```

The most unusual thing is that the conditional is written using binary operators. In fact, *then* and *else* are binary operators with the property that

```
e1 then e2 else e3
```

has the meaning we usually associate with *if e1 then e2 else e3*. Because *then* and *else* are both operators we see that

```
e1 then e2 else e3 then e4 else e5
```

must have a meaning. Because of the relative priority of then and else it has the meaning *if e1 then e2 else if e3 then e4 else e5*. The operator then used alone as in `e1 then e2` means *if e1 then e2 else undefined*. Omitting the `if` may take some getting used to.

Another familiar definition is that of *nfib*, which is written in Enact as follows:

```
nfib(n) := n<2 then 1 else nfib(n-1)+nfib(n-2)+1.
```

List processing is accomplished using *hd*, *tl* and *:* as **cons**, as the following familiar definition shows. However, it should be said that list processing is below the level at which Enact is intended to be used for modelling. The object-oriented extensions provide more powerful collection types which should be used in preference.

```
reverse(x) := x=nil then nil else
                  append(reverse(tl x),(hd x):()).
```

The following interaction shows these functions being loaded, from the file **"bench.act"** and then evaluated for various arguments. This file, which is on the distribution disk, contains the three functions defined in this section.

```
load "bench.act".
  "bench.act"
  "bench.act  3:25pm Aug 28,1992"
  aFunction
  aFunction
  aFunction
  nil
x:=(1,2,3,4,5,6,7,8).
  ( 1 2 3 4 5 6 7 8 )
append(x,x).
  ( 1 2 3 4 5 6 7 8 1 2 3 4 5 6 7 8 )
reverse x.
  ( 8 7 6 5 4 3 2 1 )
append(x,reverse x).
  ( 1 2 3 4 5 6 7 8 8 7 6 5 4 3 2 1 )
```

These functions are used for benchmarking the implementation. For example, we evaluate

```
tm:=time(). res:=nfib 20. tm:=time()-tm. res/tm.
```

to get a raw speed figure. On the above input the system responds with the answers

```
  708154325
  21891
  183
  119
```

The four results shown are respectively the (ANSI C) time, which is seconds since the start of 1970, the value of *nfib 20*, the execution time in seconds and finally the number of calls of *nfib* per sec. In this version of the implementation this figure is rather lower than I would wish it to be. Later versions will be faster. For those familiar with functional programming, functions are first-class citizens and hence currying and other higher order methods work properly, as the following definitions show:

```
inc x := x+1; twice f x := f(f x); twice twice twice inc 0.
  16
```

Various predefined functions are available. They are dealt with in a later section.

A1.3 OBJECT-ORIENTED PROGRAMMING

There is a simple object-oriented component which integrates quite well with the functional programming. There is a predefined object *Object*, which will be the root of the class hierarchy. We can define objects which will have a class and we can define new classes in terms of existing ones. Every class is represented in the system by an object. To define a new class we link it into the object hierarchy explicitly. For example, the following assignments create three new classes, and link them into the class hierarchy.

```
class Node < Object.
class Leaf < Node.
class Tree < Node.
```

Tree and *Leaf* are subclasses of the class *Node*, which in turn is a subclass of the class *Object*. We use *new* to generate instances of these classes. Thus *new Tree* is an expression which denotes a new object of class *Tree*. Objects have attributes. The expression *new Leaf with value=99* denotes an object of class *Leaf* with an attribute *value* set to *99*. So far this is all entirely functional: there are no side-effects. If *x* is an object, then *x.value* denotes the value of its *value* attribute. With this preparation, look at the following definitions:

```
leaf(aNumber):=new Leaf with value=aNumber.

Leaf.sum():=self.value.

tree(aNode1,aNode2):=new Tree with left=aNode1
                     with right=aNode2.

Tree.sum():=self.left.sum()+self.right.sum().

t:=tree(tree(leaf(99),leaf(100)),leaf(101)).
```

Here we have defined methods for each of our classes and also constructor functions. The expression `tree(tree(leaf(99),leaf(100)),leaf(101))` constructs a binary tree with three leaves. The call `t.sum()` computes the value *300* by summing over these nodes. Because the function sum has been defined as `Leaf.sum` and `Tree.sum`, we refer to it as a *method*. It must be invoked by calling it as `n.sum`, where *n* is a `Node` (i.e. either a `Leaf` or a `Tree`). In the body of a method, the variable `self` refers to the object upon which the method was originally invoked. Thus, if *t* is a `Tree` then, when `t.sum()` is invoked, the occurrences of `self` in the body of the corresponding method refer to *t*. The use of variable names of the sort `aNode`, `aTree` etc. is an idiom borrowed from Smalltalk which is very readable.

A1.4 ASSIGNMENT

You will have seen the use of assignment at the topmost level. We have also seen that it is possible to nest assignments, assigning to local or global variables or to the attributes of objects. These two sorts of assignment have subtly different meanings. The following interactions show what is possible.

```
x:=1; y:=2; (x,y).
  ( 1 2 )
program(x):=(x:=x+10; y:=y+10; (x,y)).
  aFunction
x:=3; y:=4; (x,y).
  ( 3 4 )
program(5).
  ( 15 12 )
(x,y).
  ( 3 4 )
```

The final value of *y* illustrates that the variables in *program* are local. Both *x* and *y* are local variables which are initialized, respectively, to the value of the parameter of *program* and to the value of the global *y* at the time the function is defined. This initialization is repeated each time *program* is called. Although the *y* inside *program* has the value *12* at the end, that is not the value of the global *y* after the call. Suppose, however that *y* is an object:

```
y:=new Object.
  y
x:=1; y.value:=2; (x,y.value).
  ( 1 2 )
program(x):=(x:=x+10; y.value:=y.value+10; (x,y.value)).
  aFunction
x:=3; y.value:=4; (x,y.value).
  ( 3 4 )
program(5).
```

```
( 15 14 )
(x,y.value).
 ( 3 14 )
```

The explanation is that variables inside functions behave as initialized local variables, parameters taking their initialization from actual arguments and free variables their initialization from the value they had at function definition time. This is true even of object-valued variables. But objects themselves are global. Assignment to their attributes is therefore globally felt.

Let us repeat the *Tree* example, this time using assignment, with the effect that when we assign to the value of a leaf all of the values of the nodes in the tree are recomputed. First we change the constructors so that each *Node* has a *value* attribute and a *parent* attribute. Then we ensure that when a tree with children is constructed, the *parent* attribute is correctly set.

```
leaf(aNumber):=new Leaf with value=aNumber
                      with parent=nil.


tree(aNode1,aNode2):=
  (t:=new Tree with left=aNode1
               with right=aNode2
               with value=aNode1.value+aNode2.value
               with parent=nil;
   aNode1.setParent(t); aNode2.setParent(t);
   t).


Node.setParent(aNode):=(self.parent:=aNode).
```

We can still construct a tree as before, but now the value of each node will be computed as the tree is constructed. For example,

```
leaf1:=leaf(99); leaf2:=leaf(100); leaf3:=leaf(101);
t:=tree(tree(leaf1,leaf2),leaf3).
```

constructs the same tree as before, but with the added convenience of introducing some variables which we can use to refer to each node. It is interesting to use Enact just to navigate this structure, as follows:

```
leaf1.value.
 99
t.value.
 300
t.right.
 leaf3
t.left.
 aTree
```

```
leaf3.parent.
  t
```

Note that when Enact is required to print a structure (an object) it uses the name of a global variable, if such exists (e.g. *leaf3* above), otherwise it makes up a name, such as *aTree*, by concatenating *a* or *an* to the class name.

Now we define two methods which allow us to set the value of a leaf and recompute the value of all its parent and grandparent (etc.) nodes.

```
Leaf.setValue(aNumber):=
  (self.value:=aNumber;
   self.parent<>nil then self.parent.compute()).

Tree.compute():=
  (self.value:=self.left.value+self.right.value;
   self.parent<>nil then self.parent.compute()).
```

Note that both methods inspect the parent link, and if it is set, call *compute* to recompute the parent value. The following interaction shows these methods in use.

```
leaf1.value.
  99
t.value.
  300
leaf1.setValue(102); t.value.
  303
```

A1.5 INHERITANCE

In the previous sections we have made some elementary use of inheritance. Since *Leaf* and *Tree* are subclasses of *Node*, they inherit the attributes of *Node*. For example, the method *Node.setParent(aNode)* is inherited.

Enact supports multiple inheritance. When introducing a new class one can specify a number of superclasses, as the following example shows. First we define two classes with no superclasses:

```
class A < ().
  A
A.f():=99.
  aFunction
class B < ().
  B
B.y():=100.
  aFunction
```

Then we define a class which has two superclasses.

```
class C < (A,B).
  C
```

Now we can define an object of class C and expect it to inherit from both A and B:

```
c:=new C.
  c
c.f().
  99
c.g().
  100
```

If we revise the definition of A.f as follows

```
A.f():=self.g()+99.
  aFunction
c.f().
  199
```

we see that it correctly calls B.g when invoked as c.f().

A1.6 OPERATOR PRECEDENCE

All operators in Enact have a numerical precedence. There are thirteen levels of precedence, with 1 being the highest, most binding, level. The Enact operators with their precedence are as follows:

```
1   ' new
2
3   . application
4   * / mod
5   + - :
6   = > < >= <= <>
7   with :: where
8   and loop
9   or
10  if then
11  else
12   :=
13   ; class load fix
```

All operators are either unary or binary. Binary operators at the same level of precedence associate to the left. Thus $1-2-3-4$ means $((1-2)-3)-4$. We shall list the operators here and illustrate each of them in use in the following sections.

Arithmetic operators $a+b$, $a-b$, $a*b$, a/b, a mod b, (there is no unary minus). These operators have their usual relative precedence. They compute integer values using 32 bit arithmetic.

Relational operators $a=b$, $a<>b$, $a<b$, $a>b$, $a<=b$, $a>=b$. These operators have their usual relative precedence and compute logical values $true$ and $false$. Lower precedence than arithmetic ensures that expressions like $i+1<2*j$ parse correctly.

Logical operators a and b and a or b have their usual relative precedence and meaning. Negation is defined as a unary function not and so has precedence 3. This means its argument usually requires to be parenthesized.

Function definition $f(x):=x+1$ and f $x:=x+1$ are identical in meaning. They both define the function f of one argument. Functions of more than one argument have their arguments in parentheses $g(x,y):=x+y$.

Function application $f(99)$ and f 99 are identical in meaning. Functions of more than one argument are applied as $g(1,2)$. Precedence is higher than arithmetic operators, so that $f(99)+g(1,2)$ will parse correctly. Free variables are statically bound at time of definition.

Lambda expression $x::x+1$, $(x)::x+1$ are lambda expressions and identical in meaning. Functions of more than one argument are defined as $(x,y)::x+y$. Precedence of $::$ is lower than arithmetic and relational operators, but not logical operators, so that $(x,y)::(x<=y$ and $y<=x+1)$ will parse correctly only because of the parentheses around the body. An alternative way to define functions is $f:=x::x+1$, $f:=(x)::x+1$ or $g:=(x,y)::x+y$, but this is not good style.

Currying   This is allowed, as are other higher order devices. If we define h x $y:=x+y$ then h 1 2 evaluates to 3 because h 1 evaluates to $y::1+y$.

Local definitions $x+y$ $where$ $x=99$ and $x+y$ $where$ $(x,y)=(99,100)$ have their normal meaning.

Conditional expressions   These are constructed using the operators
```
a then b
b if a
c else d
```
Both a $then$ b and b if a have the value b, assuming a evaluates to $true$, otherwise they have the value $undefined$ (so in fact, b if a is just an alternative form of a $then$ b). The expression c $else$ d has the value c unless this value is $undefined$, in which case it has the value d. Precedence ensures that, for example, a $then$ b $else$ d has the expected meaning.

Lists   These are constructed using the operator $a:b$. There are predefined functions hd c, tl c. The expression $(x,y,z,...)$ evaluates its arguments and constructs a list.

The expression *nil* is the empty list and *a:b* is the list whose head is *a* and whose tail is *b*. Precedence ensures that, for example, *hd a:b* has the meaning *(hd a):b*. The expression *atom c* is false if *c* is a list, unless *c=nil*. Non-numeric atoms are constructed with a preceding single quote, e.g. *'hello* or *'"hello world"*. Double quotes are required for atoms which are not simple identifiers.

Singleton list   Because Enact *always* takes a set of parentheses to be a bracketing structure, which, apart from their effect on precedence, can be ignored, it is difficult to denote a singleton list. The expression *(99)* is equivalent to *99*. To denote a singleton list we must write *99:()* or *99:nil* or *list 99*.

Assignment statements   The meaning of *x:=e* is to assign the value of *e* to the local variable *x*. Inside functions, free variables and parameters are local to the body. Thus assignment to a variable is local to the body of that function. An assignment statement is an expression. Its value is the value of *e*. The precedence of *:=* is very low (*12*) so care must be taken. For example in *p then (x:=y) else (x:=0-y)* the parentheses are essential. Similarly *(x:=y) if p* requires the parentheses around the assignment statement to avoid the interpretation *x:=(y if p)* which arises because *if* is more binding than *:=*.

Other statements   The meaning of *S;T* is evaluate *S* for its effect, then evaluate *T*. The iterative statement *e loop S* repeats *S* while *e* returns true. Looping in this way should be avoided, in preference for iterators over structures.

Classes   *class A < B* introduces a new class *A*, as a subclass of *B*. There is a root class *Object*. If only single inheritance is being used all new classes should be directly or indirectly a subclass of *Object*. The expression *class A < (B,C,D)* introduces a new class *A*, as a subclass of *B*, *C* and *D*.

Objects   The expression *new A* creates a new object of class *A*. The more elaborate form *new A with attr1=e1 with attr2=e2 ...* creates an object with some of its attributes initialized.

Assignment to attributes   After *a:=new A* we can assign attributes with *a.attr1:=e1* and we can access attributes with *a.attr1*. Both classes and objects can have attributes.

Methods   These are just function valued attributes of classes, for example *A.f(x,y):=x+y+self.attr1*. If this method is invoked using *a.f(1,2)* then in its body *self* has the value *a*.

Fixed point   Mutually recursive definitions can be made using the *fix* operator. For example, *(P,Q)fix(P:= ...; Q:= ...)* will assign values to *P* and *Q* where each is defined in terms of the other. The actual values of these two variables are available during the evaluation of the ellipsis in a restricted way. Usually, this operator is used only to define mutually recursive functions, as in *(f,g)fix(f(x):=... g(x) ...; g(x):= ... f(x) ...)*.

Loading files   the expression *load* *"filename"* will read a script from the file with name *filename*. This is the usual way of storing an Enact model and loading it into the interpreter for testing. A full path name can be given.

A1.7 PREDEFINED FUNCTIONS AND CLASSES

The following functions are predefined:

not x	Boolean negation
hd x	first item of list
tl x	all but first item of list
atom x	true if x is a number or a symbol, false if x is a list, if x is nil, if x is a function or if x is an object
isObject x	true if x is an object, otherwise false
append(x,y)	append lists x and y
size x	returns length of list x
map(f,y)	apply function f to each element in the list y
filter(f,y)	select those elements of list y for which function f returns true
all(f,y)	true if applying function f to each element in the list x yields true
reduce(g,u,x)	compute $g(x1,g(x2, \ldots g(xn,u)\ldots))$. For example, *reduce((x,y)::x+y,0,(1,2,3,4,5,6,7,8,9))* computes $1+2+3+4+5+6+7+8+9+0$
union(x,y)	assuming x and y are lists without repetition (pretending to be *sets*), form the set union of lists x and y. Used to implement object-oriented set operations (defined later)
difference(x,y)	assuming x and y are lists without repetition (*sets*), form the set difference of lists x and y. Used to implement object-oriented set operations (defined later)
intersection(x,y)	assuming x and y are lists without repetition (*sets*), form the set intersection of lists x and y. Used to implement object-oriented set operations (defined later)

member(x,y)	assuming *y* is a list without repetition (*set*), return true only if *x* is a member of list *y*. Used to implement object-oriented set operations (defined later)
remove(x,y)	assuming *y* is a list without repetition (*set*), return list with same members as *y* except for one occurrence of *x* (if any). Used to implement object-oriented set operations (defined later)
classof x	returns class of object *x*
attrs x	returns immediate attributes of object *x* (not inherited attributes)
time()	(ANSI C) time, seconds since 00:00:00 GMT 1 Jan 1970 (approx.)
cells()	number of list cells currently in use
maxcells()	maximum number of list cells in use this session
version()	version of Enact in use
bye()	leave Enact (or use Ctrl-C)
ask x	input–output, prompts with message *x*, returns atom typed by user as value of function (e.g. *age:=ask '"how old are you"*.) This operation should be used sparingly.

There are also predefined collection classes, specifically *Set* and *Bag*, with the following meanings. Their full definitions are included in Appendix 2. They are also to be found in the file **enact.cfg**.

Consider the following interaction, which illustrates the use of some of these collection classes.

```
s:=set(); s.insert(1); s.insert(2); s.insert(3).
 ( 3 2 1 )
s.members.
 ( 3 2 1 )
t:=s.collect(x::x+2).
 t
t.members.
 ( 5 4 3 )
s.union(t).members.
 ( 2 1 5 4 3 )
s.difference(t).union(t.difference(s)).members.
 ( 2 1 5 4 )
```

```
u:=unitset(s).union(unitset(t)).
  u
u.members.
  ( s t )
u.UNION().members.
  ( 2 1 5 4 3 )
```

Once the set s is constructed we must use $s.members$ to see its members (as a list). The expression $s.collect(x::x+2)$ computes a new set whose members are determined from the members of s using the function $x::x+2$. The $collect$ and $select$ methods are named after the same methods in Smalltalk. As you can see from their definitions (Appendix 2) they are the operations familiar to functional programmers as map and $filter$.

The expression $s.union(t)$ computes the set union of s and t. The more complex expression $s.difference(t).union(t.difference(s))$ computes those elements in either s or t, but not both. It parses correctly because function application and dot have the same precedence.

The remainder of the above example shows the construction of a set of sets u. Enact displays this as the list $(s\ t)$, the printing of the identifiers here standing for the actual sets which are members of u. The method $Set.UNION()$ always applies to a set of sets, which it flattens by forming the union of all the member sets.

Both classes Set and Bag are subclasses of the class $Collection$. The following constructors and methods are defined.

$set()$ constructor, returns a new empty set

$bag()$ constructor, returns a new empty bag

$Collection.member(anObject)$ true only if $anObject$ is a member of the collection

$Collection.size()$ returns the number of members in the collection

$Collection.insert(anObject)$ changes the collection to include the member $anObject$. If the collection is a set then repetition is avoided.

$Collection.remove(anObject)$ changes the collection to remove the member $anObject$. If the collection is a bag then all repetitions are removed.

$Collection.collect(aFunction)$ constructs a new collection of the same type, whose members are obtained from the collection by applying $aFunction$ to each of its members

$Collection.forEachDo(aFunction)$ applies $aFunction$ to each of the collection's members, purely for the side-effect that the function has.

$Collection.select(aFunction)$ constructs a new collection of the same type, whose members are obtained from the collection by selecting only those for which $aFunction$ returns true

Collection.reduce(aFunction) applies the binary function *aFunction* to the collection thus reducing it to a single item. Assumes the collection is not empty

Collection.locate(aFunction) returns an item from the collection by selecting one for which *aFunction* returns true. Assumes such an item exists

Collection.all(aFunction) applies *aFunction*, which returns true or false to every item in the collection. Returns true only if all items return true

Collection.exists(aFunction) applies *aFunction*, which returns true or false to every item in the collection. Returns true if any item returns true

Set.add(anObject) constructs a new Set, whose members are those of the given set with *anObject* added

Set.subset(aSet) true if set is a subset of *aSet*

Set.equal(aSet) true if set is equal to *aSet*

unitset(anObject) constructs a set with one member

Set.union(aSet) constructs a set which is the union of the two given sets

Set.difference(aSet) constructs a set which is the difference of the two given sets

Set.intersection(aSet) constructs a set which is the difference of the two given sets

Set.UNION() assumes the set is a set of sets, applies union to flatten this into a single set containing all the members of each member set

The final items in the Enact library are predefined functions for determining the inheritance relationships between classes and for determining which attributes are inherited from where.

attributes obj the immediate attributes of object *obj*, presented as a Set

classes obj the immediate classes of object *obj*, presented as a Set (usually a unit set)

supers c the immediate superclasses of class *c*, presented as a Set

superiors c all the superclasses of class *c*, presented as a Set

suppliers(obj,attr) all the classes which supply attribute *attr* to object *obj*, presented as a Set. The *attr* argument must be quoted (e.g. *suppliers(m,'do)*) *alphabet obj* all the attributes, including inherited attributes, of object *obj*, presented as a Set

OK obj true if all the attributes, including inherited attributes, of object *obj*, are inherited from exactly one superclass

badAttrs obj those attributes, including inherited attributes, of object *obj* which are inherited from more than one superclass, presented as a Set

As an example of the use of these functions, consider the following interaction:

```
attributes(M).members.
  ( objects labeller )
alphabet(M).members.
  ( addDependent doAllDependents do setLabel
      pick install objects labeller )
classes(M).members.
  ( Menu )
superiors(Menu).members.
  ( Event Scroller Object )
suppliers(M,'install).members.
  ( Scroller )
OK M.
  true
Event.install():=99.      % just to illustrate problems
  aFunction
OK M.
  false
badAttrs(M).members.
  ( install )
suppliers(M,'install).members.
  ( Event Scroller )
```

In fact the hierarchy here is that *Menu* is a subclass of both *Event* and *Scroller*. Initially each attribute is inherited uniquely. But by adding an *install* attribute to *Event* we can see the use of *OK*, *badAttrs* and *suppliers* to isolate the problem.

An attribute which is inherited from two different superclasses (either directly or indirectly), if it is not an error, needs disambiguation. This is achieved by redefining it in the common child so that the two inherited occurrences are masked.

The definitions of these predefined functions show something of the power of Enact when used to model complex structures. They also illustrate an unusual implementation feature of Enact, that in fact there is no distinction (in the implementation) between 'is an instance of' and 'is a subclass of'. However, the distinction can be maintained by the user of Enact, by following the style of use illustrated earlier in this manual.

These definitions will be found in **enact.cfg**.

```
attributes x := new Set with members = attrs x.

supers x := new Set with members =
 (isObject(classof x) then list(classof x) else classof x).

classes := supers.

superiors x :=
 supers(x).union(supers(x).collect(superiors).UNION()).

suppliers(obj,attr):=
 attributes(obj).member(attr) then unitset(obj) else
   supers(obj).collect(aClass::suppliers(aClass,attr)).UNION().

alphabet obj :=
 superiors(obj).collect(attributes).UNION().union(attributes obj).

OK obj :=
 alphabet(obj).all(anAttr::suppliers(obj,anAttr).size()=1).

badAttrs obj :=
 alphabet(obj).select(anAttr::suppliers(obj,anAttr).size()<>1).
```

A1.8 SOME ISSUES

One of the main concepts of object-oriented design, and indeed of good design in general, has been omitted. Encapsulation of abstractions, specifically abstract data types, has not been addressed. Far from it: all classes expose all their attributes to everyone.

This was not an oversight. I am trying not to be too prescriptive in Enact about how one should organize and present abstractions. Enact is a toolkit which can be used in various ways, which I hope to show in additional papers. For example it can be used to exercise state-based specifications or to present algebraic ones. I have used it to define a CSP interpreter and then used that interpreter to test a specification of a protocol.

I felt that the organization of all designs into simple abstract data types was too constraining, even though most of all the designs I have done do indeed fit this model. Enact users are expected to adopt design constraints suitable to their application areas and then apply a judicious amount of self-discipline when representing their designs in Enact. Some of the examples I have done illustrate the variety of such constraints and will be published in the fullness of time. In particular, a method based on developing collections of related abstract data types, which I call abstract systems, is the subject of this book. I show how such models can be implemented quite effectively in C++.

Another issue which Enact is quite liberal about is binding. Ordinary variables are bound statically. Attributes are bound dynamically. The static binding of variables extends to all free variables in the body of a function. When a function is defined its free variables are bound to the value they have at definition time. Assignment to such variables is not an assignment to a global variable with the same name. It is an assignment to the (automatically declared) local variable which has been initialized to the value of the corresponding global. Consequently, functions which assign only to statically bound variables (i.e. not attributes) are purely functional, they can have no side-effect.

The assignment within a function to the attribute of a global object is, however, felt as a side-effect. The global variable remains bound to the same object, but the value of that object's attribute changes. This liberal attitude to side-effects seems necessary for some kinds of modelling.

Finally, a word about sets. Of course these are not (exactly) mathematical sets. For a start, they must be finite (in fact they had better be quite small). But there are other ways in which they do not behave exactly as they should if they were mathematical sets. The most important is that when comparing members (for example when computing union) the equality operation used is what is usually referred to as pointer-equality. Simple values (numbers and symbols) are of course recognized as equal. But objects which may be equal, in the sense that any attempt to interrogate them through their methods would yield identical results, can nevertheless be unequal if they have been constructed separately and are thus represented by different pointers.

A1.9 AVAILABILITY

In addition to the implementation provided in the book, Enact implementations are available free of charge (or for the cost of distribution, if any) from Peter Henderson. There is a PC version and versions for UNIX™ on Sun3 and SparcStations. You may obtain these versions electronically as described below, or copy them from someone else without further permission. If you wish to be kept informed about Enact developments then please let me know, preferably by email. I am **peter@ecs.soton.ac.uk** . Please report any bugs you find.

To obtain copies of the implementation electronically you can make use of anonymous FTP. To do this you must be able to access internet with a suitable FTP program. Most universities worldwide will be able to provide such access. Use FTP to gain access to my site **ecs.soton.ac.uk** and then log on with the username **anonymous**. When asked for a password, enter your full email address (yes, give your address as the password). You should now be able to locate the Enact implementation. It is currently located in the directory **pub/peter** where a file called **README** explains the status of the other files in that directory. If this does not work, email me for advice.

Appendix 2

COLLECTION AND INTERFACE LIBRARIES

This appendix contains Enact and C++ sources for the following files:

> Collection classes in Enact (part of **enact.cfg**)
> Source of **collect.h**
> Source of **collect.cpp**
> Source of **userface.act**
> Source of **userface.h**

All of these sources are included on the distribution disk. They are included here because frequent reference is made to them throughout the book. The version of **userface.cpp** which the author has used (with Borland C++) for testing the applications in the book is also included on the distribution disk, but not listed here because is is particularly tied to the Borland text windows. Its inclusion on the disk is in the expectation that readers and teachers using this book will reprogram it for their own windowing environment.

A2.1 COLLECTION CLASSES IN ENACT

```
% (excerpt from)  enact.cfg  9:21pm Jun 20,1992


class Collection < Object.

class Set < Collection.

class Bag < Collection.
```

```
set():=new Set
   with members=nil.

bag():=new Bag
   with members=nil.

Collection.member(anObject):=member(anObject,self.members).

Collection.size():=size(self.members).

Set.insert(anObject):=
   (self.members:=anObject:self.members)if not(self.member
                                               (anObject))

Bag.insert(anObject):=
   (self.members:=anObject:self.members).

Collection.remove(anObject):=
   (self.members:=remove(anObject,self.members)).

Bag.collect(aFunction):=
   new Bag with members=map(aFunction,self.members).

Set.collect(aFunction):=
   new (classof self) with members=
     reduce(union,nil,map(x::((aFunction x):()),self.members)).

Collection.forEachDo(aFunction):=
   (self.collect(aFunction); 'done).

Collection.reduce(aFunction):=
   reduce(g,hd(self.members),tl(self.members)).

Collection.select(aFunction):=
   new (classof self) with members=filter(aFunction,self.members).

Collection.locate(aFunction):=
   hd((self.select(aFunction)).members).

Collection.all(aFunction):=
   all(aFunction,self.members).

Collection.exists(aFunction):=
   not(self.all(x::not(aFunction x))).

unitset(anObject):=
```

```
       new Set with members=anObject:().
Set.subset(aSet):=
   self.all(x::aSet.member(x)).

Set.equal(aSet):=
   self.subset(aSet) and aSet.subset(self).

Set.add(anObject):=self.union(unitset(anObject)).

Set.union(aSet):=
   new (classof self) with members=union(self.members,aSet.
                                                 members)

Set.difference(aSet):=
   new (classof self) with members=difference(self.members,aSet.
                                                 members)

Set.intersection(aSet):=
   new (classof self) with members=intersection(self.members,aSet.
                                                 members)

Set.UNION():=
   reduce((x,y)::x.union(y),set(),self.members).
```

A2.2 SOURCE OF collect.h

```
// collect.h 11:00 February 21, 1992

#ifndef _COLLECT
#define _COLLECT


class Cell;


class Collection{
protected:
  Cell* members;
  Collection();
public:
```

```
  ~Collection();
  virtual void insert(void*)=0;
  virtual Collection* New()=0;
  void remove(void*);
  void* index(int);
  int size();
  int member(void*);
  void forEachDo(void f(void*));
  Collection* select(int f(void*));
  Collection* collect(void* f(void*));
  void* inject(void* f(void*,void*));
  void* locate(int f(void*));
  int all(int f(void*));
  int exists(int f(void*));
};


class Cell{
public:
  void* value;
  Cell* next;
  Cell(void* ,Cell*);
  ~Cell();
};


extern int cellcount;
extern int maxcellcount;


class Set : public Collection {
public:
  Set();
  void insert(void*);
  Collection* New();
};


class Bag : public Collection {
public:
  Bag();
  void insert(void*);
  Collection* New();
};

#endif
```

A2.3 SOURCE OF collect.cpp

```cpp
// collect.cpp 11.00am February 21, 1992

#include "collect.h"


int cellcount=0;
int maxcellcount=0;

Cell::Cell(void* v,Cell* n){
  value=v; next=n;
  cellcount++;
  if(cellcount>maxcellcount)maxcellcount=cellcount;
}

Cell::~Cell(){
  cellcount--;
}




Collection::Collection():members(0){
}

Collection::~Collection(){
  while(members!=0){Cell* c=members;
                members=members->next; delete c;}
}

Set::Set():Collection(){
}

Collection* Set::New(){
  return new Set();
}

Bag::Bag():Collection(){
}

Collection* Bag::New(){
  return new Bag();
}
```

```
void Bag::insert(void* e){
  members=new Cell(e,members);
}

void Set::insert(void* e){
  if(!member(e))members=new Cell(e,members);
}

int Collection::member(void* e){
  Cell* c=members;
  while((c!=0)&&(c->value!=e)){c=c->next;}
  if(c==0)return 0; else return 1;
}


void Collection::remove(void* e){
  Cell* c=members;
  if(c==0)return;
  if(c->value==e){members=c->next; delete c; return;}
  if(c->next==0)return;
  Cell* p=c; c=c->next;
  while((c->value!=e)&&(c->next!=0)){p=c;c=c->next;}
  if(c->value==e){p->next=c->next; delete c;}
}

void Collection::forEachDo(void aFunction(void*)){
  Cell* c=members;
  while(c!=0){aFunction(c->value); c=c->next;}
}

void* Collection::index(int i){
  Cell* c=members;
  while((c!=0)&&(i>1)){c=c->next;i--;}
  if(c==0)return 0; else return c->value;
}

int Collection::size(){
  Cell* c=members; int i=0;
  while(c!=0){c=c->next;i++;}
  return(i);
}


Collection* Collection::select(int aFunction(void*)){
  Collection* aCollection=this->New();
  Cell* c=members;
```

```
Collection* Collection::select(int aFunction(void*)){
  Collection* aCollection=this->New();
  Cell* c=members;
  while(c!=0){
  if(aFunction(c->value))
    aCollection->insert(c->value);
  c=c->next;
  }
  return aCollection;
}

Collection* Collection::collect
  (void* aFunction(void*)){
  Collection* aCollection=this->New();
  Cell* c=members;
  while(c!=0){
    aCollection->insert(aFunction(c->value));
    c=c->next;
  }
  return aCollection;
}


void* Collection::inject
  (void* aFunction(void*, void*)){
  Cell* c=members;
  void* r=c->value; c=c->next;
  while(c!=0){
    r=aFunction(c->value,r);
    c=c->next;
  }
  return r;
}




void* Collection::locate(int aFunction(void*)){
  Collection* sel=select(aFunction);
  void* r=sel->members->value; delete sel;
  return r;
}

int Collection::all(int aFunction(void*)){
  Collection* sel=select(aFunction);
  int r=sel->size()==size(); delete sel;
  return r;
}
```

```
int Collection::exists(int aFunction(void*)){
  Collection* sel=select(aFunction);
  int r=sel->size()>0; delete sel;
  return r;
}
```

A2.4 SOURCE OF *userface.act*

```
'"userface.act 12:40pm Feb 28,1992".


Collection.forEachDo(aFunction):=
  (self.collect(aFunction); self).



class Event < Object.

Event.addDependent(anEvent):=
  self.dependents.insert(anEvent).

Event.doAllDependents():=
  self.dependents.forEachDo(anEvent::anEvent.do()).

Event.do():='"default Event.do".

Event.setLabel(aLabel):= (self.label:=aLabel).


class Prompter < Object.

prompter():= new Prompter.

Prompter.get():=ask(list('"Prompter",self,'"?")).

class Display < Object.

display():=new Display with value=0.

Display.put(aValue):=
  (self.value:=aValue;
  ask(list('"Display changed",self,self.value,'"ok?"))).
```

```
class Scroller < Object.

scroller():= new Scroller with objects=set()
                            with labeller=(anObject::nil).


Scroller.pick():=
(choice:=ask(list('Pick,
       (self.objects.collect(self.labeller)).members));
 self.objects.exists(anObject::(self.labeller(anObject)=choice))
                                                       then
   self.objects.locate(anObject::(self.labeller(anObject)=choice))
                                                       else nil
).


Scroller.install(aCollection,aFunction):=
(self.objects:=aCollection;
 self.labeller:=aFunction).



class Menu < (Event,Scroller).

menu():= new Menu with objects=set()
                  with labeller=(anObject::'noLabel).

Menu.setLabel(aLabel):= (self.label:=aLabel).


Menu.do():=
(choice:=self.pick();
 (choice<>nil)loop(choice.do();choice:=self.pick())
).



class Selector < Scroller.

selector():= new Selector with objects=set()
                          with labeller=(anObject::'noLabel).



Selector.get():=
(choice:=self.pick();
 (choice=nil)loop(choice:=self.pick());
 choice
) if self.objects.size()>0 else nil.
```

A2.5 SOURCE OF *userface.h*

```
// userface.h 9:30 February 28, 1992

#ifndef _USERFACE
#define _USERFACE

#include "collect.h"

class Window{
  char* contents;
  char* desktop;
  int tc,tr,bc,br;
  int selected;
  int row,col;
  void choose();
protected:
  Window(int,int,int,int);
  void suspend();
  void select();
  void puts(char*);
  void gets(char*);
  void locate(int,int);
  void chat(int,char);
  void title(char*);
  void clear();
};



class Event {
  Set* dependents;
  char* _label;
public:
  Event();
  void addDependent(Event*);
  void doAllDependents();
  void setLabel(char*);
  char* label();
  virtual void _do();
};
```

```cpp
class Scroller : public Window{
  int pos,size,maxsize,start,length,width;
  char buf[100];
  up();
  down();
  Set* objects;
  char* (*labeller)(void*);
  void refresh();
protected:
  int getsel();
  virtual void* pick();
public:
  Scroller(int, int, int, int);
  void install(Set*, char* f(void*));
};


class Menu : public Scroller , public Event{
public:
  Menu(int, int, int, int);
  void _do();
};


class Selector : public Scroller{
public:
  Selector(int, int, int, int);
  void* get();
};


class Display : public Window{
public:
  Display(int, int, int, int, char*);
  void put(long);
  void put(char*);
};
```

```
class Prompter : public Window{
public:
  Prompter(int, int, int, int, char*);
  long get();
  char* gets();
};

openScreen();
closeScreen();

#endif
```

Appendix 3

ANNOTATED BIBLIOGRAPHY

My purpose in writing this short annotated bibliography is to try to explain what I have learned from each of the books listed here. The order in which I have presented them seems to me to be the logical order for reading my annotations. It is not necessarily a recommended order for reading the books. That is something which you will need to work out for yourself according to your particular interests.

To a large extent I consider this collection of books an adequate reference, at the time of writing, for the topics introduced here. I have been reasonably selective. There is little overlap between the books. Where they present the same ideas, they present different viewpoints and opinions. If you wish to be abreast of the state of the art in this area then you should aspire eventually to read all of them. Even the obvious works of reference deserve a concerted browse so that you are familiar with their scope and their approach. Indeed, my recommendation is that, after reading my comments you browse each of the books where they are available in library or bookshop and decide a suitable reading order for your interests. This may of course involve ranking some of them so low that you never get round to them.

Bjarne Stroustrup, *The C++ Programming Language* (2nd edn), Addison-Wesley, Wokingham 1991, ISBN 0-201-53992-6.

This book is, of course, an absolute must for any serious student of C++. Stroustrup is the designer of C++ and therefore *the* authority on the language and how it can be used. The first edition of this book, which described an earlier version of C++, was my introduction to the language. It was the description of constructors and destructors and how they cooperate to enable the writing of encapsulated memory management that convinced me that C++ was an important step beyond C, although I confess that it was necessary for me to have this pointed out to me by a friend before I realized it and re-read the relevant passage (on a strings package). The second edition of the book is much larger, including substantial additional material on design methods and on more recent language additions (templates and exceptions).

Stephen C. Dewhurst and Kathy T. Stark, *Programming in C++*, Prentice-Hall, Englewood Cliffs NJ, 1989, ISBN 0-13-723156-3.

A concise tutorial on the use of C++ by two employees of AT&T who were part of the project which developed the language. I like it because it has the virtue of conciseness and some interesting examples. It can be read in a few hours. Some readers may prefer to read this before Stroustrup. That's not the way I did it, so I am unable to judge whether it would have been better for me. Either way, each text reinforces the other.

Stanley B. Lippman, *C++ Primer* (2nd edn), Addison-Wesley, Wokingham, 1991, ISBN 0-201-54848-8.

Another tutorial text, another viewpoint. More comprehensive than Dewhurst and Stark because it is considerably longer. One of the benefits of reading many authors on the same subject (here on C++) is that you are better able to draw the general lessons and distinguish the elements of style which are unique to each proponent. For example, C++ allows programmers to adopt a very type-secure style. Lippman illustrates that, but he also allows a relatively typeless style (witness my use of **void***). Each author defends and exemplifies his or her style to some degree. You can only understand these arguments fully by reading many programmers' cases.

Brian W. Kernighan and Denis M. Richie, *The C Programming Language* (ANSI edn), Prentice-Hall, Englewood Cliffs NJ, 1988, ISBN 0-13-110362-8.

This is the classic reference on C. The first edition was the *de facto* standard for C. Indeed, many compilers were advertised as K&R compatible. Much existing C code (legacy code) predates the ANSI standardization exercise, and for professional programmers it is still necessary to understand the relationship between K&R C, ANSI C and C++. The second edition of Kernighan and Richie revises the presentation of the language to the 1986 ANSI standard. This is (very nearly) a subset of C++. Since C is still a more universally portable language than C++ (for example it is the *target* language for many compilers) I feel it is important to understand its relationship to C++. For this purpose, the second edition of Kernighan and Richie serves as an ideal reference. It is also a source of all the standard idioms which have become commonplace in C usage and which many C programmers will transfer directly to C++ (e.g. for the implementation of **strcpy** they give **while((*s++=*t++)!='\0');**). This is C written by two master programmers.

James O. Coplien, *Advanced C++ – programming styles and idioms*, Addison-Wesley, Wokingham, 1992, ISBN 0-201-54855-0.

This is indeed an advanced book. Coplien takes C++ to realms few would imagine before reading the book. He exploits every advanced feature of C++ (such as overloading, pointers to member functions etc.) for the purposes for which they were intended. He explores idioms and paradigms for programming and demonstrates the immense power of C++. Consequently this is not a simple book, for the topics are not simple. But it is a useful source of inspiration and an important source of reference for readers who wish to exploit the most advanced feature of C++. I cannot claim to have completed the book yet, or even to have understood all that I have read. When I discovered that Coplien had developed a way of coding in C++ which was tantamount to functional programming. I was both excited and sceptical. But my scepticism was misplaced. The method which Coplien describes goes much further towards a complete functional paradigm than I imagined possible. I expect I will be returning to Coplien repeatedly in the coming years. I want that knowledge which he has committed to these pages. I feel sure that there are important ideas here which I have yet to discover.

Margaret A. Ellis and Bjarne Stroustrup, *The annotated C++ reference manual, ANSI Base document*, Addison-Wesley, Wokingham, 1990, ISBN 0-201-51459-1.

As its title suggests this is the reference manual for C++. The virgin form of the manual is included as an appendix in Stroustrup's *The C++ Programming Language* (2nd edn) but this annotated version is a valuable additional reference. The annotations (almost double the size of the original text) explain many of the design decisions behind C++ and lead to an understanding of the relationship between one construct and another. The annotations give examples of use and occasionally describe how C++ constructs might be implemented. Sometimes, when one gets to the level of detail and subtlety which interaction between language constructs involves, this is the only satisfactory way of resolving the issue. This is as true of C++, despite its careful orthogonal design, as it is of other languages.

Keith E. Gorlen, Stanford M. Orlow and Perry S. Plexico, *Data Abstraction and Object-oriented Programming in C++*, John Wiley, New York, ISBN 0-471-92346-X.

The comprehensive NIH class library for collections and many examples of its use. This is the other end of the scale from the small library described in Appendix 2. Like any professional library it is extensive. This is the way large-scale programming is tackled. Use this book both as a source of code and of inspiration.

Zortech Inc., *C++ Compiler Documentation*, 1989 and subsequently (now distributed by Symantec Corp.).

This was my first C++ compiler. It taught me a lot and is still the compiler I use for most of my development work, although having done that on the PC I have to transfer it to UNIX™ where some of my students prefer to work. The documentation which came with the compiler was my constant companion for many months and the compiler itself (on a 286 laptop) the sage which answered most of my questions. There can be few better ways to learn to use a language than to have a PC implementation which quickly responds to experimentation. Zortech provided this for me and it is a route I heartily recommend to the reader. All the code in this book was initially tested on this compiler.

Borland International Inc., *C++ Compiler and Documentation*, 1991 and subsequently.

Like the Zortech compiler, this implementation runs on my PC. For reasons of standardization (they have many Borland products) this is the implementation my university has adopted for undergraduate use. Like the Zortech compiler, it is an excellent teacher. The documentation is comprehensive and of a high standard. If you are serious about

C++ and have a PC then, if you buy nothing else, you should buy this compiler. It will be the most efficient and economical way to learn C++ to a very high standard. If you are an employer of C++ programmers, considering investing on professional training for them, you might rather consider buying them this compiler (and a machine to run it on). This investment would be amply rewarded. You would effectively have bought a C++ expert for them to consult. Then, of course, you need to invest further in giving them good design training. That's harder. Again, all the code in this book has been tested on this compiler. It is a historical accident that the order in which I became acquainted with these compilers is as it is. I currently still use both. I am aware of the arrival of the Microsoft (C7) compiler for C++ which I have not yet had time to evaluate, but of which I have heard equally good reports. If you have access to any of these compilers, then learn to use them as your teacher (going through the exercises at the end of Chapter 4 is a good start), and aspire to a style with which you are comfortable. Of course, I hope you will adopt some of the style elements which I have displayed in this book, but I am aware that a complete methodology requires much more than can be (yet) put into a single book.

Peter Coad and Edward Yourdon, *Object Oriented Analysis* (2nd edn), Yourdon Press and Prentice-Hall, Englewood Cliffs NJ, 1991, ISBN 0-13-629981-4.

I was impressed by the effectiveness of the method described in this book. I first came across it in a product design done by a company for whom I was consulting. Their designers had been on a course run by Peter Coad and adopted his methods in the design of their product. It had truly given them an understanding of their application domain. Their eventual product was built (mostly) in a 4GL but the object-oriented analysis and design done *à la* Coad and Yourdon gave it a resilience and flexibility which it might not otherwise have had. The techniques which Coad and Yourdon describe in this and subsequent books have been adapted by me to suit my purposes. If you think my methods are useful then you should certainly go back to the source and study them there, for Coad and Yourdon have considerable experience of systems analysis and their sage advice is captured in rules of usage which I have not explicitly repeated. For example, they have advice on naming classes which clearly emanates from their experiences with very large systems. But there is much more than that, including a comprehensive analysis method. They have their own diagramming methods which have clearly evolved in the light of their experience and are deserving of respectful attention for that.

James Rumbaugh, Michael Blaha, William Premerlani, Frederick Eddy and William Lorenson, *Object Oriented Modelling and Design*, Prentice-Hall, Englewood Cliffs NJ, 1991, ISBN 0-13-630054-5.

Everything you ever wanted to know about object-oriented methods is here. The point of view is data-centred, even database centred. But that is its strength, for most other authors (including this one) take a process-centred view, despite themselves. The book includes neat diagramming methods worthy of your attention, but for me the key concept which they advocate is the use of associations for the representation of relationships (see Exercise 9 of Chapter 3). This seems to be a consequence of their experience with databases. It amply illustrates that, in computing, our viewpoint reflects our history and we are yet an eclectic gathering of technologies.

Grady Booch, *Object Oriented Design with Applications*, Benjamin/Cummins, New York, 1991, ISBN 0-8053-0091-0.

There are two good reasons for studying this book. Firstly, Booch introduces a range of diagramming techniques which have become very popular for object-oriented design. Secondly, he develops five large programs in five different object-oriented languages. As well as C++ there are programs in LISP with CLOS (Common LISP Object System), Object Pascal, Smalltalk and Ada. This gives the reader every chance to generalize from the specifics of five different representations of objects. As such it is an important educational contribution.

Bertrand Meyer, *Object-Oriented Software Construction*, Prentice-Hall, Englewood Cliffs NJ, 1988, ISBN 0-13-629049-3.

This is where I really learned what object-oriented meant. I read it after I had studied Smalltalk and before C++. Meyer's style is clear and he carefully introduces all of the main concepts one by one. He uses his own language Eiffel for the clarity which it brings to the pedagogy. Although I haven't tried it, I imagine that using this book along with an Eiffel compiler would be as rapid and comprehensive an introduction to object-oriented methods as any other which I have suggested. But even without the Eiffel compiler, the book is an excellent tutorial. In the first edition, which is the edition I studied, Meyer is fairly dismissive of C++. Clearly this is not a view with which I agree. But I found everything else which Meyer said very agreeable indeed.

Adele Goldberg and David Robson, *Smalltalk-80 – the Language and its Implementation*, Addison-Wesley, Wokingham, 1983, ISBN 0-201-11371-6.

Smalltalk is an important language. It is *the* object-oriented language. There were object-oriented languages before Smalltalk (Simula 67, for example) and there have been many since, but Smalltalk it was that defined all the ground rules, exemplified the power and made us all take notice. This classic text was incomprehensible to me when I first encountered it. I know the concepts are orthogonal to traditional structured programming and that many people had difficulty with them on first exposure. But there was more to it than that. I came from a culture (Pascal, Functional Programming, Formal Specification, Program Correctness) to which object-oriented thinking was quite alien. I didn't *want* object-oriented to be the right answer. So I wasn't really receptive to the messages of this book. But then I learned to program in Smalltalk (using the Digitalk implementation on my PC) and fell in love with it. Once you know the secret, the rest is easy. And, when you know the secret, the Goldberg and Robson book is a joy to read. In fact, now I can't believe how mysterious it all was to me in the early 1980s. Read this book. If you have my experience, persevere. Trust me. You need to know what it tells you, including all the horrors of the Smalltalk class/metaclass structure. You need, for example, to see how elegantly the authors are able to encapsulate discrete event simulation. You need to see how they designed their basic class library, especially the collections. This was a significant advance for our discipline. Goldberg and Robson have recorded it for posterity.

Digitalk Inc., *Smalltalk V – Object Oriented Programming – System Tutorial and Programming Handbook*, 1991.

This was my Smalltalk teacher. Actually it was the original implementation, called Methods, which I obtained in late 1985. I spent a happy three months playing with it on a 286 PC. The manual was a comprehensive introduction to Smalltalk. Between them, the implementation and the manual taught me the basic concepts, idioms and styles of Smalltalk in an effective and efficient manner. It was after my experience with this implementation that I was ready to accept the new ideas in Goldberg and Robson. I never looked back. Now I have the latest version, which runs on my desktop PC under Windows 3. It's wonderful. And the documentation is just as comprehensive (it's remarkably similar to the original, just extended).

Greg Nelson (ed), *Systems Programming with Modula-3*, Prentice-Hall, Englewood Cliffs NJ, 1991, ISBN 0-13-590464-1.

C++ is an important language. Smalltalk is too. But we ought not to assume that either is the last word. Our technology never stands still. We build on the past by standing on the shoulders of those that have gone before. Perhaps Modula 3 is a glimpse of the future. Modula 2 was an extension of Pascal which included modules. By object-oriented standards that is not very interesting, but it also included support for concurrency, which is very interesting. Modula 3 extends Modula 2 by adding object-oriented concepts and more. Most significantly, it includes automatic memory management (expected by LISP programmers, but considered exotic by others) by the provision of a run-time garbage collector. I am sure that is the right way to go. Surely C++ will have this extension eventually. Until it does, this book of essays gives you a glimpse of the future (or a possible future). Modula 3 is an elegant language, intentionally kept small by its designers. They limited themselves to 60 pages for its reference manual, a homage to Algol 60. The idea was that they could subsume the power of Modula 2, of object-oriented programming and of other styles, including functional programming, in a language no bigger than that. They seem to have succeeded. At least they have set a target for others, in particular for C++.

Laurence C. Paulson, *ML for the working programmer*, Cambridge University Press, Cambridge, 1991, ISBN 0-521-39022-2.

In looking forward to where programming may yet go we have still to take functional programming as a serious contribution. ML is state-of-the-art functional programming and Paulson's book is a comprehensive description of the language and its use. Towards the end of the book he is able to complete examples of startling power – in particular a far from trivial theorem prover. The thought of doing such an example in any language other than a functional language is the stuff of nightmares. But there are weaknesses to functional programming still. Doing input–output and updating databases from within functional programs is not well understood and is certainly not yet near consensus among functional programmers. These are issues I expect to see resolved some day soon (please, someone, take this frustration away). My own belief is that functional programming and object-oriented programming will be combined to realize the benefits of both. Meanwhile, the best I can offer the reader is that you study each topic separately. Paulson is the best contemporary source for functional programming.

Ian Hayes, *Specification Case Studies*, Prentice-Hall, Englewood Cliffs NJ, 1987, ISBN 0-13-826595-X.

In Europe, formal methods of software design are very important. One method, Z, pioneered at Oxford, is introduced in this short book of essays. I include it in my bibliography because it has been very influential in the design of Enact. I have addressed some of the relationships in Chapter 9. The reader who found that chapter of value is encouraged to dig further by looking at this volume.

Cliff B. Jones, *Systematic Software Development using VDM*, (2nd edn), Prentice-Hall, Englewood Cliffs NJ, 1990, ISBN 0-13-880733-7.

Another influential book on formal methods. I am a firm believer that the mathematical description of systems is an important tool in helping us to simplify their design. If the maths is simple then the design will be. Jones describes another popular mathematical method, VDM. Like Z, this language holds some of the keys to understanding how to define simpler systems for complex tasks. The only reason I began with a model in Enact rather than Z or VDM is that I found it impossible to get all the way from the maths to C++ without something like Enact as a half-way house. I did not develop the route from mathematical description to the half-way point here. That is for later, or for others. I have however taken many of the examples from Jones' book and tested them by casting them into Enact models. It is this exercise which has led to the particular choice of operations on collections in Enact. There is much left to explore here.

David Turner (ed), *Research Topics in Functional Programming*, Addison-Wesley, Wokingham, 1990, ISBN 0-201-17236-4.

Finally, a collection of essays on functional programming with contributions from some of the world's foremost exponents. Turner himself describes an elegant, state-of-the-art functional language which exploits lazy evaluation, a technique for delaying computation until the result is required for use (but without recomputing it when it is required a second time). He also shows how to apply such techniques to operating systems, and hence goes some way towards solving the problem of input–output for functional languages. Also in this volume is a paper by Goguen on OBJ, an algebraic specification language. This language is at the interface of functional and object-oriented methods. Consequently, it is another important pointer for the future. But nothing in this volume is as pragmatic as C++. This is a marriage of ideas waiting to happen. Ten years from now it will be interesting to see how close languages like ML and C++ have become or how far apart they have remained. Object-oriented thinking has taken centre stage. Functional programming is still in the wings.